A KASHMIRI CENTURY

Praise for *A Kashmiri Century*

'Here is an intimate insider's look at an interesting and transformative century of Kashmir. Wakhlu belongs to a distinguished Kashmiri Pandit family and her stories explore their inner world as the social and political life changed from relative harmony to the violence of the last few decades. An illuminating read.'

Dr Mallika Sarabhai, performer, activist

'Story and history revel together to reveal the joyful intimacy of Kashmiri life. *Sambandh*, the bond that ties us, reigns supreme, whether licit or illicit, loving or traumatic, invoking courage or cowardice, horror or wonder, bringing tears of sorrow or joy. You will be touched, you will be moved. These are the magical stories of a beautiful people whose sweetness made the land wondrous until one day the music died.'

Rakesh Kumar Kaul, author, *The Last Queen of Kashmir* and *Dawn*

'Through a series of well-narrated stories covering a century of Kashmiri history, Khem Lata Wakhlu has covered an era of remarkable, and unprecedented, changes in the lives of the people of Jammu and Kashmir. In her inimitable style, she demonstrates that, at our deepest level, all of us—irrespective of which faith we may belong to—seek honesty, fairness and compassion from the people we interact with. Through her stories, Khem Lata has brought to life our innate desire to live by our highest human values.'

Anu Aga, former chairperson, Thermax Ltd and Teach for India

'*A Kashmiri Century* is a very interesting chronology of almost a century of socio-economic changes with political overtones in Kashmir. A beautifully written narrative, interwoven with interesting events and personalities and with a dash of humour; yet, it bears malice towards none. An excellent reading.'

Pran Kishore Kaul, Padma Shri and Sahitya Akademi awardee

'Written with sensitivity and compassion, Wakhlu's book gives us a panoramic view of the ethos and culture of the gentle people of Kashmir, spanning a hundred years. The gripping stories serve as beautiful reminders of the core humanistic values that we all cherish—values that are needed now, more than ever before. Khem Lata is an extraordinary woman, who has shown her grit and merit, whether in captivity or in freedom. A true heroine, and a torchbearer for Indian womanhood.'

Lila Poonawalla, Padma Shri awardee; former CMD, Alfa Laval and Tetra Pak India; founder chairperson, Lila Poonawalla Foundation

'Khem Lata Wakhlu's imaginative rendition of an era elevates the staid telling of a family memoir into a racy, suspenseful novel. Written with perception and sensitivity, she brings to life the people and incidents of a tumultuous era that her family lived through in Kashmir. It is like an epic unfolding, spanning a century of the remarkable history of the people of Kashmir.'

Siddharth Kak, filmmaker and television personality

A KASHMIRI CENTURY

PORTRAIT OF A

SOCIETY IN FLUX

KHEM LATA WAKHLU

HarperCollins *Publishers* India

First published in India by
HarperCollins *Publishers* in 2021
A-75, Sector 57, Noida, Uttar Pradesh 201301, India
www.harpercollins.co.in

2 4 6 8 10 9 7 5 3 1

Copyright © Khem Lata Wakhlu 2021

P-ISBN: 978-93-5422-327-3
E-ISBN: 978-93-5422-328-0

The views and opinions expressed in this book are the author's
own and the facts are as reported by her, and the publishers
are not in any way liable for the same.

Khem Lata Wakhlu asserts the moral right
to be identified as the author of this work.

All rights reserved. No part of this publication may be reproduced,
stored in a retrieval system, or transmitted, in any form or by any
means, electronic, mechanical, photocopying, recording or otherwise,
without the prior permission of the publishers.

Typeset in 11/14.7 Adobe Caslon Pro at
Manipal Technologies Limited, Manipal

Printed and bound at
Thomson Press (India) Ltd

This book is produced from independently certified FSC™ paper
to ensure responsible forest management.

*Dedicated to the memory of all the great chroniclers of Kashmir–past and present–who have contributed to a better understanding of the ancient region,
and
to the millions of Kashmiris around the world, who in their quiet and effective ways are working for the well-being of all people and contributing to a more wholesome, productive, prosperous, harmonious, and joyous world*

Contents

Introduction		xi
Part I: Peregrination		
1	The Lucknow Seduction	3
2	Treacherous Trips: In the Service of Humanity	59
3	Homecoming from Calcutta	77
Part II: Reform		
4	The Desire for Change	95
5	The Wood-headed Dolt	103
6	Kindred Spirits	111
Part III: Innocent People, Simple Lives		
7	Säd Makkārs	127
8	Van Buḍini	138
9	Architects of Change	156
10	A Dussehra to Remember	160
11	Drama in the Kitchen	165
12	A Windfall on Diwali	177
13	Beejān	186

Part IV: Mystics and Mysticism

14 Nandė Lāl Bab: The Clairvoyant Mystic   199
15 Graṭė Bub and the Miracle   209

Part V: Marriages, Love, Neighbours, and Brides

16 The Marriages of Rajṭoṭh and Sondhlal   221
17 Nav-sheen Mubārakh   231
18 The Peers and Dhars   244
19 Love, Life, and Death   253
20 Dramabāz Children and Lasting Friendships   266
21 The Audacious Second Marriage   272
22 The 'At Home' Blooper   285
23 The Rupa Devi Sharda Peeth Trust   288

Part VI: Phases of Turmoil

24 The Surprise Attack   295
25 The Unexpected Return   301
26 The Loss of the Moh-i-Muqaddas   309
27 The Vicissitudes of Kashmiri Life   318
28 The Kashmiri Pandit Agitation   325
29 Radicalization and Ethnic Cleansing   334
30 Armed Violence and Abductions   342

Epilogue   347
Index   355
Acknowledgements   363
About the Author   365

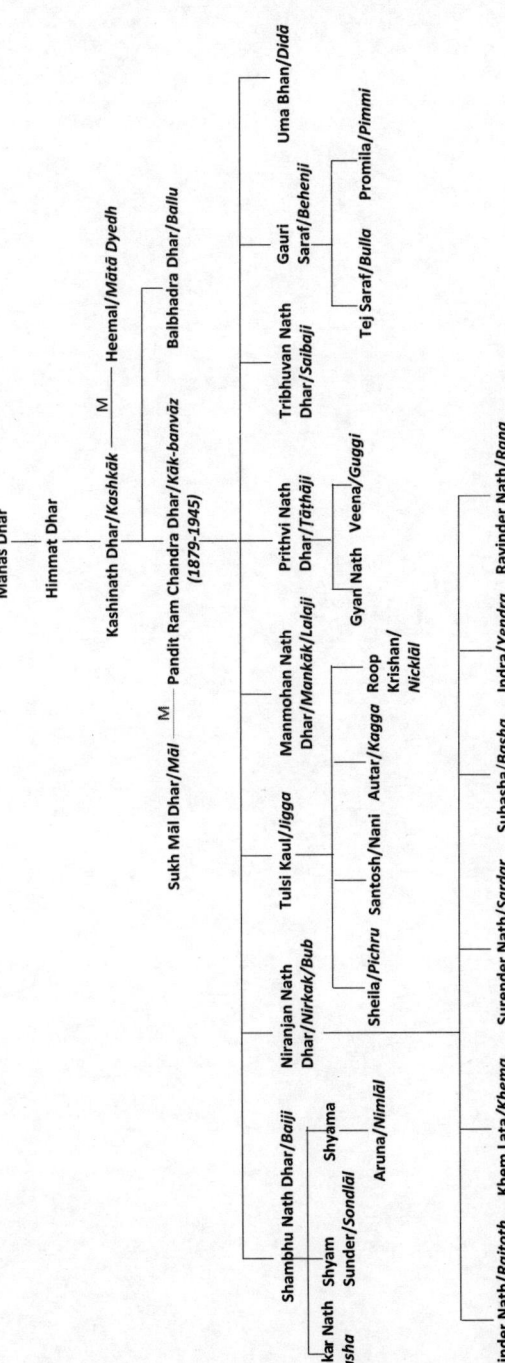

Partial Genealogical Tree of the Dhars of Rishī Vihār

Disclaimer: This is not the complete family tree, since many branches and/or descendants have not been shown. This diagram is an aid to the comprehension of the stories.

NOTES: a) **Names** / *pet names* appear next to each other in the chart.
b) The symbol M indicates 'Married to'.

Introduction

The Kashmir region has been known throughout India's long and chequered history for its natural beauty, its contribution to spiritual and philosophical thought, its lovely people, fertile soil, exuberant flora and fauna, and for being the abode of Devi Shāradā—the reigning deity of the region. Kashmir has, since time immemorial, been especially renowned for its magnificent contributions to the vast treasure trove of Indian literature as well as the first documented history of the region, the *Rajatarangini*, written by Kalhana Pandit (ca. twelfth century CE) and later updated and presented as the *Dvitiya Rajatarangini* (second *Rajatarangini*) by the historians Jonaraja (ca. thirteenth century CE) and Srivara. Srivara was Jonaraja's pupil.

Over the centuries, Kashmir has undergone cataclysmic social, cultural, and religious changes. From being the philosophical 'crown jewel' of the Indian subcontinent in the Buddhist and Hindu periods, and renowned for its open societies and liberal and erudite thinking of its elite and the relaxed life of its people, including that of Kashmiri women, it was reduced to a pale shadow of its previous self after the fourteenth century CE. Kashmir's violent subjugation thereafter, and the systematic decimation of its population—including a conscious degradation of their enormous skills, like painting, sculpture, temple architecture and more—by subsequent rulers, who were bent upon converting its innocent and simple people into Muhammedans, has had an indelible impact on all Kashmiris.

In fact, the tumultuous and violent changes experienced over the past seven hundred years have left the people of Kashmir deeply scarred. All Kashmiris without exception—those who remained Hindus and those who adopted Islam—have been affected. This traumatic phase of our collective history has resulted in the people having a unique personality that reflects an odd and complex mixture of a variety of traits, all of which are aimed at ensuring survival through difficult and dark times.

Kashmiris, however, remain innocent at heart and, despite the tragic history of the past seven hundred years, display great enthusiasm for mirth and moments of enjoyment—possibly to stay rooted and happy—despite the depressing conditions that they have had to endure for centuries. They are also the kind of people who love to hear and create wondrous stories, songs of love and pieces of satire and, lately, dark comedy. Besides, Kashmiri literature and drama as well as folklore are full of tales and songs of love, heartbreak, valour, and even hope.

This book endeavours to offer a rare glimpse into the lives of Kashmiris—Hindus and Muslims alike—and the ways in which their lives revolved around the simple pleasures of life, even as they dealt with the sociological, cultural, and political changes of the last one hundred years.

The century preceding the 1990s was no less tumultuous than the many past centuries, but the last one hundred years saw the emergence of new geopolitical alignments based on religion and identity and these have had a considerable bearing on the lives and thinking of the people of Kashmir. I have tried to capture the zeitgeist of these past one hundred years through stories and insights that provide a subtle and uncommon peek into what Kashmir has experienced and endured. This I think is a one-of-a-kind effort because, whilst so much has been written about Kashmir—its politics, the errors and omissions of governance, and the events that have led to its present state—most of these narratives give only fleeting glimpses of the simple, dignified, and mostly tough lives of its poor and innocent people. I doubt if any of the political treatises have ever delved deeply into the sociological and human sides of living in the Valley. Most writers have at best skimmed the surface of this aspect, if at all.

I was born and brought up in Kashmir, as part of the well-known Dhar family. The Dhars form a large group, albeit not all of them are related today since the branches diverged many centuries ago. The members of my family's offshoot have been residents of the Valley for hundreds of years, if not more. After the fourteenth century, as Kashmir got caught in endemic tussles between the forces endeavouring to create peace, and the greed, cruelty, and rapaciousness of invader-kings who wished to plunder whatever was worthwhile in the region, my forebears tried to play an active role in mitigating the suffering of the people. They were driven by a deep concern for the people of the Valley and an avid desire to bring an end to the miseries of the people. Not all of them succeeded, and many, including family members of my forebears, had to endure difficult times and long periods of separation—including losing their loved ones—for going against the powerful noblemen and conquerors in Srinagar. In the eighteenth century CE when a number of them intervened to stop barbaric cruelty, many presumed that the Dhars only worked for their self-interest and started to say that, 'When the Dhars are doing well, Kashmir suffers' (*Dhar ābād, Kashīr barbād*, in Persian).

This was clearly used to discredit the role of Kashmiri Pandits generally, and the Dhars in particular, for engaging those in power to make life easy for all Kashmiris. Whether during the times of the Afghans or the Sikhs, and definitely after the Treaty of Amritsar was signed in 1846, Kashmiri Pandits did their utmost with whatever little influence they had to ensure a semblance of normalcy for people.

For me personally, the work and the stories of valour of my forebears and the difficult lives that the people of Kashmir lived inspired me to join politics. In fact, but for short stints, which I spent in other parts of India and overseas, I have lived in and contributed to Kashmir for much of my life. I know the way the people of Kashmir think. I know their fears, their aspirations their enduring desire for peace and harmony, and their fundamental innocence, that yearns for the restoration of a wholesome accord within, and without.

This book is a compilation of stories from the perspective of a witness immersed in the ethos of the land that has historically been called *Reshi-Ver* in Kashmiri. *Reshi-Ver* means the 'Garden of Mystics and Rishis'. The Valley of Kashmir has been known by this name for aeons since it has been a place of great spiritual ferment and a region that has spawned and welcomed mystics, monks, mendicants, Sufis, and philosophers of all denominations and from different parts of the Orient, since time immemorial. The lives of the people revolved around hearing these great and noble saints, who preached love, oneness, and harmony as also living a life of balance. Most people would pursue their simple lives that revolved around agriculture, looking after their families, and often enduring great hardship and poverty. Because of this, most would also spend a lot of time following their spiritual practices, while simultaneously surviving against the normal hardships of life, which was hell without any of the amenities and the advances in medicine that we today take for granted.

When my grandfather built his house just off the Nalla Mar canal in the Safakadal area, towards the last decade of the nineteenth century, he named it Rishi Vihar, meaning the Monastery of Rishis. I am not sure if he was inspired by the name *Reshi-Ver* that was used to describe Kashmir or whether he actually wanted his new house to be like a monastery. Either way, the house became a landmark in the area and remains so to this day. In fact, even the locality was called *Reshan-hār*, a Kashmiri name created from a twisting of the original!

Specifically, the stories and perspectives herein start before the end of the nineteenth century and continue till the end of the twentieth. The epilogue touches briefly upon the reactions of the people of the Valley to the abrogation of Article 370 of the Indian Constitution in August 2019. Many of the stories, however, are from the 1940s and 1950s and cover the two decades of rapid change before and following Indian Independence. I have tried to give a sense of the kind of times that people lived in then, and how the feudal order—which till then was the prevailing social system—was rapidly slipping away even as many of its important outward features and elements were retained and kept intact. Despite the fact that radios and newspapers were beginning to appear in towns and villages, people still remained childlike, innocent and simple, and largely oblivious of the world outside.

Through my stories, therefore, I have also endeavoured to give a glimpse of the Kashmir that my generation, and those of my grandparents, and parents experienced. These past hundred years have been fraught with good periods and not-so-good ones, and include Partition as well as the violence that racked the Valley sporadically since 1947, but took a sinister twist 1989 onwards.

All that I have presented makes one thing absolutely clear— Kashmiris are a people who despite all the tragedies of the past seven hundred years remain peace-loving, fun, and food-craving optimists, and long for the simple pleasures of life with the primary goal to live and let live.

I sincerely hope that you enjoy the stories and the glimpses of Kashmiri life herein, and look at the beautiful people of Kashmir with greater understanding, compassion, love, and friendliness.

Khem Lata Wakhlu
Wakhlu House, Buchwara
Srinagar
5 April 2021

PART I
Peregrination

1

The Lucknow Seduction

In the sprawling neighbourhood that is today nestled between the new Navakadal (built in 1954) and the old 'clean' Safakadal bridges on the river Jhelum in Srinagar was the traditional home of the Dhar clan. The Dhars were an illustrious Pandit family from the Valley of Kashmir. They had been residing in the vicinity for over a few centuries, and their many members had played a leading role in bringing succour to the people of Kashmir over the years, including during the terrible dark years of Afghan rule.

In the late 1870s, a young boy was born to Heemal, the daughter of Divan Nand Ram Tikku. Divan Nand Ram was an influential nobleman who had served in the court of the Durrani Afghans when he was younger and had spent time in Kabul as well as in Srinagar. Divan ji was now serving in a high position in the court of the Maharaja of Kashmir, Raja Ranbir Singh. His own family now had a number of servants and was well-to-do by every standard of the day.

Divan Nand Ram Tikku's daughter was extremely pretty, literate, and talented. In fact, so accomplished was she that well before she was finally married off, all the noble Pandit families—within Kashmir and even outside of the state—would court her father, and ingratiate themselves to him so that he would agree to offer his lovely daughter in marriage to one of their sons. It is said that so renowned was Divan ji's daughter that suitors from far and wide were also known to personally appeal to the father for his daughter's hand.

But fate is a wonderful thing. Divan ji got his daughter married off to a good-looking, smart, and well-behaved, but rather carefree and fun-loving, young lad of the Dhar family in Srinagar. The man was Kashi Nath, and had done precious little with his life thus far. But since the Dhars were themselves a noble Pandit family, with lands and estates to show for it, Divan ji thought that those were sufficient conditions to ensure Heemal's marital well-being.

After her marriage, Heemal, the beautiful Tikku girl was reverentially called Mātā Dyedh (the Great Mother) and soon, much to the delight of the Tikku and Dhar families, she bore Kashi Nath three lovely boys and a daughter. By all accounts theirs was a fairly successful marriage.

The elder son was named Ram Chandra, and the youngest son was called Bal Bhadra.

These children were loved by one and all in both the Tikku and the Dhar families. From their maternal as well as their paternal sides they would receive all sorts of gifts and the choicest of eatables, like dry fruits from the plains of Kabul, delectable fruits from the far corners of the Valley, and rare mushrooms that were only served during feasts. The Dhars and the Tikkus were in fact playing a subtle game of one-upmanship with each other and strove hard, in their own ways, to make an impression on the children.

Both Ram Chandra and Bal Bhadra were thoroughly pampered with all sorts of extravagant toys, fruits and candies, and showered with out-of-season affection. Their mother, Heemal, however, was instinctively very strict in these matters, and would always take up the cudgels with her elders. She was upright, and knew that the surfeit of gifts the children were getting from their elders would eventually spoil them; and it would be difficult for them to grow into well-mannered and disciplined boys.

Deep within, Heemal was concerned. She didn't want her children to become like their father. By now, Kashi Nath had morphed into a good-for-nothing gentleman about town, who would spend time bossing over a battery of servants—all of whom were at his beck and call—and from whom he would demand the most trifling of favours. Heemal, on the other hand, was noble, gentle, compassionate, and very understanding. Every step of hers was graceful. Her words were kind and courteous. She was considerate and compassionate towards everyone. Obviously, the comparison between her husband and herself was one of extreme contrasts. She was loved and respected by everyone—not just those in her family circles, but even by those who visited them and sought her counsel.

Fortunately, the boys grew under her tutelage, and it is believed that her influence alone prevented them from becoming fickle and wayward like their father.

One autumn day, Kashi Nath wished to go to the Kheer Bhavani temple, the ancient spring and shrine situated near Ganderbal to the northeast of Srinagar. He was especially keen to undertake the trip on the forthcoming *Ashtami* day—the day during the bright half of the lunar month when the moon is halfway between the full moon and the new moon—when the shrine would be crowded with devotees and their families from far and near.

The trip was to be undertaken by boat, and Kashi Nath was very eager to take his boys—Ram Chandra and Bal Bhadra—along with him. Heemal did not want to send the children with him alone. She had the apprehension that he may give them a long rope to do things that they were not supposed to do. She knew that her children could be tempted to play with other children at the shrine and Heemal was uncomfortable with this—not only because of their status in society, but also because she was concerned about their safety. The possibility of the kids going swimming and drowning haunted her, especially because there had been multiple such cases in the past. So Heemal put her foot down, and did not agree to send the children to Kheer Bhavani.

'If anyone wants to go there, he may go,' she said emphatically to her husband, 'but I know it is not easy to handle the children while on the boat and in the crowds at the Devi's shrine, and I don't want to endanger them.'

'I'm not going alone! Prasad Ram and Kantha Ram are also coming with me. The children will be safe with us all.' Kashi Nath pleaded for his wife's consent to take the kids along.

Before Heemal could say anything, her mother-in-law entered Kashi Nath's room and shouted in a stern voice.

'I can't understand why you have to take anyone's permission to take the children to Kheer Bhavani.'

Then she looked at Heemal. 'Go and dress them up in time to go. I will also go with them, and it'll be good to visit the shrine this Ashtami.' Sensing the anxiety of her daughter-in-law, Kashi Nath's mother voluntarily took the decision to go along. She was aware that Kashi Nath was quite careless and flamboyant, and would not hesitate to flirt with any beautiful and ready-witted damsel whom he encountered. Her decision to go to Kheer Bhavani with the boys was therefore more to assuage Heemal's concerns and ensure that all parties were happy.

Kashi Nath's flirty and amorous behaviour was a fact that was known to everyone. It was something that Heemal was upset about. Heemal, on the other hand, was serious by nature and given to reserve. This not only gave her an intelligent appearance, but everyone also gave a second thought to whatever she said. She was seen as the wise lady of the household.

The children were excited the moment they heard about the picnic. Ram Chandra jumped on to a nearby chair, then on to the floor. He excitedly picked up a bolster and together he and his brother shouted, 'We're going to go to Tulmul! We're going to Tulmul!' The younger brother, Bal Bhadra, of course didn't fully understand why his brother was so excited, but he followed his brother, shouting with him in unison.

'Hey, we're going after all! Hey, we're going, with Dadi.'

The trip to Tulmul needed considerable preparation. Adequate provisions had to be taken along, and loaded on to the big tonga (horse cart), which would take the passengers to the edge of the Anchar Lake from where a boat would take them to the shrine. Servants and helpers were taken along. Prasad Ram and Kantha Ram were the main ones, but there were a couple of other men too who formed a part of the retinue. Sarvanand, better known as Sarva, was specially deputed to help with the boys, and lend a hand to the others. All of them were getting boxes of kehva tea, biscuits, Kashmiri breads and samovars (large metal urns used to boil water for making tea) from the kitchen to carry along.

The journey to Kheer Bhavani took Kashi Nath, his mother, the two boys, and their attendants over three hours to complete by tonga and boat. Once there, the men quickly set up the *vaguv* mats (woven reed mats) on the stone floor area around the spring, and placed thick namdahs (rugs) on the *vaguv* mats, creating a warm, thick sitting place for Kashi Nath and his family. Being Ashtami, many more families were already present around the shrine, and one could hear children playing and running about.

It has been a long tradition in Kashmir that anyone visiting Kheer Bhavani must savour *luchi* (a sort of thin rolled deep-fried flour roti) and fritters made of lotus shoots dipped in a batter of rice flour—better known in Kashmir as *nader-monje*. This was part of the *prasadam* prepared by the temple cooks that devotees would partake of after they had sought the blessings of Kheer Bhavani—the Mother Goddess and the reigning deity of Kashmir.

In matters of food, Kashi Nath was true to tradition. Upon seeking the blessings of Mātā Kheer Bhavani, he had returned to the padded rugs set up for his family. Upon being firmly settled on the namdahs in front of Bhavani's temple courtyard, he gave orders for the preparation of a meal comprising luchis, nader-monje and kehva tea, brewed freshly in a samovar.

Kantha Ram and his party of attendants had already got busy, knowing their master's preferences well. Very soon, hot kehva, fragrant with the aroma of ground cinnamon, crushed almonds, and cardamom, was ready to be served. The temple cooks had meanwhile prepared the luchis and the nader-monje and the entire family got down to enjoy a hearty meal, next to the divine waters of the Tulmul spring.

Kashi Nath was satisfied. The trip, so far, had gone off well and neither his mother nor his children had caused him too much irritation. He had met with other friends and acquaintances in the shrine. But now he felt full and longed to stretch his limbs a bit and stimulate digestion. He stood up and excused himself, saying, 'I'm taking a round around the temple premises.'

'We also want to have fun, we want to go with you too,' the boys said out loud, and began to move with their father. But Kashi Nath was in no mood to take his children along. He wanted to be by himself, and didn't want any hassles. But the boys kept insisting and clung to their father.

Just to avoid being with them, Kashi Nath quickly said, 'No! You cannot come with me. Sarva will take you along and you can play with him for as long as you wish.'

Kashi looked towards the senior helper who was sitting on the side by the samovars, and directed him. 'The children can have fun over there,' he said, pointing to the open fields adjacent to the temple spring. 'Some children are already playing there. Just make sure that you keep them clear of the canals and Mother's spring.' Sarva was quick to respond, and the boys gleefully followed him.

The main reason Kashi Nath wanted to be alone was to flirt with the many other young women who were circumambulating the temple spring. Kashi had a roving eye, and would glance avidly at many of the young, beautiful ladies wherever he went. This was one of his favourite hobbies. Kheer Bhavani on Ashtami was rich with opportunity.

Sarva, who was very fond of the boys, had a knack for keeping them enthralled with games and fun. In the open expanse of lush green grass that they had chosen to play in, the children were having fun playing hide-and-seek. So far Sarva had been hiding, as the two little boys, with little cloth kerchiefs tied over their eyes, eagerly looked for him. The kids loved the excitement.

It was young Ram Chandra who suggested that Sarva too should take turns to close his eyes and look for them. Sarva agreed, assured that the shrine was a safe place, and knowing that Ram and Bal Bhadra had so far clung together and had even hidden in the same spot. And so he happily tied a cloth over his eyes and told the boys to go and hide.

'Not near the spring,' he shouted, as the excited little boys ran eagerly to find a suitable hiding place. 'Call me when you're ready!'

All three of them were happily engrossed in the play.

Ram Chandra started to venture further away in search of hiding places, and in doing so he completely forgot about his younger brother. Sarva assumed that Bal Bhadra was with Ram, and stayed blissfully unaware that he may have wandered off.

It was Ram Chandra's grandmother, who had strolled towards the field where Sarva and the children were playing, who noticed that Bal Bhadra was still hiding even as Ram gleefully emerged from his hiding place when Sarva pretended to pounce on him.

When Ram asked his grandmother if she had seen Bal Bhadra, she got agitated and began to shout at Sarvanand.

'Where is Bal Bhadra, Sarva? Where is *nikka*, our dear Ballu?'

Sarva looked pale, as he frantically looked in all the places where the children had hidden only a short while ago. 'He was also playing with us, Dadi,' he said meekly. 'I'm sure he's still hiding behind one of those trees.' Ram Chandra pointed to one of the trees where he had last been with his brother. Spontaneously, all three of them began to shout in the direction of the trees.

'Beta, Ballu, where are you?'

'Ballu beta, please come out of hiding, we're going home now,' grandmother said firmly. They started to look around each tree, including those closer to the holy spring. They searched behind the sheds that housed provisions for celebrations, but Ballu was nowhere to be found. Grandmother was now in tears, as was Ram Chandra. Sarva was quickly sent to inform Kashi Nath that there was no trace of Bal Bhadra. It seemed the little boy was lost.

As soon as Kashi Nath heard the news, he too joined all the men who had by now gathered to look for the missing boy. The village elder from the hamlet just beyond the shrine had also suddenly made an appearance the moment he had heard that a little boy from the Dhar family was untraceable. Other villagers too had begun to rush in, dropping their work in the nearby paddy fields, eager to join in the search.

By now the grandmother was distraught. She yanked off her headdress and started to wail, her grey hair sticking to her face because of the tears.

'Where is my baby? Who has taken him? Where are you, my *shoosha*, my dear Ballu?' she cried loudly, as tears rolled down her cheeks. 'Come back to your grandmother, please! Your mother will die if you don't come home, dear Ballu, please come to me, darling.' She was in a desperate agony. Many village women who had followed their husbands to the shrine sat around granny in a circle, trying to console the woman. Some started to cry as well.

By now the news had spread like wildfire, not just within the temple area of Kheer Bhavani but even in the nearby villages. There was panic as people began to conjecture what might have happened to the little Dhar boy.

Everyone was sad about the turn of events, and the villagers especially were concerned about Ballu, as if he were one of their own. Able-bodied men and teenagers alike were searching for the child frantically. All were vying to be the first to find the boy, and be the bearer of good news to Kashi Nath.

However, the search at Kheer Bhavani was called off when it was too dark to look for the child. A crestfallen Kashi Nath, along with his mother and his attendants, reached home in the dead of night and broke the news to Heemal.

Now, the loud crying and shouts of Heemal, along with those of her mother-in-law, rent the night air, and the whole neighbourhood of Navakadal rushed to the Dhar household. Women of the neighbourhood joined the wailing women, and as they cried and beat their chests, one could hear a distraught Heemal crying helplessly and asking nobody in particular, 'Where is my baby? Please, please help us find him! He's my life, my little baby! I wonder where he would be right now...'

Even the men wore ashen faces, not quite sure what they could do to find the boy. The atmosphere was an odd mixture of grief and anger since people began to wonder about the tragic fate that could have befallen the child. Rumours began to spread thick and fast as people speculated about what might have happened. Everyone kept telling Kashi Nath, 'Such a thing—where a lost child, or at least his body, has not been found—has never happened in Kashmir.'

By the next morning, the whole city of Srinagar was abuzz with rumours. Crowds of people were on the roads, clogging the lanes and by-lanes, speaking with one another and eager to catch the latest bits of information about the lost Dhar child that might be forthcoming.

Heemal was still sad but had stopped wailing. Her face was all puffed up from the tearful night that she had had, but despite that both she and her husband were forced to meet the crowds of people who were eager to commiserate with the family. High officials in the state administration of the Maharaja came to Navakadal to show solidarity with the family and offer soothing words to deal with this rare calamity. Many of the ladies who came to visit Heemal and the grandmother were also doing so out of curiosity, keen to gauge how the aristocratic family was dealing with the tragedy. There was an obvious show of sympathy, but often the words were laced with questions that troubled Heemal.

'If a child of a rich and influential family such as the Dhars can get lost and then not found at all, what will happen to poor people like us?'

'Who could have done this dastardly act?' some other women would say, their voices anxious and concerned. 'May the perpetrators be buried alive under sand!' the women would curse, to make Heemal and the other relatives feel better.

Heemal's parents, especially her influential father Divan Nand Ram, had made a plan to determine what had happened to his grandson. He had also instructed a number of his trusted subordinates to scout the villages around Kheer Bhavani and secure as much information about the lost child as they could. Heemal's father was concerned about his daughter's well-being. She had stopped eating since the news was broken to her and hence Divan ji wanted an early resolution of the matter.

As the days wore on, Heemal started to look wan and weak. Her energy was sapped and she spent much of the day dazed and in a stupor not quite sure where she was or what was happening. People in the household would occasionally hear her call out: 'Has Ballu had his meals? It's past lunchtime, why doesn't he come to me for food? Where has he gone? Will somebody bring him here, to me? Why don't you bring my dear Ballu? Come, my darling, come to your mother. Don't play hide-and-seek with me, come, dear, come, your mother will die, come now.'

The atmosphere in the Dhar home was dejected and sad. Everyone was trying to pacify Heemal. Kashi Nath too was completely lost and unsure of how he must behave under these circumstances. All along he was feeling terribly guilty; almost as if he personally were responsible for his son's disappearance. He had paid scant attention to his looks ever since the fateful trip to Kheer Bhavani, and so he too was looking weak and unkempt.

Divan Nand Ram's able subordinates had in the meantime picked up some clues and speculated about how the young Bal Bhadra may have got lost. One theory was that he had been kidnapped for a ransom. Another view was that he had been kidnapped, but not for ransom. All the relatives of the family who had been camping at Navakadal found this information sufficiently meaty to get into further rounds of speculation and rumour-mongering. Most of the relatives had a perspective on the matter. After a few additional days of discussion the big, unanswered question that remained was—who could be the person or the gang that would dare to do the dastardly, uncalled-for act of abducting poor little Ballu? This line of thought brought its own share of anxieties. Young mothers were now fearful to let their children out of their sight, and many little kids were not sent to school. Everyone seemed to believe that the dark days of poor security had descended on Kashmir, and citizens were no longer safe.

Everyone obviously imagined the worst. In their minds people conjured up tales of Afghan gangs operating from faraway places, such as Kabul and Kandahar, undertaking kidnappings. One day, the town was all abuzz with rumours that it was a gang of Afghanis who were responsible for the abduction of poor Ballu. They had come to the Valley specifically to look for small children whom they could pick up and carry back concealed under their rugged cloaks and blankets. And they would then sell them in the open bazaars of Kabul to those who patronized the ancient Afghan game of dromedary racing that requires small boys to be tied to the racing animal. People loosely spread bizarre tales such as this—partly to feel better with a scary, albeit known, possibility than be completely in the dark and at a loss, and remain petrified. For many, the idea behind gossiping in this manner was to show how knowledgeable they were about the world and matters of security. It was only after considerable persuasion by the really concerned relatives that such people would eventually leave, although reluctantly. For most of the garrulous and imaginative people it was great entertainment to be a part of the calamity that the Dhar family was experiencing.

The gossip and the fanciful tales of the hangers-on would eventually find their way to poor Heemal and Kashi Nath at Rishi Vihar. And with each passing day Heemal grew weaker. Her youthful glow was gone and she now looked far older than her years.

The Kashmiri Pandits, also known as Battas or KPs, and the community to which the Dhars belonged, form a very versatile group. They have always been, and remain, an intelligent, industrious, well-educated, progressive, liberal and spiritually knowledgeable community. They are also pioneering in many ways, and demonstrate an eagerness to adopt something novel or modern, especially if it is aligned with their liberal values, and to which they take a fancy. This trait, however, also makes them copycats. Whenever they see something of utility that is different or innovative—a new device, technology, or a way of doing something—they don't hesitate for a moment before adopting it and integrating it with the way they live and work. In fact, they stand out as early adopters and take the lead in spreading worthwhile ideas.

For millennia, this quality made Kashmiri Pandits ever willing to travel outside of Kashmir and explore greener pastures and gain employment, whereby they could use their knowledge, skills, and abilities to better their own lives and make a contribution to society. What may have been a small trickle of people searching for better opportunities when conditions in Kashmir were wholesome and favourable would have become a torrent of emigrating families wishing to get away from certain death or conversion when the conditions became dark and bleak.

Over the past eight centuries, therefore, many KP families found favourable conditions of employment and life generally, in the service of kings, queens, and noblemen across the vast Indian subcontinent, who appreciated their wisdom and their knowledge of the Shastras, and provided them refuge, employment, and support.

KPs can be found all over India, and in recent times in almost every major country across the globe. At the time of Kashi Nath and Heemal, cities such as Delhi, Lucknow, Allahabad, and even Mysuru in the south and Puri in the east had a sizeable population of KPs.

Another unique quality of the KP community is their creativity and the ability to make queer fish of everyone. Pandits were quick to describe fellow Pandits on the basis of some unique features that they displayed. A devout Pandit who followed the ritual of feeding crows after his morning ablutions was given the name 'Kāv', which means crow in Kashmiri, for his love of the bird! Interestingly, over time, his surname and that of the family was changed to Kāv! Many other surnames thus changed. Today, there are some really unusual surnames amongst Kashmiri Pandits. For instance, 'Kyemū', which means insect; 'Braroo', an anglicized verion of 'Bror', which means kitten; and even my surname by marriage, 'Wakhlu', which is an anglicized version of 'Wokhul', which means a mortar (in which spices and grains are ground)!

Being smart and knowledgeable, Kashmiri Pandits have always derived pleasure from showing off their intelligence and their erudition, especially when it yielded the added benefit of 'downing' a rival. Therefore, the unresolved conundrum of the mysterious disappearance of the young Bal Bhadra was obviously sufficiently stimulating to have every adult conjecturing the possible causes of the boy's vanishing, and proffering complex theories to explain what had so far remained a complete and inexplicable mystery.

Rivals sparred vehemently on the one burning question that was on everyone's mind. 'Where and how had the poor little boy vanished?'

In faraway Lucknow, the famous city in the erstwhile region of Avadh, well known for its Nawabs and carefree lives of its prosperous citizens, there is to this day a part known as Kashmiri Mohalla. As Kashmiri Pandits left their native lands and came to Lucknow in search of opportunities and the freedom to practise their religion, they gravitated towards an elegant part of the old city, and over time a KP community was established. (KP communities could be found in many large cities in India. Delhi, for instance, had Sita Ram Bazaar that was home to many Pandit families who had emigrated and come to Delhi from the Valley.)

Kashmiri Mohalla was also home to the Kauls. A family that had probably come to Avadh close to a century ago, the Kauls had received the patronage of the ruling elite and over the next hundred years had grown and prospered. Many members of the family had become reputed lawyers and were viewed favourably by the administration.

Mrs Sumali Kaul was the wealthy widow of the late Mr Kaul, who had served as a barrister in Lucknow city. She and her husband, who had died relatively young, had no children of their own.

When Mr Kaul was alive, the couple had decided to adopt a boy from a high and noble KP family. Over the years Mr Kaul had sent feelers to KP families, not just in Lucknow or Allahabad, but even to towns and cities within Kashmir. They had relied on community priests who would travel to different KP communities to conduct pujās and ritual events to spread the word that the Kaul family of Lucknow was eager to adopt a male child.

Yet, despite their efforts to adopt a boy, the Kauls were unable to meet with success since no family obliged the couple. They tried looking for boys within their own relations, but no one wanted to give away their flesh and blood, and that too a son. After a few years of trying, the couple was very disappointed and heartbroken. Sumali remained sad and despondent. Some believe that it was his helplessness in the face of his wife's agony of being unable to channel her maternal instincts that affected Barrister Kaul's health and he passed away suddenly one day.

Sumali's zeal to adopt a boy acquired a new ardour after her husband's sudden and untimely demise. She now resolved to get herself a boy, and she would not stop until her desire was fulfilled. Soon after the mourning period for her husband was over, she started her quest for a child with renewed vigour. She was so obsessed with the idea of getting a child that she gave urgent instructions to a few priests whom she had specifically called to her home.

'It will bring solace to my late husband's soul if a boy is adopted by me,' she said earnestly. 'I would have been open to a girl child as well, but I want to honour my husband's wish, which was to adopt a boy.'

'I want you to come back to me with your ideas on how I may go about this. And, let there be no doubt that it must be done by the one who has the best idea, before the end of the month of Bhadrapada, so that when we have the prayers for my dear departed husband, my boy must be next to me. The one who sets on this mission and is successful will be rewarded amply,' Sumali emphasized.

For days after she had met with her loyal priests, she kept thinking of her recent conversation with them.

'Would anyone of them take the pains to get a boy for me?' she thought, as she fretted and waited anxiously for any one, just one, of the priests to come to her with an implementable plan. Sumali spent many sleepless nights hoping, wondering, and praying that one of the priests would take up the matter in earnest. She obsessed, 'Who would do this job without any fuss? Why doesn't anyone of the priests come back with a plan?'

A few days later, the seniormost priest of the group that Sumali had spoken to, accompanied by a few of his younger associates, paid her a visit. After an exchange of niceties, and after the priests had all been honourably entertained with sweets and *mathris* and hot cups of kehva served with liberal amounts of almonds, cinnamon, and cardamom, the priest spoke.

'We have thought of a plan. But it will also be an expensive plan to execute.' The priest sounded sombre, and he looked down at the lady's feet as he spoke. His associates nodded together as if on cue.

Sumali perked up. 'You have a plan to fulfil the late Kaul sahab's wish?' she asked, curious to know more.

'Yes, Devi ji, we have thought of a plan. But there is a problem. Which noble Kashmiri Pandit family would like to part with a child? Which is why we believe that we would have to make it worthwhile for the family, with a … ahem … a cash incentive.' The priest was now clearing his throat audibly, visibly uncomfortable with the idea of offering money for a child.

'Why, there are so many good and noble families who are very poor,' Sumali retorted, 'who would be happy to be given some money and the assurance that the child would grow up in a happy, rich family.' She sounded insistent.

'It's a very difficult task to get a Brahmin boy,' the priest continued. 'If I were to get a child from a lower caste, I would get so many boys,' he continued hesitantly, eager to gauge the reaction of the lady to this bold idea.

'How can that be, adopting a non-Brahmin boy?' Sumali retorted. 'Guru ji, would my dear husband have ever approved of such a proposition? I'm doing this only for his soul's satisfaction, and I don't want that his soul should wander any further just because we cannot get a Brahmin child, who I'll raise as our own.'

The priest let this sink in. 'We will need a lot of money then,' he said sheepishly. 'This cannot be done in either Lucknow or Allahabad, I will have to get a suitable boy from Kashmir.'

There was a serious glint in guru ji's eyes.

'I'm going on a pilgrimage to Kashmir later this month,' he continued. 'I'll use my time there to activate my contacts to fulfil your desire, Devi ji,' he said confidently. 'Also, if we have the blessings of Shārada Mātā we may be able to get a nice Brahmin child from a nice and noble family.'

On hearing this, Sumali's face brightened. Her face suddenly seemed to glow with hope and positive energy.

'How much time will it take you to fulfil this noble mission?' Sumali asked eagerly.

Guru ji indicated that he would need some time to figure that out. He looked at his associates, and whispered something to one of them. The young priest, in turn, spoke to the other one. They all opened their almanacs and pored over the pages, turning them every few minutes as if looking for the most auspicious time to have the child enter the Kaul household. Guru ji finally spoke, his chest expanding in a show of authority.

'We'll take at least six months. We will have to conduct the process with the utmost of *shuddhi* (sublimity) and care, and hence we would need to do everything according to the most auspicious times.'

Sumali had heard enough. Deep inside her she knew that guru ji was on to a workable plan. She was even willing to wait a little longer. But there was a condition.

'Guru ji,' she said firmly, 'I'm willing to wait. But you have to assure me that my dear husband's dying wish will be fulfilled.'

After a little pause, she started again, stating emphatically, 'Even if you need more money, don't hesitate to ask for it. Our mission must succeed.'

'Of course, of course, Devi ji,' Guru ji said hurriedly, the mention of money suddenly animating him.

'Money will definitely be needed. Now that's a challenge for me, but somehow I will do this task, no matter how difficult it might be.'

The priest was satisfied that his journey to Haridwar, and onward to Kashmir, would be well provisioned. In his heart of hearts he also knew that with enough money to hand out, he would be able to return to Lucknow with a suitable Kashmiri Brahmin boy for the lady.

Sumali took no time to get the money, which was kept in a tiny, neatly embroidered purse. She opened the purse and let the three shiny gold *mohurs* slip out on to her palm. Guru ji and his associates were looking on admiringly. As she handed over the purse and its contents to the priest, she said, 'Guru ji, this is *dakshina* for the noble mission you are to embark upon. You have a long journey ahead of you and one doesn't know what kind of expenses one may incur all of a sudden. Hence I've given you more than I think is needed. In fact, it's a lot more, so that you are not inconvenienced. Better to be ready for any eventuality.'

Guru ji took the purse in his hand and swiftly kept it in his pocket. It was considered impolite to count money in the presence of the lady of the household. They exchanged niceties, wished each other goodbye, and then without further delay guru ji and his associates left the premises.

With the Kashmiri Pandits leaving the Valley, many learned priests such as guru ji had become itinerant performers of pūja for their clients. For this they were paid well and treated as honoured guests in the households where they were invited to perform rituals. In the winter months, when the Valley of Kashmir was cold and often cut off from the rest of the country due to snowfall on the high mountains, many priests and their families would go to their clients' homes in the plains to stay as long as they wished. Guru ji was therefore used to travelling and had many clients whose hospitality he could rely upon.

Upon entering the Valley, guru ji didn't waste any time in focusing on Sumali's mission. He invited twenty priests to interact with him over a sumptuous meal to discuss the conundrum that he had to successfully resolve.

At the meal, guru ji made a wholesome impact on his brother priests. He spoke about the developments and goings-on in the different parts of the subcontinent that he had recently visited. He spoke about politics, the lives of the people in the provinces he was familiar with, and when he felt that he had made a good impression on the priests who were enjoying his hospitality, he decided to raise the matter that had been weighing on his mind.

Pausing for attention, he spoke first about Kaul sahab, the judge and Sumali's husband, whom he had always admired.

'It was because of Judge sahab that I got interested in the politics of our vast country. Kaul sahab was a great man with a big vision and enormous intellect. May his soul attain *sadgati*. He is no more now. His passing has indeed left a void not only in his home but for the whole of Kashmiri society.'

He heaved a big sigh and began to raise the main topic for which he had called the audience. He continued his conversation and said, 'He has left a fortune for his wife. She has everything worth the name but alas, she does not have a child.'

'Why doesn't she adopt a child?' one gentleman asked him.

'Yes, that is what we want,' he said, with a little pause. 'In fact, the purpose of my coming to the Valley is mainly this. I am indebted to them so much that I don't know how to repay them in this lifetime. Judge sahab was a noble soul, peace be to his memory, in fact it was his wish to adopt a child. But God's ways are unique; he suffered a heart attack that took him away in such an untimely manner. Now it is his wife's duty to fulfil his wish so that he can rest in peace.'

While speaking he sighed deeply. 'Now you have to help me in this task otherwise I will not be able to show my face to the noble lady.'

Guru ji requested the priests to compile a list of Brahmin families with little boys whom he might interact with. He asked for details of the parents of the children. Had any family lost a young mother in childbirth? Was the father alive? Who was responsible for the welfare of the children?

With the help of his brother priests he began to collect the information he needed. Soon he had a KP who's who within Kashmir.

With all the information at hand—with what was known generally and with the additional details he had meticulously compiled—guru ji finally zeroed in on one family. From his records as well as intuitively he knew that a boy from *this* family would please Devi ji in Lucknow no end.

It had been almost four months since guru ji had arrived in Kashmir. He was now getting a little desperate to find a suitable boy to take back to the lady in Lucknow because he felt obliged to fulfil his promise. Besides, he had spent quite a big sum for his wife's and his *yatra* to Haridwar and other places.

Guru ji had played his cards well. By engaging and sharing his mission with his brother-priests in the Valley, he had enlisted them all. Any delay in achieving the objective that fired them all now would be a slur on their collective prestige, and not merely a loss of face for the head priest. The ball was squarely in the court of the Pandits now; the situation was a problem for all of them. They were all committed to finding a solution to the matter without any further ado.

'Who will give away their child to an unknown family—even if they are Kashmiri Pandits—who live in such a faraway place?'

one of the priests asked emphatically, apparently to drive home the complexity of the task.

'Kashmiri Pandits outside the Valley lose many of their samskaras,' another piped in, highlighting one of the less obvious reasons why a family might be reluctant to give their child for adoption. 'Besides,' he added quickly, shaking his head sombrely, 'Lucknow is so far, the family will never be able to see their boy again.'

'There is no doubt that the situation is a complex one,' Guru ji said in his sonorous voice. 'But together we should be able to find a solution compatible with our Shastras.'

The mention of the Shastras had a few young priests looking at each other with some consternation. One of them spoke, his voice cracking with nervousness.

'Sir, I ... I ...' he stammered. 'I ... I think that if ... if ... if we are going to go by the prescribed rules and conditions in our Shastras as well as other regulations imposed by the Maharaja, nobody will be ready to give their child for adoption. Definitely not some ... someone from a ... a noble family.'

The entire group looked at the young priest who had just spoken. The attention from his senior associates made him self-conscious. However, he also felt emboldened and continued: 'There's only one way out ... to ... to solve the problem.'

Guru ji was listening intently. 'Speak up! How can we solve our problem?' All the priests were curious.

'Sir, there is no other way.' The young priest looked at guru ji, hoping that he'd know what he was suggesting.

'What is the way, dear Shambhu Nath? We are all eager to know what's on your mind,' Guru ji was echoing the mood of the group. Everyone was interested to know what solution Shambhu Nath had in mind to get their revered guru ji out of his predicament—a mission that had by now energized the entire group.

Shambhu Nath took a deep breath and paused for effect. 'Sir, the only way is … is … to … to do as King Ravan did. Kidnap. Kidnap a suitable child.'

He uttered these words in one breath and almost stood up after he was done, as if to run out of the carpeted room lest anyone kill him for even thinking of such an inappropriate solution.

'Kidnap a child? Shiva! Shiva!' All were shocked to hear this. 'Are you in your right mind? Isn't there any other way? There must be someone who'd be willing to give up his baby for adoption.'

Almost an hour was spent in the arguments that followed, and the proferring of pros and cons of Shambhu Nath's bizarre idea. There were some in the group who vehemently countered the suggestion.

'If we were to do as brother Shambhu Nath suggests, the entire clan of Brahmins will be brought to shame when people find out! In fact, not only learned priests like us but even the entire Kashmiri people will denounce us for emulating Ravan! Not to mention that such an act will banish our souls from *devlok* and even our ancestors won't forgive us for such a horrible deed.'

When the meeting was finally over, no satisfactory solution had still been found. All the priests bowed, paying their respects to guru ji, and left. Guru ji too was tired and eager to go to bed.

Guru ji was, however, unable to sleep. He tossed and turned in his cot. The thought, the very idea of kidnapping a child, stuck in his mind. He seemed obsessed with it. Try as he might, the thought kept clinging to his mind. He tried to sleep and only managed a few minutes of slumber before he was awakened by his relentless thoughts.

Somewhere during his fitful sleep guru ji began to rationalize the idea. 'If we were to get a boy picked up, I would not be doing it for myself. I'm indebted to the Kaul family. I have to repay them for their patronage. Besides, the child will not remain in the Valley. He will have a wonderful future and of course I will also be able to repay my debt to the family. This is not a sin. This is not for myself.'

In a little while, guru ji's breathing became relaxed. He was sound asleep. His mind was calm, and he had found a workable solution to his predicament.

The next few days were busy ones for guru ji. He was his decisive self once again. He had already contacted Shambhu Nath, the young priest with the slight stammer. He had promised Shambhu a handsome reward if the task was done discreetly and without the knowledge of too many people, and definitely not the brother priests who were part of the gathering at guru ji's home a few days ago. It was also understood that the plot was not to be made public under any circumstances.

'People will forget this event sooner than we think,' Guru ji shared with Shambhu confidently. 'Go forth boldly, and let's do what needs to be done.'

The intrigue had been hatched. It was also executed flawlessly. Guru ji's wife had accompanied brother Shambhu to the Tulmul shrine (aka Tulla Mulla) a few days before Ashtami, the time when Tulmul was teeming with ardent pilgrims and devotees from all over the Valley. Around Ashtami devout KP families assembled at the shrine and set up camp for almost a week, and that situation would provide the conspirators ample opportunity to carry out their plan. The logistics and resources for the kidnapping had all been lined up and the stage had been meticulously set.

As soon as the child was picked up and hidden beneath a large blanket, the tonga (horse cart), which was already in place outside the shrine, took them all to another destination. Instead of going to Srinagar they went towards Awantipora, on the way to the less used Jammu road. Guru ji and his band of trusted confidants too had assembled at Awantipora. With the child in their custody they embarked on the difficult journey to the plains—trekking over the high Pir Panjal mountains—hastily leaving the Valley behind.

From there onwards, God alone knows how many months the band of conspirators took to reach their final destination, Lucknow. It was definitely long enough to have the young boy Bal Bhadra completely forget his parents and his home.

When guru ji and his wife took Bal Bhadra to Sumali Kaul's home, the lady was ecstatic. She was so happy to see the sweet little boy, she hugged him and held him close to her. At one point she even called out to her late husband, forgetting for a moment that she was a widow.

She rewarded guru ji handsomely for his resourcefulness and for having kept his word. The priest was careful, however, not to divulge the exact manner in which Bal Bhadra had been brought to her. Instead, he had fabricated a fairly credible tale, which he shared with the lady and all the other people around her. A consistent theme in his narration was how much effort he and his brother priests had to make to bring the boy to Lucknow. The Kaul family, and Sumali especially, believed the loyal old priest and got busy in caring for the young lad.

Meanwhile, back in Srinagar, the search for the missing boy was still on. It had been over six months since young Bal Bhadra had gone missing, and since his body too had not been found everybody was still hopeful. Heemal and Kashi Nath looked a little weak and older than their years, but had regained their poise and seemed to have reconciled to the loss of their young boy. They became especially doting towards Ram Chandra and ensured that they spent a lot of time with him.

Prayers were held regularly for Ram Chandra's well-being and that of his siblings, as well as for the safe and happy return of dear Bal Bhadra. There was still hope in the Dhar family that providence would help find the young lad.

Around this time, the rumour mills in Srinagar and other main towns of the Valley were working overtime. In hushed tones, it was being surmised that the young Dhar lad had been abducted. Soon more details were emerging from the buzz of gossip. The grapevine was agog that the dastardly deed had been done by none other than a renowned and erudite priest who had come to the Valley in connection with a pilgrimage.

Divan Nand Ram and his resourceful subordinates were quick to pick up leads and hunted for whatever additional facts and details they could get. Once a few leads were acquired much more valuable information was collected, which seemed to confirm that Bal Bhadra had indeed been abducted. Finally, it was the horse-cart driver who gave Nand Ram and his spies a clear account of how he had carried a young boy along with a woman and a priest from Tulla Mulla to Awantipora. The dates were tallied and by now it was clear that Bal Bhadra had been carried away by someone known to the Brahmin priests in the Valley.

Very soon the whole town of Srinagar knew all about Bal Bhadra's disappearance. In order not to be seen as being complicit with the kidnapping, all the Brahmins who were part of the *Mahamandal* of priests and had dined with guru ji a few months ago came to meet the elders in the Dhar family and gave them all the information that they too had acquired. Soon the name of Sumali Kaul of Lucknow was known to all the KP families in the Valley, and more rumours flew thick and fast about what the Dhar family would do to get back their lost boy.

Kashi Nath and Heemal were reassured with all the developments and the news that had been forthcoming. The fact that Bal Bhadra was hale and hearty, albeit in faraway Lucknow, was a source of great joy to Heemal and her face started to show the initial signs of relief and joy.

The Dhar family, along with guidance from Divan ji and other community elders, decided to send some responsible persons from the community to Lucknow to bring back Bal Bhadra after speaking with Mrs Kaul and explaining the circumstances under which the boy had been brought to her. Three persons were identified. They all had the gravitas as well as a good command over the Urdu language, which was essential to ensure that the communication with people in Lucknow, including the police and the administration, would be flawless. It was imperative that Bal Bhadra be brought back and the job completed without any hindrance.

At this stage Kashi Nath put his foot down. He insisted that he should also go with the three people who had been identified to bring back the boy. His argument was simple—as the boy's father it was his primary responsibility to ensure the child's safe return. Besides, he would also bring pressure on the Kaul family and get them to give up Bal Bhadra. Somehow Kashi Nath's point made an impact and it was agreed that he would indeed go to Lucknow, accompanied by the three senior members of the KP community.

The preparations and the journey of the four gentlemen to Lucknow from Srinagar took a couple of months. By the time Kashi Nath was in Lucknow, Srinagar and the Valley were in the midst of a bitter cold and the forty days of *chill-e-baccha* were well under way. Lucknow, in contrast, was pleasant, bright, and cheerful in a way that would appeal to Kashi Nath's temperament.

The party of four reached Kashmiri Mohalla in Lucknow late in the evening. They had travelled a long way, over a span of many weeks, but were glad and relieved to be where they had set out to be. They had enquired from the local temple priest where the community elder lived, and had decided to meet him even though it was late. The group knew that a meeting at a late hour would drive home the importance and urgency of their mission.

Much of the mohalla was quiet. Feeling a little awkward, one of the men took courage and knocked on the door of the head of the KP community in Lucknow, one Pandit Sharga, and waited for a while for the door to open. The four were embarrassed with the din they were making in the dead of night.

'Who's there so late in the night?' someone shouted from inside.

'We've come from Kashmir,' Kashi Nath spoke, looking towards a window where he thought he'd heard the voice come from. 'We're here on an important mission,' he volunteered further, 'and wish to meet you, sir, please.'

The householder could be heard moving around the house, shuffling down what must have been a flight of stairs. Finally, the door opened, and a man wearing a nightcap and carrying an oil lamp emerged.

He was surprised to see the four strangers, who were definitely from the Valley. Curiously, he asked Kashi Nath, 'Whom do you want to meet?'

'We are here to meet Mrs Sumali Kaul and her family,' Kashi Nath replied. 'We've all come in connection with an urgent matter that concerns us and her family. However, before meeting the Kauls, we were keen to share with you, sir—the head of our biradari in Lucknow—some facts which are important for you to know.'

Before the still groggy Pandit Sharga was able to respond, one of Kashi Nath's companions added sombrely, 'The matter is very pressing and we could not have waited till tomorrow.' Then after a slight pause, and hesitantly, he said, 'We've just arrived in Lucknow from Kashmir.'

Pandit ji was surprised.

'You mean all of you have just come into Lucknow just a little while ago? You must all be tired and hungry. Have you decided where you intend to stay?'

'Yes, we've just reached,' Kashi said, 'but no, we haven't had time to think about where we might stay. But with the blessings of Bhavani Mātā we'll manage somehow. Maybe we'll stay in the nearby *sarai*.'

By now Pandit ji's son, a young man in his thirties, had joined his father, probably concerned about who had come to their home at such a late hour.

'Father, who are these people? And whom do they want to meet at this hour?' the son asked Pandit ji, his irritation apparent even to the visitors.

'Son, these gentlemen are from Kashmir,' Pandit ji answered quietly, 'and I wish that they spend the night in our outhouse, and maybe a few days more thereafter till they find a place of their own.'

Pandit Sharga was a well-built man. Tall, fair, and with a mop of grey hair, his appearance inspired obedience. When his son heard his father suggest that the strangers from Kashmir stay in their outhouse, he chose to say nothing but went into another room to get the man-help in the house to guide the visitors.

Pandit ji continued to be gracious. 'Before you retire for the night, we'll make sure that you've had something to eat. I gather that you've come directly from where you were dropped of.'

Kashi Nath was touched by Pandit Sharga's warm and generous hospitality. 'You, sir, are truly a saint and a rishi! We didn't want to waste anyone's time, but the nature of the situation is such that it demanded urgency.'

The group was properly fed a hearty meal, and as they were done eating, Pandit ji ensured that they were made comfortable for the night. Noticing the relief on the faces of his visitors, he reiterated that the travellers stay with him as long as they required to be in Lucknow.

'Please do stay in our commodious outhouse for as long as needed. Those rooms are kept only for the purpose of accommodating visitors.'

After a little pause he added, 'You are our very own people, and since you're coming from afar, it is our utmost duty to make you comfortable.'

Pandit ji was doing what most well-to-do Kashmiri Pandits would do for other Kashmiri Pandits. It was customary to demonstrate kinship among the Kashmiri Pandits. They would go to any lengths to favour other Pandit friends and kin who needed help. It was well known that all the Kashmiri Pandits were interrelated and hence lending a hand was something that was done in the spirit of community kinship.

Pandit Sharga had another reason to keep the visitors at his place for a few days more. Being a curious man, he was eager to extract some more information about the goings-on in the Valley, and was especially interested to know what business had brought Pandit Kashi Nath all the way to Lucknow. Now that the guests were to stay at his place, the conversations continued unabated.

Kashi Nath needed no persuasion to share his story. He narrated all that had happened from the very beginning. As he shared the troubles and the travails that he and his family had endured, tears welled up in his eyes and he sobbed like a little boy. The story was sufficiently interesting and intriguing to elicit the interest of many other members of the host family. Knowing that Kashi Nath and his companions were from a reputed KP family in the Valley, the story acquired a special poignancy and sharpness that gripped the attentive listeners all the more.

The story was narrated till the early hours of the morning, and nobody wanted to stop Kashi Nath midway from giving every fact and nuance of the saga. It seemed that the pathetic and heartbreaking tale of the visitors from the Valley was serving to bond the Sharga family with the Dhars.

By now everyone knew who the boy was, and who the adopting family happened to be. Kashi Nath and his companions were relieved that the Shargas had swiftly determined that the boy was the very one that Sumali Kaul had 'adopted'.

'We were told that the boy was adopted legally,' Pandit ji said with some concern, 'and that the adoption had occurred with the full blessings and consent of the child's parents. Obviously, from listening to Pandit Kashi Nath, the case is altogether different. We need to do something about it.' Pandit ji sounded stern as he spoke.

It was his son who spoke next.

'That is true, Father, but the matter, as you can imagine, is very sensitive. The Kaul family is very influential, and we need to be clear about how to tackle this unusual situation.'

Pandit Sharga pondered over his son's suggestion. The matter was indeed a tricky one and no drastic steps could be taken or else the whole KP community in Lucknow, Kashmir, and elsewhere in the country would face criticism and disfavour. That would bring a bad name to the entire community, and a loss of face for Sumali and her family. Pandit ji was too wise and perceptive to let that happen.

'In the light of the sensitivity of this matter and the potential it has to bring dishonour and undue negative publicity on to our community,' he finally said with considerable gravitas, 'I propose that we handle the matter tactfully. In fact, we should bring all the elders of the community to weigh in and ensure that we arrive at a solution that both the concerned families consider fair and satisfactory. I'm clear that we will need to convene the Kashmiri Pandit Sabha forthwith.'

When the news of the special meeting of the KP Sabha spread, the KP community in Lucknow was all agog. The need for an emergency meeting of the KP Sabha regarding the bemusing situation that Mrs Kaul was in was enough to excite the imagination of the community, and rumours about possible solutions flew thick and fast in the days leading to the meeting of the Sabha.

Meanwhile, Kashi Nath's first few days in Lucknow were spent getting acquainted with the community elders at Kashmiri Mohalla. Kashi Nath and his three companions were all treated with utmost respect. Many asked him for the details of what was now referred to in hushed tones within the community as the 'child abduction' matter. By the time of the emergency meeting of the Sabha, Kashi Nath and his companions knew most of the biradari (clan) elders in attendance.

The meeting of the Sabha was a sombre affair. Most key members of the group had come to attend the meeting. The Sabha had a rule that all matters affecting the KP community had to be discussed together, and the outcome too had to have the support of all members present. This was indeed a unique set of rules governing the meeting, and everyone present therefore was attentive and eager to discuss the outcome.

There were even some senior KP government officials in the gathering whose views and opinions would have a bearing on the matter. These people were respected in the clan and people were walking past them deferentially, with folded hands.

The opinion-makers within the Sabha were broadly divided into two groups. One group held the view that little Bal Bhadra's future was safe and assured within Lucknow due to the good availability of modern education and the fact that he had already come to accept his new home, and any further disruptions in his life at such a tender age would impact his well-being. The other group held an opposing view. The child had first to be restored to his rightful parents, and it was for them to decide what they would like for him.

As expected, the Sabha meeting was fractious. There were arguments from every side, with the pros and the cons of every possible option being discussed thoroughly. Yet after considerable time, and with many divergent perspectives being presented, everybody still remained puzzled and unable to take a final stand on how to deal with the tricky situation, and present a satisfactory outcome to ordeal of the little Bal Bhadra.

Since Sumali Kaul was a respected member of the biradari in Lucknow, no one was keen to openly go against her wishes and thus alienate themselves from her favour. This added yet another dimension to an already complicated problem.

A senior member of the Sabha spoke up.

'In my considered view, in this unusual case, there is no evidence to lay blame on or fault our dear Sumali Devi ji. She was given to understand that the child had been legitimately brought for adoption, isn't it? I am convinced that she has had nothing to do with the kidnapping of the boy.'

'We'll have to find a way out of this conundrum, for the sake of our community,' another senior member said, as he stood up for effect. 'Both the parties need to be satisfied. Nothing short of an amicable settlement will be acceptable to the Sabha.'

Another gentleman then stood up to proffer his perspective.

'I agree that the child's well-being is paramount. Let's not forget that the little boy is feeling completely at home in the Kaul household now. I've heard that he has settled in nicely by now. And considerable time has passed already, more than seven months if I'm not mistaken?'

The meeting lasted for four hours. But a settlement was still not forthcoming.

It was evident that both the parties at the Sabha wanted to have their cake and eat it too. They wanted to keep everyone happy, and not disappoint anyone.

Finally, after much argument and more counterarguments, it was decided that Kashi Nath and the rest of the men in his group would shift to the home of Mrs Kaul, ascertain the reaction of the boy and observe whether he recognized his father.

All through the past few weeks, Sumali had been kept fully informed of the developments by her contacts and relatives in the Sabha. She knew—from her own understanding, and from the comments that had reached her from other members—that hers was indeed a murky situation. There was one thing that she was quite clear about though, that she would not let little Bal Bhadra return to Kashmir. That would leave her heartbroken, and she would forever harbour the guilt of not having been able to fulfil her late husband's wishes.

Soon after the Sabha took the decision to have Kashi Nath visit his child at the Kaul residence, word was sent to Sumali that the boy's father and his fellow-travellers would be visiting her home the next day.

Sumali welcomed Kashi Nath and the others very graciously. She was a wise and charming lady, and as she was unwilling to lose Ballu she decided that she had no option but to greet Kashi Nath and his relatives warmly. This behaviour of hers baffled Kashi Nath. He expected Mrs Kaul to be bitter and angry at the way things had turned out with her 'adopted son'. Her behaviour seemed most unusual under the circumstances.

Kashi Nath turned on his charm as well.

'My son brought me here,' he said politely, 'and it's been nearly eight months since we saw him last.' Kashi wasn't quite sure how to start the conversation.

Sumali responded politely.

'You rest, eat something, get refreshed, and we'll talk later.' Then, after a brief pause she added, 'All will be sorted out in due course of time.'

Kashi Nath noticed Sumali for the first time that day. He had heard that she was very cultured and a woman with good manners. He understood why she was so well respected in the clan. But he also noticed that she was a beautiful woman, with a vivacious spirit and an intelligent, endearing look. Kashi Nath, who had never seen a woman speak so boldly to a stranger, was deeply impressed.

Kashi's mind was racing. 'As a lady she is managing all matters by herself, with not a soul to help her. She is not even ruffled that my son will be taken away from her.'

The little boy Ballu had verily forgotten his parents and his Kashmiri moorings. He no longer had a clue of his home in Kashmir and within the past few months had begun to feel at home in Lucknow.

When Kashi Nath saw him, he could not recognize the boy immediately. He had grown into a very sweet little boy. His hair was longer than in Kashmir, and he looked plump, well fed, and well dressed. Kashi Nath could not believe his eyes. He was equally amazed to see the whole edifice that the lady was handling. 'How is she managing her affairs?' he thought to himself.

Kashi Nath now found himself caught in a very awkward situation. He was completely unsure how he should proceed further in the matter. When he saw Ballu, he went forward to hug him and to take him in his arms. But the boy did not respond at all, which was a shock. He spoke out loud.

'How is it that he behaves like this with me, his own father? Has he really forgotten all of us?'

He was looking towards Sumali with a look of utter confusion and despair.

The lady could read his thought process and gauged the anguish in his disturbed mind. She attempted to console him and reassure him even as she tried to explain little Ballu's behaviour.

'Don't you think that the boy is still very small, barely three years old? How can a boy of this age remember anything about anybody, especially since he's been away for close to eight months?'

Sumali was sympathetic towards Kashi, but it was evident that she'd become possessive about the boy, whom she had come to love very much. Eight months had been enough to stir Sumali's maternal feelings for the child, and she had therefore developed a strong bond with little Ballu.

She was sufficiently wise so as not to offend the boy's father. She paused a bit and then spoke once again.

'Pandit sahab, don't you think we are expecting too much from dear little Ballu? We want the poor boy to behave in a way that's too much for him to grasp in such a short time! These things take time to get settled.'

She was trying her best to handle a difficult situation.

'I am sure,' she continued, 'you must be quite hungry by now. Lunch is ready. I would be honoured to have you join the family for a meal. May we go to the dining room, please?'

With this Sumali got up and strode towards the dining hall. Kashi Nath and his friends had no option but to follow her.

The lady was determined and perseverant. She had a way with people and could influence anyone with ease. Even little Ballu had taken to Sumali like a fish to water. The boy too was, by now, attached to Sumali, and would happily spend time with her, playing as any child would with a loving mother.

It was obvious to the visitors that the boy was very well looked after and had a very bright chance—being in a wealthy household in Lucknow—of growing up in a wholesome, open atmosphere. Even for his studies, Lucknow was a far better place to be in than Srinagar, given its many limitations. Deep within him, Kashi Nath was happy for Ballu, and had even acquired a positive fascination for the place himself.

Sumali was a gracious hostess. Before long, Kashi Nath and his accompanying friends had already been living with the Kaul household for a week, enjoying the hospitality of the grand dame of the house.

Sumali and Kashi Nath had also begun to enjoy each other's company.

'Do you like it here, Kashi ji?' Sumali asked him one morning, soon after they had finished breakfast and Kashi's friends had gone to take a look at the famous La Martiniere School, which Sumali had suggested one evening was the school that she would like little Ballu to attend.

Kashi Nath was touched. He had been deeply impressed by this unusual KP woman, and by now he had started to look at her with a warm, unusual affection—something that he hadn't felt for a long time, and a feeling that he associated with the intimate moments he'd spend with his wife and the many other women that he liked.

'I really love it here,' he said, blushing. Sumali noticed that he was being truthful and smiled.

'Really?' she answered, smiling coquettishly.

'Yes, very much. You've been so gracious to us, and I am truly very obliged and appreciative. You've also taken such good care of our dear Ballu,' he added quickly, eager to make a good impression on his hostess.

That night Kashi just couldn't sleep.

He was happy that Ballu had been found, and was well. He was also assured that Ballu's future was far more secure in Lucknow—in Sumali's loving care—than in Srinagar, with its relative meagreness and hardships. He was also enjoying being in Lucknow, and being close to both Ballu and Sumali.

'What should I do, O Shankar Bhagvan?' Kashi Nath implored Lord Shiva, as he tossed and turned in bed. 'Please show me the way to solve this intricate problem of my son. What should I do, O Bhagvan!'

The warm feelings that Kashi Nath was harbouring for Sumali did not go unnoticed. Kashi's friends from the Valley, who'd accompanied him and had now spent the better part of four months away from home, were getting homesick and wished to return. They were also keen to report about the abducted boy's welfare, and return the boy to the Dhar family with whom they had not been in touch since their arrival in Lucknow.

They broached the topic of their return, along with Ballu, to Srinagar.

'We've been here for a long time now. We should pack up and leave this place, along with dear Ballu.'

Kashi Nath reacted with irritation. 'What are you saying? Do you think, Sumali ji will allow Ballu baby to go with us? We shouldn't forget that she's taking good care of the boy, more than a real mother would. Besides, the boy is attached to her and is unlikely to come with us at all.'

The men sensed that Kashi was himself reluctant to go back home. In their own minds they justified his behaviour, knowing that the boy was, after all, his own flesh and blood and that Kashi would be unwilling to leave him in Lucknow and return to Kashmir without him. That would be a significant loss of face.

Kashi himself was flustered. He needed a strong enough reason for his friends to *understand* why he had to stay back in Lucknow. He struggled to find a plausible excuse that would convince his friends. Finally, he announced emphatically.

'You would agree that our dear Ballu baby should not be taken back to Kashmir. The trauma of relocating to Srinagar, after all that he has been through, would be heartbreaking for us all and will affect him too. He seems to be destined to grow up in Lucknow. Besides, the gracious lady will never ever allow him to go with us.'

Kashi's friends nodded in assent.

'That's what we too have sensed. But we can't stay here indefinitely, can we?' they asked, concerned.

Kashi was relieved. At least a major part of his worry was gone. All he needed to do now was to convince his friends that it would be beneficial for Ballu if he too stayed back for some more time, and returned home when Ballu's affairs were fully settled between him and Sumali ji.

'I'm glad you see my perspective and agree with me,' Kashi said seriously. 'If we all return to Srinagar, Ballu will cease to have any connections with Kashmir and his real home. In a few years he won't recognize anyone of us, let alone his mother and grandparents.'

'So when we get to Srinagar, should we then share with your family that you've had to stay back because of the boy? Is that how you wish it to be conveyed?' asked one of his three friends with a mischievous look on his face.

They all understood Kashi's inner conflict, and wanted him to be comfortable. They had decided to leave for Srinagar at the first opportunity.

When the decision was shared with Sumali, she was overjoyed and relieved of much of her anxiety. The Sabha was suitably informed. Kashi Nath would remain as a guest with Sumali for a little longer, for the sake of the young boy, and all would be amicably settled. The KP biradari heaved a collective sigh of relief.

In her heart of hearts Sumali Kaul was delighted that Kashi Nath would be staying back with her. Her affinity for the handsome man from Kashmir had grown further over the past few weeks, and it was for the first time since the passing of her late husband that she had felt a lightness in her step, and a sense of joyous fulfilment and contentment in her heart.

It took Kashi Nath's three companions almost two months to return to Srinagar. By this time spring had set in in the Valley. The Valley of Kashmir looked as if it had been transformed into a bride adorned with garments of lush green and emerald jewels and colourful ornaments of almond and peach blossoms. The waters of the Nagin and Dal lakes shimmered in the sunshine and reflected the snow-capped peaks of the beautiful mountains around the Valley.

The two men lost no time in reporting back to the eager members of the Dhar family. They presented a very positive picture of how things were in Lucknow and reassured all concerned that the little boy Ballu was being very well looked after. They also explained how Kashi Nath was *forced* to stay back, to keep an eye on the boy and remind him of his roots and his true family in Srinagar. Everyone was relieved and celebrated the good news.

Only Heemal was sure that her husband had found some other interests, aside from his genuine concern for their child that would have prompted him to stay on, away from her.

Days went by, months passed. Heemal's health began to deteriorate due to her worries about her younger son and husband. Ram Chandra and the other children were at her side, but watching them grow up without their father being around was also a cause of concern. Her poor health was quite visible to all in her family.

Despite the news that had been received from Lucknow, the situation within the Dhar household was still fluid and uncertain. What had started as a search for Ballu, had now morphed into one where even Kashi Nath was no longer at home. Nobody knew what was *really* going on out there and this was causing uncertainty and anguish to Heemal in particular. As for others in the family, they were at a loss to determine what course of action would be appropriate to take.

Communication in those days was very difficult. It would take ages to get messages across and usually required letters to be physically carried to the intended destination. The Kashmir postal system was still nascent, having been started by the Maharaja's government only in 1866, but which was not very popular among the common citizens of the Valley around that time.

Kashi Nath's absence was beginning to rankle. Heemal's parents insisted that some action had to be initiated to mitigate the stalemate. Heemal's mother was upset that her dearest, virtuous daughter had virtually become a widow even when her husband was alive.

She would nag her husband.

'You are a powerful man, or so you say. Can't you do anything to bring Kashi back to this place? Do you want our dear Heemal to spend her life yearning for her lost son and husband in this way?

And for how long do you think she can live in this condition? I really can't face people when they ask me about our son-in-law! They ask me strange questions for which I don't have answers!'

Divan ji too was perplexed.

Back in Lucknow, Kashi Nath was living a happy, carefree life. He was in one of the finest cities in India, and revelled in the culturally resurgent atmosphere. For him, a new dawn had risen, and all his charm and many wonderful qualities were suddenly being appreciated.

Sumali's affection, her generosity, and her lifestyle had succeeded completely in luring Kashi to feel at home. He had got well settled in the Kaul household, and all the help in the house had started to refer to him with deference.

In the process, Kashi had forgotten Kashmir, his *real* home, as well as his wife, his other children, and his parents, many uncles, aunts, and cousins who were all part of the large joint family. He was happily engrossed in the spirited and lively atmosphere of Lucknow. He was sharp and quickly picked up the prevalent styles of the noblemen. He mastered the subtleties of the Urdu language, and got fully acquainted with the culture of the elite.

Kashi Nath had always been very fond of Urdu poetry since it was customary for sophisticated gentlemen—aspiring to serve prosperous noblemen in the plains—to learn and appreciate the refined things of life. Kashi too had imbibed the right capabilities. But now, Lucknow provided him the space and many platforms, for someone of his calibre and cultivation, to show his talent.

Within no time he was quite familiar with the poetry-loving gentry and got access to *baithaks*, clubs, and galleries. In his own way, he became quite famous in all the pertinent circles. He was quite impressed with what was referred to as the Lucknawi culture and the

Mughal way of life. In his own humble manner, he even made a small contribution to the prevailing norms of poetry at that time.

Whenever Kashmiris travelled and settled in other geographies, they were always quick to learn new ways of living, lifestyles, nuances of new cultures, eating habits, dress codes, and anything worth emulating. In much the same way, Kashi Nath did not leave a single stone unturned to assimilate the Lucknawi style of the Nawabs. He got busy in business as well since he was already well versed in land matters.

In less than eighteen months after Kashi Nath came to Lucknow he was well immersed in the life of the great city. Sumali and he were now pretty close and he was even behaving like her husband. His presence had made a difference to her life as well. She felt happier than ever—she had a son and a man who loved her by her side. Kashi had also helped Sumali retrieve some of her properties that had been usurped by some people after the demise of her husband. Kashi's cachet had increased considerably within the KP community as well, especially after he secured the lands for Sumali, and many considered him to be fit to be their advocate, their *munsif*, for other such disputes.

Lucknow was treating Kashi well and he was also making money by resolving the land disputes of his clients. Together with Sumali, he was living a happy, contented, and comfortable life.

In Kashmir it was now common talk that Kashi Nath had left his wife Heemal and had remarried in Lucknow. Not just that, other bizarre stories too were floated. Srinagar was always a fertile place for rumours, and juicy, scandalous gossip was quick to get around.

'If this can happen to Heemal, the daughter of a rich and influential man, then any man can dump a poor man's daughter,' was a common refrain.

Other wags had other views, and spoke with derision about Kashi Nath. 'That errant womanizer Kashi is absolutely without any shame! He went to fetch his little boy and was completely taken in by the sweet talk of a woman. She must be some *ḍāyan* [meaning witch, *ḍän* in Kashmiri]!'

In those days public opinion played an important role in the lives of people. The public was, in a strange way, the safe deposit box of the reputations of the high and mighty, and hence anything adverse was something to be avoided at all costs. Those who had reputations to shield would go to great lengths to gag the mouths of vocal people.

The rumours about Kashi were bringing a bad name to his family. The family had agonized on the matter long enough. Action was now imperative. Under the guidance of Divan Nand Ram, the family members agreed that just as Kashi Nath was sent to Lucknow to locate little Ballu, Heemal too should go and join her husband. It was also decided that two trusted persons—Sarvanand and Prasad Ram—who cared for Ram Chandra—would go along with her.

When Heemal heard of this decision, she was overjoyed. Her mood lifted and she felt happy after a long, long time. The absence of any action so far as she had brooded on her fate had left her despondent. Now she saw a glimmer of hope at the end of a dark tunnel.

Preparations for her journey commenced without delay. It was agreed that there was no time to inform Kashi Nath, since Heemal was likely to reach Lucknow well before any mail got to her husband.

Even as the preparations were under way, the family cleverly spread the word that Heemal had been *summoned* by her husband to Lucknow along with their other son, Ram Chandra. This news too spread like wildfire and well-meaning people started to visit the Dhar household to congratulate the family, almost as if poor Heemal was going to get married again!

Within the family, there were mixed feelings of happiness and sadness. Nobody knew how long Heemal would be away. Would her parents and her in-laws see her in their lifetimes again? How would she be received by her husband? Even the journey was long and arduous. Besides, she had a little boy to look after.

There were apprehensions about her being alone amongst strangers in Lucknow. There were also so many unanswered doubts and questions born out of a complete lack of reliable information regarding Kashi Nath.

Yet everyone was clear that Heemal's being in Kashmir and spending her years as a faux widow for no fault of hers was far worse than taking the risk of going to an unknown place like Lucknow.

Finally, all the arrangements were done. Food for the long journey, clothes, water, and some goodies for Kashi Nath were taken along. Little Ram Chandra was excited to be visiting a new place and meeting his lost brother again. Ram Chandra's enthusiasm and excitement along with the wisps of hope in her heart were the only silver lining in the otherwise tough situation that Heemal found herself in.

The day Heemal and Ram Chandra left Srinagar, all their near and dear ones accompanied them up to Qazigund, which the party reached after four days of travel. All the relatives even stayed at Qazigund for a couple of days.

Reaching Qazigund had not been easy. The journey was done on a horse-drawn cart. The road was a muddy, beaten track, which looked like a serpent when viewed from the mountains nearby.

When it was time for Heemal, her son, and the two fellow travellers to proceed from Qazigund, the accompanying family members couldn't control themselves any longer. At the time of parting everyone was weeping, yelling, and sobbing like little children. They all seemed sure that this was their last meeting with Heemal.

Heemal's parents were the last to leave Qazigund. That's when Heemal suddenly felt the pangs of separation and felt overtaken by a sense of unease. For the first time she felt apprehensive about her future. With her parents around she was reassured, but now she felt as if she'd been pushed into the ocean without any guidance or clear directions. She began to weep bitterly. Seeing Heemal in utter distress, Sarvanand and Prasad Ram, who were accompanying her, went near her and began to console her, reassuring her with their kind words. But little Ram Chandra, seeing his mother weeping, and not knowing the reason, began to cry too. The two poor men, Prasad Ram and Sarvanand, were doing all they could to comfort the little boy and get him to calm down.

'You are not alone,' Sarvanand finally said lovingly to the boy, as Ram Chandra rested his head on Sarva's shoulder. 'We aren't dead yet. Why are you worried about anything? We will see to it that you and dear Ram Chandra are settled properly in Lucknow, along with your husband. Till then we won't return.'

Prasad Ram put his hand on Heemal's head, showing great affection and concern. 'You are dear to all of us. No harm will befall you. And until we achieve our mission we won't show our faces to anyone,' he said to her emphatically.

Heemal was soothed and lightened by the kind words of both Sarvanand and Prasad Ram, and was grateful that they were with her. She was appreciative that they were doing all that was necessary to make the trip for her and little Ram Chandra a comfortable one.

Kashi Nath was unaware of the fact that his wife and child were on their way to Lucknow. He remained engrossed in his poetry, his successful enterprise of land dispute resolution, and other extracurricular activities. He was not bothered about his family at all nor was he interested to know about their welfare. He was finding himself like a free bird, one that had been freed from a cage. In Kashi's case, it consisted of the suffocating clutches of his parents and his in-laws.

In Srinagar, he was always overawed by Heemal's father who was an influential man with a big post in Maharaja Ranbir Singh's administration in Kashmir. But in Lucknow there was no one to taunt him or nag him.

Heemal and her retinue took nearly two months to reach Lucknow. While travelling they crossed a few friendly kingdoms and always stayed in the homes of reputed Kashmiri Brahmin priests, who usually maintained a record of the entire KP community within the Valley and outside of it. These priests had maintained these big books for a long time and each subsequent generation furnished details of their family, ensuring that a lineage could be traced back to hundreds of years.

In the course of her trip, Heemal was given considerable information about Lucknow by the many families that she stayed with. She was given tips on the etiquette of the noblemen and women of Avadh, and a few basic dos and don'ts to prevent any embarrassment. She was told to discard her *pheran* (the traditional long gown worn by Kashmiri women) and given a sari to wear instead. The ladies of the host families even taught her how to wrap a sari around her waist.

Despite being educated and lettered, the culture shock for Heemal was considerable. The heat of the plains made her feel weak and listless. Many of the things that she had been taught and those she had observed and picked up seemed strange to her. She felt like she was in a completely alien land and couldn't fathom why her husband had stayed back in the heat and the dust, leaving the cool climes of Kashmir behind. She was yearning to go back to her home, in her heart of hearts. Yet she dared not express her feelings, lest people think that she was either self-centred or mad or both. Besides, having come thus far, she was eager to be with her husband and see her dear Ballu again. Deep inside her, however, there was a gnawing sense of disquiet about her husband's motivations and actions, especially since she was well aware of his frivolous and philandering nature.

It was a bright Sunday morning in the month of October. People in Lucknow were making the most of the weekly holiday. Heemal and Ram Chandra had finally made it to the Kashmiri Mohalla in Lucknow. The Kashmiri priest of the locality, Pandit Shyam Nath, who knew Heemal's father Divan Nand Ram, was deferential and courteous. He and his wife had warmly welcomed them on their arrival and had made Heemal and her son feel at ease and welcomed.

'Beti,' he had said to Heemal, 'please consider this to be your father's home. You are absolutely welcome to stay here till you are united with Kashi Nath ji, and then feel free to visit us whenever you wish.'

For Heemal these words were quite soothing to hear. Yet, she was getting restless and was keen to meet Kashi Nath.

Sensing her restlessness, her host, Pandit Shyam Nath, suggested that she be sent to meet her husband following the traditions of the community.

'We won't just send you to your home like this! You'll have to wait till tomorrow, and we all will accompany you. You haven't forgotten the customs of your birthplace, have you?'

Heemal managed a weak smile. In her lovely cotton sari she looked beautiful, but like someone from a faraway land.

Word of Heemal and her party's arrival, all the way from Srinagar, spread within the Kashmiri community in Lucknow like wildfire. Everybody from the community began to visit the 'newcomer' from Kashmir. Heemal met them all amiably and looked innocent and beautiful as she made polite conversation with many of the members of the community who'd come to meet her. Many knew her illustrious father well, and were curious to see his daughter.

When Kashi Nath heard about Heemal having arrived in Lucknow he was dumbfounded. His mind was racing.

'She's here? How? Why? What should I tell her? How can I explain why I've not been in touch with her?'

Sumali Kaul too was caught completely off guard. She was very disturbed for a few days after the news of Heemal's arrival reached her. She was now concerned, once again, about *her* boy. She was fiercely attached to him and could not fathom parting with him.

She strode into Kashi Nath's room and spoke to him angrily.

'Do you know that your wife and son are in Lucknow?'

'Yes, I heard the news too,' he said sheepishly. 'She's been staying at the home of Pandit Shyam Nath for the past few days. She is accompanied by my very own Sarvanand and Prasad Ram.'

'So why is she here?' Sumali responded, her anger still evident.

'I don't know, really! I had no clue that she and Ram Chandra were coming. In fact, I was hoping that you'd tell me what I should do now.' Kashi Nath's helplessness, frustration, and annoyance were writ large on his face. Sumali could read his expressions easily and knew that he was genuinely in a quandary.

'Don't waste any time now. You should go to Pandit ji's house and bring her here.' She was now commanding Kashi. He had become dependent on her, which she knew. There was no point in arguing about this topic, since he himself was unaware about the whole thing.

'What!' Kashi responded incredulously. 'You want me to bring her and Ram here?'

He was cursing Heemal in his heart of hearts, but could not express his inner feelings to Sumali or to any of his friends.

Sumali was emphatic. 'Yes, bring her and Ram here without further delay.'

'Are you sure?' Kashi asked, unable to fathom Sumali's mind.

'Yes, I'm very sure,' she said firmly.

While Kashi was getting ready to leave, Sumali nudged him.

'Welcome Heemal wholeheartedly. Hug your son. Don't show that you're unhappy to see her. I don't want people to spread any more slanderous rumours about us than they've done already.'

Kashi knew that Sumali had a unique way of welcoming people whom she didn't know, but he was still a little puzzled. She was now relaxed and completely in control. As Kashi was about to step out of the house, she spoke out, 'I'll keep everything ready to welcome her.'

As Kashi Nath was being driven to Pandit Shyam Nath's home in a horse-drawn phaeton, his mind was racing.

'How can I pretend to be so relaxed and happy to see Heemal and Ram? I'll have to do a bit of a drama, that's what Sumali has suggested. How will poor Heemal respond? She was always good to me. It was her domineering father who was always naggiwng me. That's why I hated him. And Heemal, she'd always take his side.'

Once he entered Pandit ji's home, Kashi Nath was surprised to see many pairs of shoes on the threshold of the outer door. This could only mean that Pandit ji had a lot of visitors. The thought that there'd be many others inside made Kashi nervous.

But as soon as Kashi took off his shoes and stepped inside, Ram Chandra came forward running and laughing and hugged his father with innocent enthusiasm. Kashi Nath was amazed to see his son who had not just grown taller, but seemed so much more mature. Kashi forgot everything that he had been imagining and tightly hugged his son. One by one the guests in Pandit ji's home came out and hugged him and offered him their blessings.

Prasad Ram and Sarvanand were also overjoyed to see Kashi Nath. They shared all the news about the loved ones back home, and proudly gave him the details of their journey to Lucknow.

When Kashi Nath had heard from them, he enquired, 'So, even as you were diligently planning for the journey, didn't you think it would be important to inform me beforehand?'

'The journey was meant to be a quick one,' Prasad Ram said, 'and frankly there was barely enough time to prepare fully. We were also told that the postal system would have taken longer than us anyway, so we didn't send any information.'

Kashi Nath was relieved and glad to have had a chat with Prasad Ram and Sarvanand. He was brought up to speed on all that had happened in his absence in Kashmir. Both the men also gave him the lowdown on the rumours that were circulating in the Valley in his absence.

'In fact it was the endless rumours that prompted Devi Heemal and us to leave Kashmir hastily,' Sarvanand added for effect.

Kashi Nath spent much of the day at Pandit Shyam Nath ji's home. He had seen Heemal and given her a weak smile. Much of his attention was on Ram Chandra, who was also delighted to be with his father again.

Pandit ji's gracious wife was warm and courteous and made sure that they all had lunch together. The sumptuous meal was followed by the traditional pink salt Kashmiri tea—*sheerchai*. The conversation eventually revolved around Heemal and Ram Chandra joining Kashi at his home, to which the tutored Kashi readily agreed.

At six in the evening, Kashi Nath, his wife Heemal, Ram Chandra along with the two attendants as well as Pandit Shyam Nath and his wife all proceeded to Sumali's place. Seeing all the people in a procession, a congenial Sumali, who was also temperamentally quite amiable, welcomed the visitors kindly. When she saw the innocent, cherubic and beautiful face of Heemal, she was quite reassured.

She knew there and then that there would be no threat of conflict between her and Heemal.

In the days that followed, Sumali's home had a string of visitors. Members of the Kashmiri Pandit Sabha made sure to tell her that they had a role to play in the manner in which the complex case of Ballu had been settled. At the same time, Heemal was bombarded with suggestions. Sumali knew that all these were well meant and wished to make Heemal feel comfortable in the new environment. Yet she wanted to know what Kashi Nath had in mind. So far she had no clue.

'Beti, Lucknow is your home now,' an elderly member of the Sabha said to Heemal genially. 'You have to forget Kashmir for some time, at least till your sons' education is over. It is their future you need to focus on.'

Like an obedient girl Heemal would nod her head in affirmation. She had ideas but she was still getting used to the place and dared not let her mind be known.

Fortunately, it was without any hesitation that Ballu hugged his mother and stayed in her lap till she told him to go and play. Both the boys met each other as if they had never parted. They were friendly, unaware of what had befallen the entire family during this whole period.

―――⁂―――

For about a week the visitors came.

By now Heemal had again forged a loving bond between Ballu and herself. She had taken pains to have her two boys also connect with each other and play together again, like they would in Kashmir. Heemal and Sumali had also developed a strange acceptance of each other that was simultaneously respectful but not fully open as yet, and the conversations were still stiff and infrequent.

One evening, after the boys were asleep and dinner was over, Kashi Nath walked into Heemal's room. He sat down next to her on the divan where she was seated and started to have a conversation with her. Unlike in the past when he would speak to her in Kashmiri, he queried her in Hindustani.

'*Aap ko yahan theek lag raha hai?*' (Are you comfortable here?)

But before she could answer or before even Kashi could ask her more, Heemal began to weep and cry out so loudly that her sobbing was heard all over the house.

Poor Kashi Nath stood up nervously. He was anxious to pacify Heemal, lest anyone—especially Prasad Ram and Sarvanand—should think that it was he who had brought her to tears.

He began to cajole her. He spoke to her reassuringly.

'Now, now! Please don't cry! All will be fine now that you are here, with me, with us.'

Heemal was quiet now.

Kashi continued.

'All along I'd been thinking of bringing you here. My problem was really about how I could return home without our dear Ballu, whom Devi Sumali loves and takes care of so well.'

While Kashi uttered these words Heemal stiffened and gave him a stern look. Just through her body language she was making it known to him that she knew he was lying.

Kashi Nath sensed her anger rising and thought it prudent to keep mum. He didn't want to throw himself into an ugly argument.

The lives of Kashi, Heemal, and Sumali as also those of Kashi's and Heemal's biological children were now intertwined through a strange act of providence. The aim of this 'new family' in Lucknow was to ensure that the children were educated in the best possible manner and in the relatively modern ambience of Lucknow. With more members—his wife and children—with him and Sumali in the household, Kashi Nath started to become even more responsible and devoted his energies to earning more than before. That was a wise decision since the needs of the family only grew with time.

Both the boys now attended a good school nearby. It was also decided that Heemal should learn the official language of Avadh, which was Urdu, and which was also largely used for documents prepared by the administration. A retired KP teacher proficient in Urdu was accordingly engaged for Heemal to learn, read, and write in the new script.

The days passed, months and years too, and the family stayed happy and comfortable even as the boys grew up into teenagers, and Heemal and Sumali grew closer and bonded like sisters.

During these years, Kashi Nath's parents and Heemal's parents passed away. The news of the passing on of their loved ones took time to reach them. While they knew that there was nothing that they could do about the sad news, the pertinent rituals were still followed.

The Dhars in Lucknow saw many springs, monsoons, and summers pass by. The large estates in Kashmir were forgotten. News would trickle in that the lands were being usurped by relatives and others. Kashi Nath was also older now and couldn't imagine himself going back to Kashmir to secure what was rightfully his. Another reason was that Kashi Nath by now was earning well. He had also burnished further his reputation as a poet and as a nobleman. To maintain his status it was necessary to spend money, and this he did without let or hindrance.

Heemal by now was reconciled to the ways of her husband. She yearned for Kashmir much more than Kashi did and still maintained the values from her *real* home. Hers was a frugal and dignified lifestyle, which was a complete contrast to the jaunty ways of her husband. She hoped that when Ram Chandra, whose affection for her was immense, graduated he would take her to Kashmir.

Ram Chandra was now a strapping young man. Polite, gentlemanly, dignified, and intelligent, he had acquired the good looks of his parents and was always at the top of his class. Despite his youth, he possessed the maturity and wisdom of one who was older, and many sought his opinion on crucial matters.

Bal Bhadra, in comparison, was peacockish. Over the years Sumali's fondness for the boy had resulted in his getting pampered by her and he had begun to identify himself as the 'rightful' landlord of the house. Besides, he was mediocre and would not give importance to studies. He was quite satisfied emulating the ways of his easy-going father.

Suddenly one day, Prasad Ram's son, Maheshwar, came from the Valley to surprise all of them. No one was expecting him. Like Heemal, almost twenty-odd years ago, he too arrived unannounced.

When he met with Heemal, she didn't recognize him at first.

'I'm Maheshwar, the son of your Prasad Ram.' Heemal's eyes brightened as she realized that the older boy whom she knew as Ram Chandra's playing companion, especially after Ballu's abduction, was right there in front of her in Lucknow. Maheshwar had become a young man and had many of the same features as his father.

Heemal smiled at him.

'Look at you! You've grown into a man!' she said fondly. 'After how long am I seeing you? You were just a boy when I left Srinagar.'

She hugged him like she would hug her own children.

'How are our loved ones in Srinagar and elsewhere in the Valley?' she enquired. It was evident that she was really happy to receive Maheshwar. It had been ages since someone from her home in the Valley had dropped by. Heemal too had grown into a middle-aged woman but her beauty had not faded.

After Maheshwar had rested he shared the news that he had actually travelled to Lucknow to convey.

'All's not well in the Valley,' he started. 'Your *jāgeers* and the orchards in different places have been usurped by your [Kashi Nath's] cousins. After the demise of your esteemed father, respected

Divan ji, all went downhill. Till my dear father was alive, the other side of the family dared not do anything. But after the demise of Divan ji as well as the passing on of your loyal Prasad Ram, they got emboldened and openly grabbed the entire estate.'

This news hit Kashi and Heemal like a rock.

'My own cousins usurping our lands and orchards?' Kashi Nath was incredulous. 'Why would they do such a thing? I'm still alive! How dare they do this!'

Tears welled up in Heemal's eyes as she saw her husband's face. She sensed that Kashi too was burdened by the thought of being betrayed and defrauded by none other than his own kith and kin. His forlorn look stirred her to the extent that she began sobbing like a little child.

Poor Maheshwar was sad that it was he who had to be the harbinger of the unhappy family tidings. He was duty-bound to do what he did. He knew his father, Prasad Ram, had been a loyal and trusted part of the Dhar family and he was keen to continue to be of service to the family he too loved very much.

With the developments pertaining to his family's landed properties, Kashi Nath was in a quandary. He grappled with how best to deal with his land-grabbing cousins, while not affecting the well-being of his family.

Once again, the KP Sabha was convened. All the elders of the community came to give them their perspectives and the pros and cons of taking action as well as of letting things be. From his own experience, Kashi knew that if he did not return to Srinagar permanently, his family would have to forfeit any claims that they had on the lands. Many in the Sabha too reinforced this point. The lands were valuable and too big a stake for his family to relinquish their rights to them.

Fortunately for the family, it was only a few months later that Ram Chandra graduated with honours from his college in Lucknow. In the course of meeting his principal, an Englishman, he had shared his family's concerns about whether it would be prudent for him to return to Srinagar. His father had expressed that his prospects were far better in Lucknow than in Srinagar.

Yet, fate works in strange ways. The principal, moved by Ram Chandra's situation, wrote a recommendatory letter to the Divan of Maharaja Sir Pratap Singh, the King of Kashmir, suggesting that the young Ram Chandra could be of immense help in improving the quality of school education in His Highness's territories.

In those days such letters were like appointment orders. Kashi Nath was now relaxed about his eldest son's prospects, and decided to return to Srinagar with Heemal, Ram Chandra, and Bal Bhadra. Sumali was to stay in Lucknow, but she extracted a promise from Heemal that they would visit her as often as they could.

It was twenty years after Kashi Nath set out in search of his abducted son that his family and he, accompanied by Maheshwar, undertook the journey to return to Kashmir.

Back in Srinagar, matters moved quickly. Ram Chandra was appointed to a position of importance, looking after education in the state. However, the home that Kashi Nath had left a quarter of a century ago didn't feel like home any more. Ram Chandra also decided that it was time for his parents, his siblings, and him to have a separate home of their own.

Keshav Lal Kak, who was a dear, albeit older, friend of Ram Chandra, and well versed in dealing with matters related to construction, civil works, and contractors was entrusted with the task of planning and supervising the construction of the new house not far from the banks of the Jhelum river and very close to the old Nalla Mar canal. The house was finally ready sometime in the early 1900s and was named Rishi Vihar.

Around 1893, Keshav Kak too was blessed with a boy, whom he named Ram Chandra. Interestingly, Ram Chandra Kak grew up to become a renowned archaeologist who conducted numerous excavations within the state. He also served as the Prime Minister of the state of Jammu and Kashmir from 28 June 1945 to 11 August 1947.

2

Treacherous Trips: In the Service of Humanity

It's well known that Kumārajīva, the son of Kumārāyana—the Kashmiri monk in ca. fourth century CE—was responsible for the spread of Buddhism through much of western China and the rest of the kingdoms to the east of the Taklamakan region. Kumārāyana, who was a learned young monk, travelled to Kuchea (the regions that are east of modern-day Aksu in the Xinjiang region of China) along some of the prevalent trade routes from Kashmir to Central Asia. Once the Pamir mountain range—near present-day Tajikistan—has been crossed and one heads in an easterly direction across the Taklamakan plains, one reaches the beautiful and peaceful region of Kuchea.

In a short span of time, after Kumārāyana reached Kuchea, he became the chief priest of the king of the region. He must have been very impressive in his erudition, because soon after he was offered the hand of the king's sister Jivaka in marriage. Kumārajīva was born to them.

Young Kumārajīva and his mother—the Kuchean princess—travelled to Kashmir for his education. In the benign presence of his grandfather, fondly known as Tāthya (the loved one) and an array of renowned teachers led by Bandudattā, Kumārajīva attained mastery of the Buddhist scriptures in a little over three years. He returned to Kuchea thereafter, and took the entire region by storm with his wisdom and insightful understanding of the Buddhist doctrines and canons. He translated most of the notable Buddhist texts into the language of the region, and helped spread the teachings of the Buddha across the length and breadth of China.

Since time immemorial, travelling away from Kashmir and traversing difficult routes to reach newer destinations has been a way of life for many Kashmiri men. Kashmiri Pandits, in fact, have been conscious travellers for over two millennia, if not more. Our forefathers would wilfully travel to regions beyond Kashmir, seeking the patronage and backing of wise kings whose kingdoms would benefit from the scholarship, learning, and administrative acumen of the Pandits. Peregrinations were undertaken in small groups, but mostly solo.

Before the advent of Islam, when Kashmir was populated by Buddhists and Hindus and when the population was akin to any Hindu samaj (community) across the subcontinent, the motivations to travel were many. Some would leave the confines and security of their homes to seek better fortunes outside; some others would go on to spread their knowledge or their extraordinary skills in temple architecture, sculpture, painting or whatever else they were adept at; while many others would be invited by learned people elsewhere (to Kasi, Ujjain, Leh, Puri or Lhasa, for instance) to provide guidance in writing books and for translating Sanskrit or *Shārdā* texts into the local languages of the respective regions.

Our forefathers were intrepid in their commitment to *Dharma* and would go forth boldly to different lands. History is full of tales of brave, learned, and determined Kashmiris (see the aforementioned short glimpse of the life of Kumārajīva) facing utmost risks to pursue their goals—not just for themselves or their loved ones but for the well-being and betterment of humanity.

The movement of Kashmiris outside of the Valley became a flood of migrations during times of misfortune. The conversion of Kashmiris to Islam happened through waves of unspeakable brutality, spanning about two to three hundred years. Starting from the twelfth century CE, it saw many Pandits and Hindus move lock, stock, and barrel from the Valley. All were driven by a desire to flee persecution and the extreme penury that had befallen them, especially as the temples, the gifts to the deities, and the temple lands that they and the larger community looked after and depended upon got destroyed and usurped. In fact, many gifted and renowned sculptors had their hands and arms chopped off by overzealous conquerors because idol worship is prohibited in Islam. Many such people were therefore forced to flee. Priests too were prohibited from praying at riverbanks and other sacred places, thus reducing a vibrant samaj to utter hopelessness, despondency, and poverty. Besides, with no patron kings to use their services and with the Hindu samaj—the people who venerated and supported the priests and the learned ones—having mostly become Muslims, the dangers of survival were genuine and dire.

It is said that during the darkest period of the persecution of the people of Kashmir, so great was the migration from the Valley that only eleven Pandit families (*kahey garè*) were left across the length and breadth of Kashmir.

The states of Jammu, Kashmir, and Ladakh were unified and formed as a well-demarcated kingdom in 1846 as a result of the signing of the Treaty of Amritsar on 16 March 1846 between a wealthy and powerful commander (as well as an erstwhile prime minister) in the late Maharaja Ranjit Singh's service, Raja Gulab Singh Dogra of Jammu, and the British officers loyal to the British East India Company. This was the second Treaty of Amritsar that the British signed, the first one having been signed in 1809 with Maharaja Ranjit Singh, curtailing any expansion by the powerful Sikh king south of the Sutlej river. Following the signing of the first treaty in 1809, the British troops maintained a continuous presence on the southern bank of the Sutlej and remained there till the time of Maharaja Ranjit Singh's demise thirty years later. Throughout the three decades, the British forces extracted tributes from the local rajas and communities that they were ostensibly protecting from Maharaja Ranjit Singh.

Raja Gulab Singh became the first Maharaj of the new kingdom of Jammu, Kashmir, and Ladakh. He was already familiar with the territories that were now a part of his kingdom, since he and his general, Zorawar Singh Kahluria, had subdued the regions to the east of the Punjab, and in the north all the way to Skardu and Gilgit, on behalf of Maharaj Ranjit Singh some years earlier. Besides, Gulab Singh was a Jamwal Rajput from Jammu and had familial and community affiliations with many of the families in the region.

The administrative and economic restructuring of the new kingdom of Jammu and Kashmir (also known historically as Kashmir) would have started soon after Gulab Singh subdued the rebellious Sikh Durbar–installed governor of Kashmir, Sheikh Imamuddin, and some of the lesser rajas of Rajouri and Rampur. It was only after November 1846 that Gulab Singh's reign began in earnest.

Gilgit and the northern regions of the kingdom, however, continued their rebellion and till the end of the reign of Gulab

Singh, in 1857, the Indus river formed the northern frontier of the kingdom.

It was only during the reign of Gulab Singh's son and successor, Maharaja Ranbir Singh (1857–85) that Kashmir forces under General Devi Singh advanced beyond the Indus and captured Gilgit in 1860. The regions further north and bordering the western regions, comprising Chitral and Kafiristan, were included through military action only by the 1890s.

Administration of the far-flung areas of the kingdom required educated, articulate, trustworthy, and capable officers to manage the affairs and maintain contact with key people in these areas. Health centres, police stations, post offices (introduced as modern message-sending services in the state of Jammu and Kashmir as early as 1866 during the reign of Maharaja Ranbir Singh), revenue collection and land record centres, and schools (however rudimentary) required people to man them and ensure that some basic level of the administration's writ was discernible. Since the Kashmiri Pandits were relatively better lettered in Persian, Hindi, Urdu, and Sanskrit (and later English), and could also speak Kashmiri fluently, many of the critical positions created within the administration were occupied by them. These were not easy positions to be in since in most cases the incumbent would be posted all alone, with a limited staff of both Hindus and Muslims to provide the services to the people on behalf of the Maharaja's government. Family members would always be left in the bigger cities (Srinagar, Anantnag, Sopore, and later Jammu) to look after ageing parents, uncles, and the children. Contact with the breadwinner was limited to no more than a visit or two per year, but it was still preferred because it provided sustenance to an entire family and ensured that the large family could make ends meet without difficulty.

The regions to the north and west of Gilgit were in a state of constant flux for several decades preceding the subjugation of Gilgit by the Kashmir forces in the 1860s. Russia, using the Cossacks as their allies, had started to attack and make inroads in various parts of Central Asia. By the time Maharaja Ranbir Singh was reigning in Kashmir, Russia had become even more active, and was trying to enhance its influence in both the Central Asian regions and further south into Afghanistan and the western frontier of India.

These were alarming developments from the perspective of the British in India, and the intelligence reports gathered by its military personnel, notably Captain John Biddulph of 19 Hussars, in the early 1870s, convinced the British that the 'insatiable maw of the Muscovites' could only be curbed by having the kingdom of Kashmir allow the functioning of a British political agent in the Gilgit region, so that the interests of the British government could be directly managed. The political agent was to work with the local chieftains and tribal heads in the neighbouring regions, and ensure that suitable alliances were formed that would serve the best interests of Her Majesty's Government in India. Maharaja Ranbir Singh was consulted in a series of meetings in Madhopur (Jammu) in November 1876, and with his acquiescence, the state of Jammu and Kashmir leased Gilgit and the adjoining areas to the British in 1877. Major John Biddulph, who had by now been promoted for his services, was appointed the first political agent of the Gilgit region. This arrangement continued all the way till India became independent in 1947. The British agent relied on trained and committed officials and soldiers from the Maharaja's administration and troops to carry out his duties.

It must have been the winter of 1934. The Valley of Kashmir was cut off from the entire world during those cold months. Despite advances in telegraphy and the investments made by the state in having more runners and postal centres along key routes from Jammu and Srinagar, communication was still rather poor and definitely inaccessible to most of the common citizens. News about the goings-on in the world would trickle into the Valley at a snail's pace and by the time people got the news, it would have become stale and lost its currency.

There was, however, one (and the only) reliable means of receiving news and information, and that was through the radio. The British government had allowed private broadcasting from Bombay and Calcutta in 1927, but just three years later the Indian State Broadcasting Service was set up. It eventually became All India Radio in 1936. However, radios in Jammu and Kashmir were a rare commodity, and not everyone could afford them. Only well-to-do families had them, and they used to receive transmissions from powerful stations all over the globe. Radios in those days were large and bulky, and therefore kept in a big hall so that everyone in the mohalla would come at a particular time to hear the latest news about the goings-on in the country as well as around the world. Listening to the radio was also a time for family members and neighbours to get together, gossip, and comment on the news, almost like one would do in a coffee house or a club. The elders would typically comment on the politics of the world and the actions of well-known leaders, while the children—listening in keenly—would pick up titbits of valuable information on politics and the behaviour of world figures.

This was the time when the people of the Valley were generally peaceful and not touched by the many vagaries of the outside world. They were living in their own little worlds, making the most of the time, pursuing the simple pleasures that they would encounter in their daily lives.

Kashmiri Pandits, since time immemorial, have given education considerable importance and attention. It was erudition that enabled Kashmiri Pandits to find employment in kingdoms far from home. It is also what sustained them after other means of income from the traditional work of praying and conducting spiritual rituals and rites for society no longer remained an option.

With the advent of the British, the study of English gained importance and many KP men, and a few women too, would go to places as far away as Lahore, Lucknow, and Allahabad to study subjects in that language and gain mastery over them. Knowledge of English was seen as an essential competence for young people looking for employment, and therefore it caught on. With it, an interest in English literature started to emerge and a whole class of Pandits, and erudite Muslim families as well, emerged, who not only spoke English like Britishers but also started emulating their ways of life. By the mid-1930s, it became very prestigious to know the English language well. Maharaja Hari Singh, who was coronated in 1925, made education an important state policy, and hence the language was taught in government schools and colleges and became the medium of education as well.

Not surprisingly then, in the early twentieth century, Shakespeare's plays and poetry and those of other renowned English writers were known to the English-educated class of people, and quotes from these works were routinely used to make an impact during conversations. By exhibiting their knowledge of the literary works of English writers, educated Kashmiris would demonstrate that they were quite modern and adept in the latest in English literature.

Maheshwar Nath was an intelligent young Pandit boy, just out of college, who was bubbling with ambition and a host of modern ideas that he had picked up from the many books that he had read as a student. He was a voracious reader and could read English, Urdu, Hindi, and Sanskrit with ease. He had recently graduated with good grades and was eager to go outside of Srinagar to further his education. He wanted to pursue a master's degree in English literature. He had planned to go to Lucknow to study further, but his father was opposed to the idea and didn't approve of Maheshwar Nath's proposal.

Not being able to study further rankled Maheshwar Nath for a really long time. In fact, this was one of his bigger regrets in life—being unable to go to Lucknow for an MA degree.

Once he reconciled with his circumstances, he applied for a job in the newly formed Department of Irrigation in the Maharaja's administration. At that time, the department was headed by an Englishman, Mr Thomas. He had been specifically brought in by the Maharaja to ensure that the state could make full use of its ample water resources for the sake of enhancing agricultural productivity.

Mr Thomas was an engineer by profession and was looking after the entire department. He was looking for an able and energetic personal assistant, who would do a good job of writing proposals, managing the office and all the correspondence, and typing. Young Maheshwar Nath, who had applied for the position, was eager to start his career and contribute to his family financially.

During the interview for the position, Mr Thomas took an instant liking to Maheshwar Nath who was lucid and articulate. Mr Thomas could also discern that the young man had a sharp mind, was a voracious reader, and well versed in English literature. Maheshwar Nath was also gifted with a sturdy common sense and that became very useful in helping him interpret engineering project proposals and prepare summaries for his superior's attention.

In a short span of working together, the two of them developed a good equation and worked effectively as a team. Maheshwar Nath's grasp of matters and his ability to draft memos, issue orders, and send letters on behalf of his boss to the heads of various divisions in the state enhanced the department's productivity and delighted Mr Thomas.

A couple of years later Mr Thomas was asked to work out of Gilgit for a period of three years. The British agent had committed to the local tribal chiefs that he would improve the lot of the people in the region, and enhancing the area of arable, irrigated lands was an effective way to go about it.

Mr Thomas had to choose the staff for his new office at Gilgit. It was quite challenging because Gilgit was seen as an unruly place (which it was), where the Maharaja's writ was limited and the British political agent and his people held greater sway. Finally, after having cobbled together an able team, Mr Thomas also chose his trustworthy assistant and requested him to accompany him to Gilgit as well.

Despite the risks—from going on a long, arduous journey from Srinagar to Gilgit, and the difficult life in the remote part of the state—going to Gilgit was akin to going to the UK or America in the 1950s. For young people like Maheshwar Nath this was an opportunity that would come by only rarely and could not be wasted. One of Maheshwar Nath's friends had gone to Gilgit only the year before in connection with his official work, and when they had met his friend had spoken of Gilgit as if it were London! Working in Gilgit also meant working with British superiors and that in itself broadened the prospects for ambitious young people.

When Maheshwar Nath declared that he had been transferred to Gilgit on a promotion, there was a mixed reaction within his family. His father, who was still working but had married a second time after Maheshwar's mother had died in childbirth about fifteen years earlier, was concerned that the household needed all the income of earning members to be run effectively. Theirs was a joint family, like most KP households at that time, and to run the household was also a joint responsibility. Now the problem was that if Maheshwar Nath were to miss this opportunity, he would never get such a chance again. At home, Maheshwar also played the role of a strict elder brother to his stepbrothers and stepsisters and was therefore an important person when it came to controlling the reins of the youngsters in the large family. Everyone in the family was respectful and in awe of him and despite his young years he was seen as the 'glue' that held the entire family together.

After many hours of discussion on the pros and cons of going to Gilgit, it was decided that one of Maheshwar's stepbrothers and stepsisters would also accompany him, along with his wife and his eight-month-old son (his first child), to Gilgit. For the sake of family unity, and yet to allow Maheshwar Nath the autonomy that he craved as a young man rising in his profession, this seemed the best way out. The economic dependence within the family made it seem normal to tie down a young professional with family responsibilities.

In the early 1930s, going to Gilgit from Srinagar required travelling for days together, mostly on horseback (and on horse-cart where the terrain was flat) over treacherous mountain routes that were not just dangerous, but scary as well. The journey would take the travellers to Bandipur by boat, on the northern edge of Wular Lake, and then the caravan would proceed on horses, with the luggage on packhorses and mules in a north-easterly direction towards Minimarg. Before reaching Minimarg the travellers would go over the beautiful Rajdhani Pass and travel through dense forests on to the Gurez valley. Thence the group would travel northeast along the mountain ridge, below which the treacherous Burzil river would flow. From Minimarg, the group would traverse in the north-westerly direction, following the Burzil and Astore rivers till they reached the Indus river valley. That route would take the travellers to Bunji, on the banks of the Gilgit river. From Bunji the travellers would have an inspiring view of the towering Nanga Parbat peak to the west, its snowy ridges and peak glistening in the sunshine. Thence, following the Gilgit river and proceeding north by northwest, the travellers would finally reach Gilgit. As the crow flies the distance is a mere 205 kilometres. But along the treacherous mountain routes, the journey would take over a month if all went well and there were no mishaps along the way.

Maheshwar's wife, Lila, was quite apprehensive about the travel they were going to undertake, especially with their first surviving infant being just over eight months old. But at the same time she had tremendous faith in her caring husband and knew that he would look after everything. So she chose not to bother her head about her concerns and trust her husband.

She was not alone to think like this. In those days and in that era, all the ladies would depend solely on their husbands for planning and decision-making. As a matter of fact, the husbands used to have an upper hand in decision-making, and in planning for anything in the home or even outside. Ladies, who were neither as well educated nor financially independent, willingly played second fiddle.

Lila was a very gentle, pious, and obedient wife. Whatever her husband told her, she would take as God's command to her, and without questioning the order or the intention would simply go about following it. The journey to Gilgit therefore had to be taken, and Lila was happily going with what her brave husband Maheshwar had suggested.

The journey started on the due date. The parting and goodbyes with the other members of the family were so emotional that all were weeping and crying as if some calamity had befallen them! At some level the elders must have been concerned about whether they would see the departing family members again in their lifetimes.

In those days, such long and arduous journeys were done in groups, much like caravans. Not less than ten families would travel together to break the monotony of the journey. They used to carry along all the requirements of a full-fledged kitchen, food items, and half a dozen cooks to make food on the way to their destination. All the ladies of the caravan would help to cook, clean, and chop the vegetables. In conversations with one another they used to learn so many new things and the experience of the journey was indeed unique. They were all novices, inexperienced, and ignorant about so many things, but there were inevitably a couple of ladies who were quite clever, experienced, and intelligent. They would automatically boss over the others and become leaders of the group. They would brag about their husbands' jobs and would never hesitate to say that the English bosses of their husbands were so fond of them that they wouldn't leave them (their subordinates) even for a moment!

As soon as the caravan reached a major stopping place, all would get energized. They used to fix up tents and camp in the stunningly beautiful meadows and the mountain flats. Once the tents would be ready, the horses would be left to graze, while the cooks and the ladies would get busy in preparing the food. All together, the caravan would be quite large, and with the horsemen, the labourers, and the help brought along by the families, the staff would often outnumber the family members travelling.

Riding on horseback and covering long distances over hilly and rocky terrain can be quite a pain in the bottom! In those days the saddles were made of hard leather, and with the kind of clothes the men and women wore, it was quite common to get pretty sore in the legs and the back after a day's journey. The labourers were often asked to press the backs of the travellers for extra payment, and make sure that the travellers were all fed and rested by the next day.

For small babies and toddlers in the group, arrangements were done separately. For young mothers with their infants, it was akin to going to another world, away from the security, support, and the safety of their homes, where help from family members was always forthcoming. Everyone was apprehensive about the new place they would be visiting, the people they would encounter, and the overall atmosphere. At the same time there was excitement too about the bright future they were all envisaging.

Travelling together in a group, over a long period, fostered a strange and warm kinship amongst all the travellers and their horsemen, the cooks, and the help and the labourers who formed the entourage. It was as if they were one big family or related to one another. They would care for each other in a way that showed their innocent and mutual affection in many ways. If one got hurt or bruised, the whole caravan would endeavour to get the right medicine or balm. Even labourers would bring some native medicinal herbs for an appropriate cure. These gestures would be appreciated and they forged tight bonds of trust, love, and mutual affection for one another.

Through the journey, while the adults were on horses or walking, all the toddlers were tied to the backs of the horsemen in thick and sturdy woollen blankets. That was the safest and the most secure way to take an infant over a long journey, and the horsemen, as also the labourers, were adept at this. One of the persons was carrying Lila and Maheshwar's son, the little baby Omkar. During the journey north of Minimarg, as the caravan was following the Burzil river, the baby grew very hungry and started crying and flailing his little arms on the back of the man who was carrying him. His mother Lila was keen to have the baby to pacify him and suckle him. But while handing the baby with the woollen covering to his mother (who was on horseback), and before she could settle the baby and hold him firmly, the baby slipped out of her hands and fell into the raging Burzil river! Fortunately the baby fell with the thick blanket covering his body, but Lila screamed in panic and soon the entire entourage knew that baby Omkar had fallen into the river. The other women started to wail.

The alarm bells rang, the whole caravan got panicky and there were shouts all over. 'Amma, Momma, Ahada, Nabba,' Lila and the other ladies pleaded with the horsemen and the labourers, 'Please help the baby! He's in the river!' They were crying helplessly. The whole caravan had to stop.

The moment the baby had slipped into the river, a dozen or so men from the caravan had jumped into the icy waters of the river and were quickly swimming towards the baby, who was fortunately floating in the water due to the woollen blanket around him. Wrapped in a blanket, with his head covered in a woollen baby cap, the infant looked like a small bundle floating on the surface of the water. Before the water could soak the blanket and freeze the child, the baby was picked up by the intrepid Amma. Amma was all wet but was beaming as he brought the infant out of the river safe and sound. Everyone heaved a sigh of relief and soon it was time for jubilation and thanksgiving for everyone. Amma became the hero of the day. He got all the praises and the rewards for this deed from all the members of the caravan.

The caravan proceeded forward towards its destination. Maheshwar Nath was quite upset with his wife and admonished her for being so careless as not to hold the baby properly. He probably wanted to give her a dressing down but it was not possible to do anything of that sort in front of other people as it would have made them look like fools and undermined their prestige. So he thought that he would give her a piece of his mind in private, after they reached Gilgit.

From that point in the journey, the group took one more week to reach their destination. At long last they all were relieved to reach the town of Gilgit. Maheshwar Nath's luggage was put in a big bungalow, which was too big for his family. He was not the only one to have a huge place to live in. There were others too who had huge houses to live in. It was all according to the official status of the incumbent. Since Maheshwar Nath was directly working with an English official as his assistant, his status was a bit higher than that of his other colleagues who were not reporting to an English boss.

Being in Gilgit was as good as being abroad. There were so many English officers along with their wives—strolling in the parks, on the high mall roads with their children, with toddlers in prams being pushed by young girls from the local tribes, and so on. Young Kashmiri men, bubbling with new ideas, wanted to emulate the lifestyles of Englishmen. Their wives, however, were tradition-bound and would not cooperate on that account. But they were not bothered about their husbands going out to play cricket or tennis and other games with their office colleagues, who were Englishmen and were well versed in these games. Most of the young KP men were very intelligent, hard-working, and obedient. This quality of theirs was appreciated a lot by their officers and that brought many of them quick material gains. With this kind of interaction between the Englishmen and the youngsters from Kashmir, the latter not only learned how to be good at the games that they were exposed to, but were able to polish their English-speaking skills as well.

The English, however, despite occasional interaction, would behave like superiors to the Kashmiris and locals in Gilgit, and would always exude a disdainful sense of superiority. It was part of the job for many Kashmiri Pandits to be given a horse to ride on. Maheshwar Nath too was assigned a horse and a syce to look after the animal. Maheshwar was very fond of animals and took an immediate liking to his horse and would care for it lovingly. He would also make sure that when he went to work, he would always be properly attired, and would ensure that he wore breeches and boots while riding to work.

On one bright Sunday morning, Maheshwar Nath was on his horse riding to his friend's place. On the way a hefty middle-aged Englishman was also on horseback, coming from the opposite side. Maheshwar stopped his horse, and wished the English rider, whom he possibly recognized: 'Good morning, Mr Jones! It's a beautiful day, isn't it?'

However, even before he could finish his words, the Englishman was furious, and his face grew red with rage.

'How dare you wish me good morning? Don't you know who I am?' the man said angrily, snorting as he spoke.

'Sir, sorry, I didn't mean to ... I was ...' Maheshwar tried to respond politely. But even before Maheshwar could respond, the Englishman spoke.

'Shut up, you, and just keep quiet! You insolent man, you! I'll see you tomorrow, and make sure you're taught a lesson!'

Maheshwar was disgusted. He was feeling bad that for the first time in his life, for no apparent rhyme or reason, an Englishman had humiliated him. He felt the pangs of a direct insult to his dignity and was deeply hurt.

He thought to himself. 'What triggered the man to behave like this? Was it racism? Is this what Mohandas Gandhi experienced in the train in South Africa?'

The next day when he went to his office he saw the burly Englishman who had admonished him the previous day coming out of the office room of his boss. He felt sad that the man might have told the boss a bunch of lies and fibs to discredit him. 'Would Mr Thomas believe him? Knowing my boss, he will surely enquire about this whole episode from me. I'll tell him the whole truth,' he thought.

As soon as he entered his room, one of his colleagues told him that the boss was eagerly looking for him. He went to meet his boss immediately.

'Good morning, Maheshwar Nath.'

For once Maheshwar felt too diffident to respond because of the previous day's incident.

'Ahm, good morn.' He was unsure whether he should reciprocate at all. Till now, he had always responded cheerily. But today he was conscious, unsure about what he ought to do. He kept quiet for a while.

'Good morning, Maheshwar Nath.' It was his boss who was repeating the greeting, warmly.

'Good morning, sir,' Maheshwar promptly responded. It was as if someone had injected a dose of energy into him.

'Would you please get file number 738? I have a dictation to do.' Before Mr Thomas could say anything further, Maheshwar Nath went to get the file. 'He may be an Englishman, but he's a gentleman par excellence,' he thought to himself. 'Like with all humans, there'll always be variations.'

3

Homecoming from Calcutta

As I've shared earlier, the Dhars formed a large family. In fact there were many family members to start with and together with their respective spouses, their children, the relatives who would stay at Rishi Vihar for extended periods, and the house help, the atmosphere was more like that of a commune.

Ram Chandra passed away in 1945. However, all his children were well read and accomplished and had very good and respectable government jobs. That meant the family was well heeled and there was financial stability in the family.

In the mid-1950s, when the Jammu and Kashmir Constituent Assembly was drafting the rules for the state (which had already become a part of the Union of India in October 1947), it also introduced an Act called the Landed Estates Abolition Act. With this, the large landholdings of all absentee landlords of arable lands were formally given to the tillers, mostly Kashmiri peasants who were actually working on the lands. The original owners of the landed estates—most of whom were Dogras from the Jammu region and Kashmiri Pandits who had received *jagirs* from the maharajas from the mid-1850s onwards—were all given small landholdings (not exceeding about 180 kanals; a kanal is 5,400 square feet) and no compensation. The logic was that the lands were largely received from the state and included villages and public lands for which no compensatory benefit was payable.

When the system of land to the tiller was finally implemented by 1951, it did not impact the Dhar family at Rishi Vihar very much. Since they were well qualified and held good positions, they happily gave up whatever cultivable lands they had owned for a few generations.

Ram Chandra's youngest son, Tribhuvan Nath, was living in Calcutta in those days. He had left home as a teenager to study engineering at the Banaras Hindu University. After completing his studies he started his career from Calcutta.

While Ram Chandra had returned to Kashmir after his studies in Lucknow were completed, Tribhuvan chose to work outside the state. He therefore became the first person in the family to go to the plains to earn his livelihood. After he got a job, he got married and took his bride along with him to Calcutta.

In the early part of his career, Tribhuvan would visit his family in Kashmir once a year. But as he rose through the ranks in the company that he worked for, he got busier, his responsibilities increased, and his visits to the Valley not only got shorter, but also reduced in frequency. Many months and years would elapse between his visits home, especially after his father passed away.

Since communication in those days was only through an occasional letter (which would take two to three weeks to reach Srinagar from Calcutta), Tribhuvan's mother, Māl, as well as his brothers and sisters, who were all in Srinagar, would pine to meet him. Time went by and it soon dawned on Māl that it had already been over four years since she had seen her son.

One Sunday, when all the members of the family were having their lunch in the big room, a postman appeared with a telegram and went into the room to deliver it personally to Māl, the grand matriarch of the family. She was seated at her usual place, which was fixed for her for as long as I remember.

'This is for you, Mother,' the postman said with reverence, as he handed the telegram to her.

'Is all well?' Māl asked apprehensively, concerned that there shouldn't be any bad tidings in the telegram.

'All's well, all's well,' the postman said reassuringly. 'In fact there's good news for you. Congratulations!'

His words were reassuring. Grandmother, who was now excited, ordered one of her grandsons in the room to open the telegram and read what it said. The postman stood by politely, waiting for the message to be read.

When the telegram was opened, Ajnath jumped and said excitedly, 'Saibaji, our uncle Tribhuvan is coming to Srinagar very soon.'

On hearing this news the grandmother was delighted. We could all make out that she was unusually happy at having received this news. She took out a small purse from her wooden box, which served as her desk and her portable safe, and opened it to present the postman with a silver coin.

'Thank you, thank you, Mother! I told you that the telegram carried good news. That is why I came here to deliver it personally.' The postman too was elated to receive a coin from Māl. Everyone hurried through their sumptuous lunch since all were curious and wanted to see the contents of the telegram for themselves.

In the four years that Tribhuvan was away, some more additions had been made to the family. Those who were born when he was last in Srinagar were now four years older. And all those kids had absolutely no idea about this uncle of theirs. Yet, touching the telegram that had brought the news of this adventurous uncle became a ritual for all the kids, almost as if touching the paper would magically bring back images of his avuncular countenance.

Much like what happened in Rishi Vihar, the mohalla was soon fully clued up on the developments of the afternoon. This message of Tribhuvan's homecoming spread like wildfire. The elderly folk from the entire mohalla came to congratulate Māl on the big, happy news. It was after four years that uncle was coming to Kashmir to meet his family members. This was indeed a red-letter day!

In due course, relatives, friends, subordinates of other brothers of Tribhuvan, and even friends and acquaintances from the neighbourhood were all visiting the household to ascertain how they could help in the preparations for the homecoming of the 'son from Calcutta'.

In the next few days many people were given one task or another, as part of the preparations for the forthcoming visit of Tribhuvan. The master-craftsmen, *vosta* (which means 'master' from the word *ustād*) Razāq and *vosta* Sullā were entrusted with the tasks of painting and carpeting Tribhuvan's room, and a few other rooms in the house. For days thereafter, the men and their assistants were everywhere, fixing things and sprucing up the rooms in preparation for the big day. They too were feeling important since readying the rooms of the guest and his spouse, as also ensuring that the project was completed on time, was entirely their responsibility.

Razāq and Sullā did a wonderful job. The big room on the ground floor and the room for Tribhuvan and his wife were beautifully painted with oil paint. The ceiling of the rooms—done in the traditional style known as *khutumband* (a kind of woodwork parquetry made by tongue-in-groove fitting of geometric pieces)—was then varnished, giving a beautiful sheen to the elegant woodwork.

The rooms were furnished with thin durries, which were then covered with thick and elegantly embroidered woollen rugs. The sitting room was furnished with the new *vaguv* mats (special mats that are made of lake rush-grass by weaving the dry stalks together; such grasses are found almost along all the waterbodies and lakes in Kashmir). On top of the *vaguvs* were spread plain woollen rugs, which were then partially covered with a thick and elegant Kashmiri carpet.

The sitting room with the fresh painting and with the new furnishings looked like a posh hotel room. It was Māl who had supervised the details of the project, with help from her sons of course. Of her sons, however, it was Niranjan who had a remarkable aesthetic sense and being a curious person would imbibe diverse ideas from books and the places he'd visited. His mother often consulted him for ideas and to approve of something that she had in mind. Niranjan himself enjoyed being the consultant to the family in matters related to architecture and decor.

It was now merely two days before Tribhuvan, his wife, and their little daughter would arrive in Srinagar. All the children in the household were excited about the frenetic, last-minute preparations that were going on in the family. The older boys got busy making buntings to decorate the road outside their home.

Travelling from Calcutta to Srinagar in the middle of the twentieth century was a long, tiring journey. The 1,900 kilometres from Sealdah station in Calcutta to Pathankot cantonment station was a slow forty-hour-long journey that required passengers to prepare almost as if it were an expedition into the wilderness! Food had to be carried for the journey, especially if you were picky about what you ate and would rather rely on home-cooked food than what would be served along the way. In addition, bedding rolled in a canvas holdall with leather straps had to be carried to ensure some sleep on the hard wooden berths during the night. Sufficient water had to be carried as well, which was usually done in earthen *surahi* to keep the water cool and clean during the hot and dusty journey. This was the era of open-window trains that had no air conditioning and where the loud *clackety-clack* of the journal bearings and the steel wheels on the rails would echo and boom across the coaches all through the long journey.

After the forty-hour train journey, the train would reach Pathankot cantonment station. This was a busy station, not more than a few kilometres from the city in those days. This was also the last railhead in the plains before the hills in the north and the east had to be ascended, and hence there would always be a milling crowd of people at the station, scurrying around, carrying large pieces of luggage, like metal trunks, holdalls, gunny sacks of provisions, and bundles of stuff tied in cloth to carry to the villages on the upper slopes of the Himalayas and the Shivaliks. Then there'd be horse-drawn carriages, tongas, cycle rickshaws, and even a few rickshaws pulled directly by strapping men—all calling out to passengers to be taken to various parts of the city.

In order to reach Srinagar from Pathankot, however, a twelve to fourteen-hour bus journey would have to be undertaken from the bus terminus in the city. Buses to different towns and cities in Kashmir were usually run by a few private entrepreneurs. I recall that the only Parsi family in the state of Jammu and Kashmir, the Pestonjees, had an interest in the transportation business and ran a bus service from Srinagar to Pathankot under the aegis of Pestonjee Transport. Another enterprise was N.D. Radha Krishan and Company, which also operated buses to different parts of the state.

By the time travellers reached Srinagar from faraway places, they would be exhausted, not to mention how dusty and grimy they looked! Sensible travellers not hard-presssed for time would therefore break their journey and arrive at a leisurely pace—looking better and definitely less tired than if they would have travelled non-stop.

With just a day left for Tribhuvan and his family to arrive, the planners now began to work out the logistics of getting the travellers from the bus station in Srinagar to Rishi Vihar—a distance of about six kilometres. Detailed checklists were made to name and identify a suitable person to receive the travelling members of the family at the main bus stand in Srinagar. This person, along with the accompanying house help, would also be responsible for placing them on the Dhar family-owned tonga along with one of the brothers, and also load their luggage on additional tongas that would be hired for the occasion. There would also be lookouts and runners at key points along the route just to make sure that if there was any help needed it could be given. The runners would also make a dash for Rishi Vihar and bring the news of the actual arrival time of the travellers.

Not only were these elaborate details discussed and finalized between the members of the family, the high points were also shared with the venerable elders in the entire neighbourhood. Many of them insisted that they too would receive Tribhuvan and his family at the bus stand rather than wait for them at the bridge leading to Rishi Vihar.

'Tribhuvan ji's homecoming is a special occasion for all of us as well,' the elders would say, in support of their plans. 'After all, he belongs to us all and is the son of this whole area, he is our own nephew, and we've all been a part of rearing him. He too should know that we too have been waiting for him eagerly.'

With those words, it was settled that they too would receive their beloved 'nephew' and his wife and daughter at the bus station itself.

Baiji, the eldest of Māl's and Ram Chandra's sons, was touched. 'There is no doubt that my younger brother is your nephew and a part of our extended neighbourhood family, and you have every right to receive him at the bus terminus itself. So from our side, we'll only send Prath Kak and my eldest son, Gasha. Together, you will form a truly elegant reception assemblage.'

Baiji's words were reassuring to all. Thereafter, everyone left the interactions happy and excited at the prospect of going to the bus station as a part of the reception group.

That evening it was also agreed that all the little children in the locality would receive small paper flags to wave at the arriving family members as they'd enter the gate of Rishi Vihar. The children were delighted.

On the day Tribhuvan was to arrive, the plans were meticulously executed. Everything was going as per schedule, and the minutest of details were attended to.

Tribhuvan's mother and his brothers and sisters were visibly excited on the day of his arrival. After all, they would all be meeting Tribhuvan after a gap of more than four years. It was obvious that every one of them was trying to demonstrate that they loved him dearly.

There was a reason why the family was going overboard in its display of affection. It seemed that while Tribhuvan was enrolled as a student in the Banaras Hindu University, he had not fared very well in his studies. This declension from the high academic expectations of the family had not been taken too kindly by his father. Even Tribhuvan's elder brothers had shown their annoyance and must have scolded him at that time.

Tribhuvan took the family's displeasure to heart, and left his parents' home in Srinagar in disgust. He was determined that he wouldn't return to face them until he had made a mark in his career.

Driven by a desire to prove that he had the smarts to be successful, Tribhuvan secured a very good position in a public sector organization in Calcutta. He also rose rapidly within the company.

The family in Srinagar was obviously keeping an eye on how things were shaping up for him and had been urging and pleading that he pay his ageing mother a visit. No wonder then that such a fuss was made about his visit to Kashmir after a gap of four years.

Homecoming from Calcutta

In a few hours, Tribhuvan and his family were to arrive. Everyone in the family was dressed up in elegant clothes. The atmosphere was cheery and festive, filled with an excited chatter of well-dressed children holding small paper flags and waiting patiently for the guests to arrive. The ladies of the family too were adorned in wonderful saris, colourful and elegant, with wide embroidered borders.

The older boys in the family had also arranged crackers for the occasion. The plan was to burst a strip of squibs as soon as Tribhuvan and his family alighted from the tonga that was to bring them to the gate of Rishi Vihar. Some of the business owners of the locality had also erected decorated archways all the way from Nawa Bazaar up to the gate of the Dhar home.

'They've reached Nawa Kadal,' someone was heard shouting. 'Within ten minutes they'll be here!' One of Baiji's sons too came in running to share this information. This news galvanized everyone as they hurried towards the main gate to receive the visitors. Soon two long rows of people lined up in front of the main gate, with garlands of fresh flowers in the hands of the elders. While waiting, some ladies were busy tucking in the pleats of their saris, while the older women were checking their pherans, straightening any unwanted creases.

As Tribhuvan entered the gate amidst the loud bursting of crackers, his mother Sukh Māl was the first to garland him. She hugged him and as she did so both the mother and her son shed tears, weeping like little children. Other elders of the family followed, after which it was the turn of his brothers and sisters to welcome the guests.

For many of us who were still very young, it was difficult to understand why all of a sudden even other members of the family began to weep, even as they hugged Tribhuvan, his wife Bibi, and their little daughter, Rita. On the one hand there was jubilation, on the other hand everyone's eyes were moist. Probably Pandit Ram

Chandra's absence—who'd passed away a few years earlier—could be a reason. It was a tearful reunion, which lasted for some time. Tribhuvan was hugging all those who had assembled to receive him, including the many people from the neighbourhood. Even Bibi was busy hugging the family members one by one. There were so many children standing in front of them but they just couldn't recognize them because some of them had been born over the last five years.

All the children were equally surprised to see their uncle, Tribhuvan. He was a tall, handsome man with sharp features. He had a neatly trimmed moustache and excellent sartorial taste, which made him stand apart from his brothers. Living in Calcutta also ensured that he had access to the latest fashions of the day, quite unlike how it was in Srinagar then. His wife too wore a sleeveless blouse to match her elegant sari. She too was a tall, slim lady with good looks, and in her well-draped sari she looked beautiful and from a faraway, different land.

All the children were overawed to see them. All the fuss about them was worthwhile and made for some wonderful entertainment. When the welcome hugs were done, they all walked towards the big room, making it seem like a procession for a dignitary.

That evening, after everyone had had time to relax, the family reconvened in the presence of Māl. The elders settled down in their usual sitting spaces on the thickly carpeted floor, with Tribhuvan being given a place of honour, close to his mother. His wife, Bibi, and daughter, Rita, sat close by.

Māl began to introduce all the little children to Tribhuvan, Bibi, and their daughter one by one. They must either have been toddlers at the time they'd left Kashmir, or were born within the five years that he was away.

'This is Bulla, and the other one is Sardar,' Māl said as she gestured towards the children.

'My god, they've grown into such lovely little boys!' Tribhuvan said cheerily. 'Come to me, come,' he said fondly, as he opened his arms to hug them. They both got up and together hugged him with joyous innocence. Then Kagga and Nani came forward, and hugged him. In this manner, in groups of ones and twos, all the little kids got to hug their Tribhuvan uncle.

In the following days it became clear that Tribhuvan uncle was a fun-loving person, who neither wanted to quiz the children about their studies nor impose his will on them. This was so unlike the other elders! That's why all the children liked him instantly. There was no fear, just the mutual bonds of love and affection between him and the children.

Within three or four days it felt as if Tribhuvan and his family had never been away from home. From day one, so many relatives, friends, and colleagues of the other uncles came to meet them. Even, a high-profile client of Baiji, who was visiting Srinagar, paid a visit. With Tribhuvan's coming, it seemed as if Rishi Vihar was in a state of perpetual festivities!

One day, after lunch was over, Tribhuvan made an announcement. He requested everyone to be present in the big *vot* room after the evening meal.

Looking at his mother, he made it all the more clear.

'All in the family have to be present in the *vot* after dinner.'

Māl was curious. 'You can talk to them even now, dear Tribhuvan. Why does it have to be in the evening?'

Tribhuvan laughed joyously. 'It's a surprise. It'll have to be done in the evening.'

'Oh! A surprise?' Māl exclaimed. However, she didn't press for any further information. She must have understood why the family had to assemble in the big room after dinner.

At the centre of the big *vot* room, a long wooden bench was placed to partition it into two seating arrangements: one portion was for all the men and the other one was for the ladies of the house and the children. Children being the way they are, many climbed on to the bench and made themselves comfortable there.

As dinner got over, the levels of curiosity began to rise. The ladies especially could not contain their eagerness any longer, and began to coax Tribhuvan and Bibi to tell them more about what they had planned for the evening.

'Please tell us why you want us to be present in the room, dear Trubha Kāk?' his sister-in-law, Sati, asked. Bibi just smiled as she heard her sisters-in-law pleading with her husband.

'There must be a very valid reason for this, I'm sure!' the younger sister-in-law, Benigashi, said emphatically, trying to sound clever.

'Come on, now, give us a clue! We won't tell anyone,' Benji, the other sister-in-law who was younger than Sati but older than Benigashi, also jumped in the fray.

By now Bibi was laughing hard and deriving utmost pleasure from the intense curiosity of her sisters-in-law.

Bibi was the youngest daughter-in-law of the family. She was outspoken and talked to everyone in the family freely, including her older brothers-in-law—Baiji, Bubji, Lalaji, Ṭāṭhāji and the others in the family. Most KP women in Kashmir at that time would hesitate to speak freely with the elder male relatives from the husband's side of the family. So interactions between them and their fathers-in-law or brothers-in-law were relatively rare.

But since Bibi had been living in Calcutta for some years now, she was more open and outgoing, and her behaviour was visibly different. I'm not sure all were comfortable with her candour and openness, but out of love and respect everyone took her approach to interactions in their stride. She was the youngest of them all, and was therefore allowed some liberties.

Watching Bibi laughing loudly, her youngest sisters-in-law, Umaji and Bahinji, strode up to her.

'Can you please tell us why you're laughing so? Is there nothing you can share with us, please?' They pleaded.

'She is being naughty. She does not want to divulge anything about the surprise tonight,' Sati said, reassuring Umaji and Bahinji and confirming that there was no secret pact between Bibi and them from which Tribhuvan's younger sisters had been excluded.

'She is so secretive, nothing ever comes out of her belly,' Benji added.

The women were all in a jovial mood. The overall atmosphere was congenial and cheerful. Having Tribhuvan and Bibi back after a long gap had greatly contributed to the overall felicity in Rishi Vihar.

At the appointed hour, all the members of the family had assembled in the *vot*. Even the children were wide awake. Māl was happy to have her whole family together in the room.

'Haven't you slept till now?' she addressed the children.

'How could they? After all, there is going to be a magic show,' said Jiglal, Māl's eldest daughter who had also come visiting. Her words made everyone break into laughter.

As soon as all of them were settled, two of the men working in the family, Sidha and Sarvanand, entered, carrying a big steel trunk. The trunk had two fat padlocks, one each for the two hasps on either side. The presence of the locks and the way the two men were walking—their faces were flushed and sweaty—made it evident that the box was bulky and contained something valuable. The men placed the trunk deftly in the middle of the room, wiped their brows, and smiled at everyone around. The trunk's presence in the centre of the *vot* was to enable the family members to take a good look at the box from all sides and speculate about what it might contain.

The conversations in the room were loud and animated. Everyone was keen to see the trunk opened. At long last Tribhuvan got up from his place next to his mother, strode to the centre of the large room, and sat down in front of the box. He asked his wife Bibi to hand the keys of the trunk to him. Bibi got up and handed the keys to him. All eyes were fixed on the padlocks and the bunch of keys that had been handed over. Tribhuvan chose a fat, long key from the bunch, and proceeded to open the locks. As soon as the locks were opened, and the hasps released, he opened the lid. The trunk must have taken quite a beating because it opened with a shrill, creaky noise. All the children got up eagerly to see what the trunk contained. Their curiosity prompted their mothers to scold them. 'Can't you all sit still until Saibaji opens the box fully? Naughty children, sit down, now!'

With the box fully opened, Saiba and Bibi now began to gingerly take out the packets of gifts, like magicians pulling things out of a hat before an eager, curious audience. It was fairly late at night, and yet everyone was wide awake with curiosity.

'This is for Mother,' Saibaji said smiling, as he pulled out a colourful roll of cloth tied with a string, his sonorous voice booming in the room. 'Here, please pass this on to her,' he said to his wife.

Mother appreciatively received the roll. She placed her hand on the cloth and moving it gently across, nodded happily. Then handing it to her older daughter-in-law, she remarked, 'Isn't it beautiful?'

'Yes, yes, it's really good material. In a colour that will suit you too! This is the ideal cloth for making an elegant pheran,' she said excitedly.

After this, one by one Tribhuvan and Bibi began to pass the gift packets around. Everyone was keen and curious to see what kind of clothes and gifts the other people were getting. They were comparing the colour and the texture of the different pieces of cloth that were presented. Mother and Sati—who still wore the traditional pheran and had chosen not to wear saris—got the same type of cloth but the colours of their respective pieces were different. Similarly, Benji, Benigashi, and Dulabhabi—the younger daughters-in-law, who had started to wear saris when the transition was made in the reformist years of the 1930s—got elegant saris in different colours. There were gifts for everyone. Children got their share of gifts as well, creating a ripple of joy across the whole room despite the late hours.

Finally, Mother spoke up. 'Trubh-*kāk*, you must've spent a fortune getting us all these gifts. It's akin to a full-fledged dowry given to a daughter when she's married.' All of Tribhuvan's elder brothers nodded in assent, and smiled appreciatively at his and his wife's gesture.

The events and emotions of that evening were indelibly etched in everyone's minds. To this day, that special reunion of the family seems like it happened just yesterday. Everyone was happy that Saibaji and his family had finally returned home after a long gap.

Before retiring for the night, Saibaji called all the family helps into the room. Saibaji handed over ten packets of gifts to his mother and said, 'Māl, please distribute these gifts to all of them. There is cloth for shirts and pyjamas for all of our trusted help.' Then looking at Sarvanand, Siddha, Prasad Ram, and the others in the room, he smiled heartily and asked, 'Hope you all are happy and satisfied?'

Spontaneously they all smiled and uttered blessings to the Dhar family and to their own. Then Sarvanand, the eldest of them all, said with tears rolling down his face, 'We're so glad that you're back.'

Part II
Reform

4

The Desire for Change

The return of Kashi Nath, his wife Heemal, and his two grown-up sons to Srinagar was a momentous one for the KP community as well as for the Kashmiri elite. A renowned family that had been away for over twenty years in a 'foreign land' had chosen to return. This was, in many ways, as much a vote of confidence for the prospects in Kashmir as an inspiration to others that one need not permanently forsake one's motherland, even if one is desirous of acquiring new skills and a better education outside.

The Dhar family had also brought along a new way of looking at the world. Together, they had a fresh, new, and modern perspective on the many social ills that had for generations remained unquestioned, and which were therefore considered to be the norm in Kashmir. Issues of women's health and education as well as social ills related to dowry and ostentatious weddings and other ceremonies—all of which had become millstones around the community's neck—were no longer sacred cows that could not be questioned.

The home of the Dhar family thus became a magnet for people who were keen on change and who questioned prevailing norms. Kashi and Heemal were always warm and welcoming, and Rishi Vihar soon became known for the eclectic and diverse mix of people who would gravitate there—much like a club or a cafe—for conversations, perspectives, ideas, or simply to test the waters for a new direction for the community.

The Dogra rule in Kashmir started when Gulab Singh—an energetic and crafty warrior-administrator belonging to the Rajput Jamwal clan of Jammu—bought the territories comprising Kashmir, Jammu, and Ladakh from the British East India Company for a sum of seven and a half million *Nanakshahi* rupees in 1846. Gulab Singh became the first Maharaja of Kashmir and established the Dogra dynasty that stayed in power till 1947.

Gulab Singh had made his fortunes and enhanced his influence systematically through his years of service with Maharaja Ranjit Singh, at his court, in Lahore. Together with his two equally influential brothers in the Sikh court, he developed and commanded considerable clout over the years. When Maharaja Ranjit Singh passed away in 1839, it is said that Gulab Singh played an active role in the protection of Prince Duleep Singh and his mother Jindan Kaur, and used them—they possessed the brilliant Koh-i-noor diamond—to his advantage while negotiating with the British East India Company after the First and Second Anglo-Sikh Wars.

Gulab Singh died in 1857 and was succeeded by his son, Ranbir Singh. Maharaja Ranbir Singh ruled till 1885.

It was during the rule of Ranbir Singh that the administration of the princely state improved and a new organization was established for the purpose. One of the reasons for this was that the state expanded its frontiers. Apart from the regions of Jammu, Kashmir, and Ladakh that were already a part of the state, new trans-Himalyan territories such as Gilgit and Hunza were also added during the reign of Ranbir Singh, which called for a better way to collect revenues and administer the regions.

Ranbir Singh accordingly followed the Mughal system of having 'pergunnahs' as the basic unit of administration, and hence divided the state into a number of *parganas* that were managed by *parganadaars*. Under each parganadaar, in turn, there were subordinate government employees, such as those in charge of security (*thanedaars*) and land titles (*patwaaris*). The head of a number of *patwaaris*, was known as a *kanungo* and was typically responsible for ascertaining the quality of agricultural lands and if they were fit for tilling (*girdawari*) and revenue collection.

Fotedaars (pronounced foh-tey-daars) were also employees of the government of His Highness the Maharaja, and were entrusted with keeping stock of the inventory in the royal treasury. Kashmiri Pandits who worked in this capacity often adopted their function as their surname—possibly because it differentiated them from other Kashmiri Pandits and bolstered their family status.

During the reign of Maharaja Ranbir Singh, two Kashmiri young men—Pandit Hargopal Kaul and Pandit Saligram Kaul—had raised the banner of revolt against the king and had made provocative speeches against Ranbir Singh in Lahore. When they returned to Srinagar, they were promptly arrested and put into jail for sedition.

Hargopal Kaul was later released, albeit he continued to speak, write, and work actively for the betterment of the people of Kashmir. His daughter Padmavati, who was a contemporary of Pandit Ram Chandra Dhar, was also an active promoter of women's education amongst Kashmiri Pandits. Padmavati was self-taught and had mastered Persian, Sanskrit, and Urdu entirely on her own. She opened a school for women in her own home and encouraged women to study and learn skills that would make them economically self-reliant. She housed a number of young KP widows who were ill-treated by their in-laws and were unwelcome in the homes of their brothers. She cared for orphans and worked hard to improve their lot, encouraging them through their education and ensuring their adoption. Like her illustrious father, Padmavati too brought about a big difference in the mindsets of the women of Kashmir in the late nineteenth century. She showed them a new direction and helped them, and the KP community as a whole, to tide over some of their superstitious taboos and orthodox, unscientific ways related to health and reproductive hygiene.

Padmavati herself was widowed young, when her husband, Pandit Prakash Joo Fotedar, died prematurely. She had no children of her own, so she adopted a young boy whom she named Shiv Narain.

Young Shiv Narain Fotedar's formative years were thus spent in the inspiring and enlightening ambience of his home, under the loving care and tutelage of his mother. His grandfather, Pandit Hargopal, too played an active role in his upbringing and ensured that he was given a fine education.

Shiv Narain was a bright student. He completed his master's in history at the Foreman Christian College in Lahore in 1928 and had already become a bit of a celebrity with his extraordinary debating skills, oratory, and flawless diction in English as well as in Urdu. Back in Kashmir, he took up his first job as a professor of history at the Prince of Wales College in Jammu.

Shiv Narain, who was eager to serve society as best he could, came in contact with two stalwarts of the KP community at that time—Shri Kashyap Bandhu and Justice Pandit Jia Lal Kilam—both of whom were in their own ways spearheading a movement to bring in certain social reforms within the community. By the early twentieth century, as education and other scientific discoveries were improving health, hygiene, and longevity, social reformers like Kashyap Bandhu and Kilam, among others, were endeavouring to make the KP community progressive in their outlook and ready for the modern world. In the early years their emphasis, also inspired by the work of Pandit Hargopal Kaul, was on issues like widow remarriage, eradication of dowry, and the prevention of ostentatious and wasteful expenditure on marriage ceremonies. In fact, every Sunday, Kashyap Bandhu would organize a meeting of the community at the historic Sharika temple on the Hari Parbat hill and share his ideas with the congregation.

In the early 1930s he was emphatic that modern KP women would have to switch over to wearing saris and blouses, instead of the pheran, along with its matching headdress, the *taraga*. This was his way of promoting modern ideas among Kashmiri Pandits and sensitizing them towards looking 'globally' smart and elegant.

Pandit Shiv Narain Fotedar, grandson of reformer and iconoclast Hargopal Kaul, took to the task of serving the community as well. Following in the footsteps of Kashyap Bandhu and Jia Lal Kilam, he became a member of the Sanatan Dharam Yuvak Sabha (SDYS), a Kashmiri Pandit social reformation organization that met regularly at the Sheetal Nath temple. By sheer dint of his work and his many wonderful qualities, he was soon elected to the executive body of the Sabha. The year was 1931.

In the years just preceding Independence, the SDYS was given a new name, the All State Kashmiri Pandits' Conference (ASKPC), and it continued with its agenda of social, cultural, and political reform of the KP community. Many leading professionals of the younger generation, inspired by the likes of Kashyap Bandu, Justice Jia Lal Kilam, Shiv Narain Fotedar, Dr S.N. Peshin, Justice J.N. Bhat, Shambhu Nath Dhar, and Prem Nath Bazaz continued to serve the community. The magazine of the group, called *The Martand*, was widely read and was an instrument of social change for the KP community. In the 1960s, Amar Nath Vashnavi played a role in leading the ASKPC and guiding the community.

Around the same time the Muslim community in the state was also undergoing changes. A broad-based, scientific education that was beyond the narrow confines of religious texts was encouraged by community leaders, especially by the young men who had been educated in Aligarh and elsewhere in the country. Many were also educated overseas, having been identified by the Maharaja and sent abroad at the expense of the state.

These men would assemble in their homes and share ideas and thoughts on how to reform their community and broaden the opportunities available to them. Many in the group (sometimes called the Fateh Kadal Reading Group, FKRG) viewed the Maharaja as the cause of the troubles of the Muslim community. Sheikh Mohammad Abdullah, a member of the FKRG and a fiery, ambitious young opponent of the monarch, was especially vocal in stating his views.

It was this sort of thinking that led to Sheikh Abdullah forming the Muslim Conference in 1931. His doing so, however, undermined the authority of the Mirwaiz of the Jama Masjid, Mohammad Yusuf Shah, because Abdullah was probably more charismatic and had cultivated the image of someone whose job it was to right the wrongs that people had endured. The Mirwaiz, whose authority (as the leader of all Muslims) was repeatedly challenged by Sheikh, got increasingly desperate and formed his own political party, the Azad Conference.

Despite the overt differences, both Sheikh Abdullah and the Mirwaiz were endeavouring to create a strong political foundation for themselves, based on a Muslim identity. Their focus was the emancipation and advancement of Muslim interests. In the pursuit of their goals Mirwaiz Yusuf Shah's followers and those affiliated to the Muslim Conference of Sheikh Abdullah clashed a number of times. The tensions hardened, when the Mirwaiz, whose authority as the religious head of Kashmiri Muslims was approved by the

Maharaja's administration, was also paid a montly stipend. Sheikh Abdullah on the other hand was viewed by the administration as a community organizer, eager for power and who was in conflict with the regime.

Sheikh's followers were called *shers* (lions) while the Mirwaiz's were known as *bakras* (goats). Many violent clashes between the *shers* and the *bakras* occurred across the Valley from time to time for almost fifty years, starting from the 1930s till as recently as the mid-1980s. In between, around the summer of 1939, the Muslim Conference was rechristened National Conference because some say that Sheikh Abdullah was actually keen to make his movement (against the monarchy and for social justice and the rights of all) a broad-based movement, rather than one confined to Muslims alone. I'm of the view that while this may indeed have been the intention for the resolution to change the name of the Muslim Conference, the creation of Pakistan in 1947—a nation that was formed specifically on an Islamic identity—created a bit of dissonance in Sheikh Abdullah's mind, and he remained ambivalent and unsure about Kashmir's identity at critical phases in his life. The result was that while he became the first prime minister of the state of Jammu and Kashmir in 1947 (just eight years after the adoption by his party of the *Naya Kashmir* vision document and the broadening of the membership of the National Conference), by 1953 the Government of India had to dismiss him from his position and incarcerate him.

In 1947, the Mirwaiz, Abdullah's arch-rival, moved to Pakistan and lived the rest of his life there. His nephew, Maulvi Farooq, was made the new Mirwaiz of the Jama Masjid. The National Conference was led by Farooq Abdullah after Sheikh Abdullah passed away in 1982.

It was only in 1987 that the nephew of Mohammad Yusuf Shah, the then Mirwaiz of the Jama Masjid, Maulvi Farooq, joined hands with his old enemy, Farooq Abdullah, son of Sheikh Abdullah and president of the National Conference at that time.

That era of 'Double-Farooq', as the unusual and unprecedented coalition of the *shers* and the *bakras* was then known, resulted in a hardening of the Muslim identity in Kashmir.

5

The Wood-headed Dolt

Shiv Narain Fotedar rapidly emerged as a towering leader of the Pandits in the Valley. Much like his contemporary, Sheikh Mohammad Abdullah, Shiv Narain was also a man full of ideas for change and modernization. Sheikh Abdullah and Shiv Narain Fotedar were both viewed as leaders of the Kashmiri people.

It is said that Shiv Narain—who grew under the benign shadow of his wise grandfather, Hargopal Kaul, and his loving mother, Padmavati, acquired many of the wonderful gifts and traits of his grandfather. He was sharp and witty, and used humour and his razor-sharp intellect to defuse even complex issues. He was urbane and suave, and endeared himself to one and all.

Since he was the only son in his mother's family, he was brought up with fondness and care. He would spend much of his time with his grandfather and learned various nuances about the politics of those tumultuous times directly from Hargopal Kaul.

From his childhood, Shiv Narain would visit the Dhar household at Rishi Vihar. He was about the same age as the young boys of

Pandit Ram Chandra Dhar. The young boys and girls of the Dhar family were fond of him, and he was treated like one of the family.

Ram Chandra's eldest son, Shambu Nath (Dhar, aka Baiji), and his immediate younger sibling, Niranjan Nath (aka Bubji), were especially close to Shiv Narain, who was about the same age as Niranjan Nath. Shiv Narain was affectionately called Bhaijānji (brother dear) by them. Because that was the term that Shambhu Nath and Niranjan Nath used for him, all others in the Dhar family used the same endearing name for him, including, funnily, the children of Shambhu Nath, Niranjan Nath, and their other brothers and sisters!

The friendship between Shiv, Shambhu, and Niranjan as well as the other Dhar brothers was based on a deep bond of mutual affection and respect. Many people actually thought that they were all real brothers! He was treated as one of the members of the Dhar family, and even Shiv felt that way, and was not merely invited to, but was actually always involved with family events and celebrations.

After the completion of their education, Shambhu became a lawyer while Niranjan took up a job with the state administration. Shiv, however, plunged straight into politics, and started to improve the lot of the Kashmiri Pandits. He continued to work as a very effective and successful community organizer with the SDYS. Around this time, the Maharaja's administration, finding in Shiv Narain a dynamic and competent young man, nominated him as the provincial head of the state's census operations. Shiv, true to his capabilities, conducted the census efforts with dedication and aplomb.

Shiv Narain's visibility as a young leader was on the rise after the success of the census operations. Community elders, in fact, selected him to lead a delegation of Kashmiri Pandits to meet leading political leaders in New Delhi to discuss the impact of the freedom struggle on the KP community and on the people of Jammu, Kashmir, and Ladakh in general.

The delegation travelled to Delhi and had a good number of meetings with some of the prominent and influential leaders who were a part of India's freedom struggle. Shiv Narain, with his flawless Urdu and English (he spoke both these languages and Kashmiri brilliantly) had a very salutary impact on many leaders, including Sir Tej Bahadur Sapru, Raja Narendra Nath Raina, Pandit Madan Mohan Malaviya, Pandit Govind Ballabh Pant, and Kailash Nath Katju.

In 1933 Shiv Narain fought the elections to the Srinagar Municipal Corporation and was elected a member with a four-year term. He worked diligently in this role, helping to improve the infrastructure, the cleanliness, and the public health services available to the denizens of the city. He became quite popular with the people of Srinagar and was easily re-elected in 1937. The Maharaja's administration, which definitely had an eye for talent and young leaders, also included in 1934 the young Shiv Narain as a member of the Maharaja's Praja Sabha—the forerunner of what was to become the Jammu and Kashmir Legislative Assembly after 1947. Shiv was re-elected to the Praja Sabha in 1938 and again in 1947.

The Praja Sabha—a body of eminent citizens—was the Maharaja's response to the agitation by Sheikh Mohammad Abdullah insisting that the monarchy 'Quit Kashmir' because of what was perceived to be the 'anti-people' orientation of the Maharaja's administration. On 13 July 1931 the state's forces had fired at a group of rioting protesters within the Srinagar jail premises, where a trial was under way, and about twenty-one people had died. The Praja Sabha was the administration's response for a greater involvement of the Kashmiri people in the functioning of the state.

Meanwhile, Shiv Narain's work as a community organizer with the SDYS was also picking up. There was a general view that the lot of Kashmiri Pandits needed improvement, and much more had to be done to reform the community of its ills and prepare young KP members for a future that remained fuzzy and uncertain in the light of the developments in the rest of India. In 1935, therefore, Shiv Narain was elected as the president of the SDYS and the community continued to harbour great expectations from him.

―⚭―

As Shiv Narain's responsibilities increased with the passage of time and he became more actively involved in the affairs of J&K after the state's accession to India in 1947, his confidants and sounding boards for many of his political dilemmas were Shambhu Nath (who was endearingly called Baiji), Niranjan Nath (Nir-kāk, aka Bubji), and their younger brothers.

One day, Shiv Narain came to the Dhar household all red and furious. Apparently, his detractors in the SDYS had, in a recent public meeting, called him *hache-kale* (a wooden-headed dolt). That meeting had been a fiasco for Shiv Narain and he had had to eat humble pie that day.

No one is sure what had triggered this insult the first time, but it must have rattled Shiv considerably because any time people were annoyed with him they'd shout *hache-kale* and malign him thus and watch him fume and walk away. Some believe that he had shown obduracy while discussing a sensitive matter in public, and then had said something in a huff, which had drawn the ire of people opposed to him and hence they had hurled this epithet at him. This view, however, is doubtful. Shiv was a man who'd speak with considerable thought and reflection and was very unlikely to be heedless or disrespectful to others. Yes, he could be unyielding on matters of principle, but that was one of his endearing qualities as well.

Shiv Narain was very disturbed by the name-hurling episode. When he met his confidants and friends, the Dhar brothers, he divulged everything to them presuming that they had no knowledge of how his critics had been taunting him. However, by now the whole of Srinagar was fully conversant with the event, and Niranjan

Nath could no longer contain his amusement as he heard what had actually happened. Even before Shiv had finished, Niranjan started to laugh like a child.

'What makes you laugh like this? Is this something to laugh about?' Shiv Narain retorted, a little irritated at the flippancy being shown by Niranjan Nath.

'No! No! This is definitely not a joke!' Niranjan replied, still smiling. 'I couldn't help laughing because your critics have chosen a very strong and nasty word to annoy you,' he continued, becoming serious.

'The question now is, how can this be countered?' It was Niranjan's younger brother Prithvi, who spoke. Everyone was upset to see Shiv Narain so sullen.

All of a sudden, Niranjan Nath stood up and as Shiv Narain looked at him a little surprised, he announced with emphasis: 'You're going to use the same whip to beat your opposition with! That is the only way to teach them not to mess with you.'

'Tell us what's on your mind, Niranjan,' Shiv implored, knowing that everyone in the room was quite curious and eager to know about Niranjan's plan.

'You convene a big meeting at the Yuvak Sabha, where you will deliver a lecture and will admit that you are indeed a wood-headed dolt!'

'What?!' Shiv retorted in surprise and with considerable shock. 'You want me to admit that I'm a wood-headed idiot? Are you in your senses, Nir-kāk?' Bhaijānji was furious to hear this.

But Niranjan didn't stop. He continued to speak and began making a speech as if Bhaijānji was speaking at the meeting that Niranjan Nath had suggested.

'I, Shiv Narain Fotedar, am indeed called wood-headed, and people further say that I am headstrong to the point of idiocy. Yes I'm wood-headed because it is essential to be steadfast for the sake of my people. I am not the kind of person to barter the well-being or the rights of my people for petty, personal gains. Like a strong, upright tree I might break in a gale, but I shall never bend. If I were to bend and buckle and show none of the wood-headedness that gives me resolve and makes me what I am, then blood will flow in the river Jhelum.'

Niranjan Nath sat down, satisfied, albeit a little breathless.

'You have to start your speech with these thoughts. That's your strategy for the coming meeting, dear Bhaijānji. Do you get what I'm suggesting?'

As soon as Nir-kāk finished speaking, Shiv Narain stood up and hugged Nir-kāk fondly. It was evident that Shiv Narain was relieved and a weight was off his chest.

'I think this approach will work very well,' he said, smiling. 'This will break their bones in a non-violent way.'

All in the room burst into laughter.

A meeting was arranged in the Sheetel Nath temple compound, where the members of the SDYS would frequently congregate. All those who had assembled were especially curious to know what their leader was going to say after the recent debacle he had had, when he was publicly called a 'wood-headed dolt'.

Just to make fun of him and to rattle Shiv Narain further, the faction opposed to him sent their cronies in large numbers to scuttle the meeting, and they had been advised to throw rotten tomatoes and spoilt potatoes on him if he were to say anything critical of the opposition leaders.

At the appointed hour, the compound was filled with people, including large numbers of people comprising the opposition to Shiv Narain. There was tremendous apprehension about serious trouble brewing in the ground. The police was all around the complex and the air was surcharged.

But the meeting started normally. The workers of the opposition, with their rotten tomatoes and potatoes in their hands, but concealed within their pheran sleeves, were waiting for him to speak and say something provocative so that they would start their work of ridiculing and dishonouring him with systematic precision.

However, that just didn't happen. In his sonorous voice and flawless oratory, Shiv Narain didn't utter a word about his opponents. Instead, he started his speech the way he had rehearsed it beforehand.

'I, Shiv Narain Fotedar, am indeed called *hache-kale* ...'

Nobody in the audience was expecting him to speak in this manner. With each word that Shiv Narain spoke, people grew even more curious to know what he was *really* up to.

What is he going to say next?

People kept thinking and asking one another. As Shiv Narain spoke, those who were apprehending trouble and who had been sitting on the wall near the exit gate, jumped to the ground eager to hear Shiv's enthralling speech.

By the time Shiv was halfway through his speech, it was apparent that even his opponents had been won over and the tables had turned in his favour. As news spread that Shiv Narain was lecturing powerfully, the whole ground swelled up with more people hurriedly walking in. People thronged in hordes to hear him. Men, women, and children now joined the *jalsa*. For his supporters and friends, the event was a matter of victory and jubilation. For Shiv's opponents, this event became a signal for their impending defeat in the forthcoming elections. The opposition members also got a good rebuff for the nasty manner they had adopted to ridicule a person of his stature.

From that event onwards people were unanimous in their view that all the qualities that make for a great leader were possessed by Shri Shiv Narain Fotedar. Privately, Shiv Narain would laughingly suggest that while Kashmiri Pandits had a great many wonderful and endearing qualities, they also displayed some unusual traits, and he would then say this in Sanskrit:

Nishkārna vairi, nishkām nindya

Implying that Kashmiri Pandits show animus without a reason and will be critical without being involved in something.

There are many who quote these lines of Shiv Narain to this day!

6

Kindred Spirits

Shiv Narain was a religious person. Yet, he was liberal and quite modern in his thoughts and deeds. His upbringing, with an iconoclastic grandfather and an educated liberal-minded mother, had definitely contributed to his being the way he was. Even his constant contact with the open, progressive, and liberal Dhar family from his childhood would have played a key role in shaping the way he viewed the world and in his overall development. As a young boy, he as well as the other Dhar children of his age were often regaled with stories by Ram Chandra, who as a keen educator took special interest in the growth of all young children who were a part of the extended Rishi Vihar family.

In the Rishi Vihar home of the Dhar family, another young man—also a contemporary of Shiv Narain, Shambhu Nath, and Niranjan Nath—Dr Gwasha Lal Kaul would spend considerable time, almost like a member of the family. Much like Shiv Narain, he too had grown up with the Dhar siblings and they were all very close to and fond of one another.

Many outsiders visiting the household would never know the difference between the Dhar boys and their friends as they were all treated alike, and the fondness between them was not based on something transient or superficial, but was solidly based on mutual love, trust, and a real and abiding concern for one another.

Dr Kaul was from a religious and pious Kashmiri middle-class family. He was brilliant right from his childhood and chose to become a doctor. He was amongst the first group of people who, sometime in the mid-1930s, were sent abroad for higher studies by Maharaja Hari Singh's government as part of the state's policy of developing talent in order to man and lead the institutions that would serve the people of the state.

By the time he returned to Kashmir from Britain, as a qualified Fellow of the Royal College of Physicians, Dr Kaul was one of the few members of the KP community who was 'foreign returned'.

Studying in London, Dr Kaul was quite influenced by the life and habits of the Britons he came in contact with. He obviously took a liking to some of the good things that he observed in Britain, so when he returned he tried to emulate habits that he had observed and attempted to bring about changes within his home.

Obviously, it was not easy to completely emulate the lifestyle of the English in toto, given the prevailing milieu in the Valley at that time. So, it became a trend to adopt what could conveniently be introduced within the home without disrupting the existing ethos too much. It was relatively easy, for instance, to adopt some of the fancy British names and to acquire modern furniture such as a dining table and chairs to go with it. Sometimes this was done to impress the people around, while at other times it was also a matter of convenience since eating on neat little individual tables close to the floor (as was the tradition) wasn't convenient when dressed in English clothes!

Dr Kaul named one of his daughters Nancy, after one of his English friends in London. As I've mentioned before, Kashmiris are quick to adopt new things, especially if it somehow adds to their cachet, and so it wasn't long before many newborn girls in Srinagar were also named Nancy!

Dr Gwasha Lal Kaul had a very pleasing personality. He was tall, good-looking, and, like most Kashmiris, fair of skin. It was said that in London he passed off as an Englishman and the only thing that ever gave him away (if at all) was the accent with which he spoke his otherwise flawless English. He was quite fond of music and was also spiritual. Despite being a famous, competent, and successful doctor, he enjoyed being in the company of mystics and sages for hours together. In those days there were innumerable mystics, saintly people, and rishis in Kashmir, and reaching out to them wasn't difficult, unless of course the mystic discouraged visitors.

Some say that Dr Kaul would get so engrossed in his work that many of the things that he would ordinarily have done would slip his mind. Sometimes he would remain at the hospital treating patients, including those who would just walk in, and in doing so he'd often forget that he had given time to a few patients to come to his home clinic!

Once he had a boil on his neck, which was giving him tremendous pain, and it wouldn't allow him to concentrate on anything. Niranjan Nath, his friend, suggested that he have it checked.

'You go to the hospital for work every day, why don't you do something about it? It's causing you so much pain, and you continue to suffer, to the extent that others feel bad for you. As the head of the department, you can definitely order someone from the apothecary to make you a poultice.'

But Dr Kaul was a different kind of man.

'I don't remember my boil when I'm in the hospital,' he responded to Nir-kāk.

'What? You don't remember the boil? Even though it gives you extreme pain?' Nir-kāk retorted incredulously.

The good doctor avoided looking Nir-kāk in the eye and turned instead to his assistant who was standing quietly nearby. Pointing to the boil on his neck he said, 'As soon as we reach the hospital, remind me to attend to this first, will you please?'

With this he looked towards his dear friend Nir-kāk, his body language making it seem as if he was asking him, 'Are you happy now?'

Dr Gwasha Lal was renowned for his extraordinary ability to heal his patients. What he would accomplish in a mere five minutes with his patients, many other physicians couldn't do for months. As the word of his *shapha* (his healing touch) spread, people would bring their ailing loved ones to his clinic in large numbers, or would implore him to make a house visit, especially if the patient was quite unwell and couldn't travel the distance to the hospital.

Since he had been trained in modern medicine, he disregarded some of the traditional methods that other doctors would employ. For instance, starving patients to regulate their 'habitus' was quite common among the traditional doctors. But unlike the traditionalists, Dr Kaul offered a unique type of treatment, which was not at all conventional. While most doctors were starving their patients for months together, he would allow his patients to be fed small quantities of food even if they still showed symptoms of their disease. This was quite a departure from the norms of those times, but Gwasha Lal's patients would invariably get better and would be back in health much sooner than others.

After work, Dr Kaul would also visit the Dhar household for relaxation and to meet his friends. But since the Dhars were a large joint family, there were always a couple of patients for him to treat. In the presence of the matriarch of the family, Ram Chandra's wife, Māl, he would politely take the patients aside and take a look at them. With this done, he and his friends, as well as the older members in the family, would sit, chat, and laugh for hours on end.

Because there was a lot of love and affection between the members of the Dhar family and Pandit Shiv Narain and Dr Gwasha Lal, the latter two would spend considerable time at the Dhar household. Not only that, during the winter months, when the state capital moved to Jammu (as part of the Maharaja's Durbar relocating to the winter capital for about six months), the friends would stay for weeks with Nir-kāk and his family. They shared the accommodation that was provided to Mr Dhar, who worked for the revenue department, for the winter in Jammu. Looking back, it seems amazing that the friends behaved as if they were a band of blood brothers! So close were the friends that the youngsters in the household were of the impression that they too were members of the family, and blood relations, like the other uncles and cousins! To this day I wonder how they all lived harmoniously in a community system with multiple small family units. At one level, joint-family living contributed to the enhancement of mutual tolerance, trust, respect for one another, and an abiding love for one and all. Although the Dhar family was quite large—by and within themselves—they would graciously open their hearth and home to welcome those whom they called their own. Some relatives would send their sons and daughters to the Dhar household because of either financial difficulties, or they wanted the child to study devotedly and hoped that the ambience in Rishi Vihar contributed to their learning.

Once part of the household, all the relatives, near or far, it didn't matter, were treated as esteemed members of the family who were showered with affection and care without any discrimination. So much so that the whole family warmly adopted all such relatives and made them feel completely at ease.

The wife of Pandit Shambhu Nath Dhar was called Sati, while my mother—wife of Niranjan Nir-kāk Dhar—was known as Benji. When their nephews or sisters came to live in the Dhar household, they were considered to be a part of the family. Benji's nephew, Brij Lal Kaul, became the adopted son of the entire Dhar family when his aunt brought him home after his father died young. He was everyone's darling and considered as one of the sons of the family. Benji's sister, Maciji, was everyone's aunt 'maci'! Sati's sister, Liljigri, was dear to everyone. Similarly, Pran Bhaijān was the brother of Prem Nath Dhar's wife, Benigashi, and was treated like a brother. Mithan Lal was Liljigri's son, and was part of the household at Rishi Vihar for years together, and like all the others was treated like one of the dear members of the extended family. All cousins, near or distant, were like real brothers and sisters in the family.

The mutual love, affection, and consanguineous atmosphere that prevailed at Rishi Vihar, in my view, was due to the matriarch of the family, Māl. She was the one who spoke about and lived by the values of familial kinship and thereby set the tone on how the entire family would conduct itself. She was beautiful, wise and intelligent, and a very gracious woman. In spite of not being formally educated, she was versed in the poems and writings of philosophers and mystics, and would remember the verses—in Persian—of people like Jalaluddin Rumi and Hafiz. She could recite—in Sanskrit—the poetry of Kalidas as well as the *bijaks* of Kabir, and would use them in her conversations to emphasize a point at the most appropriate times. She would often use her knowledge and her vast repertoire of Persian couplets at gatherings and parties giving the impression of being a highly educated woman!

Her demeanour and sagacity ensured that Māl had immense influence not only within her large family but also through the family to their relatives across the Valley, and the community of Pandits and Muslims alike. It was Māl who was very fond of adding more members to the family, especially if she got to know that members of the extended family living elsewhere were going through difficult times. It was she who would suggest that the children or nephews or nieces be brought in to continue their education or until adverse conditions in their own homes improved. It was also Māl who would make sure that all such young members were loved and treated as true members of her family, with no discrimination by anyone. Hers was a unique way of making any and all guests to her home feel comfortable and welcome.

Like her husband Ram Chandra, she too was in favour of educating girls, and for this she had the support and admiration of her contemporary, Padmavati, the mother of Pandit Shiv Narain. Yet, she was also tradition-bound and would often boast about being the only daughter from four mothers. Her grandchildren would tease her on this account.

'How come you have four mothers?' we would all ask, almost as if we wanted to know more of the fairy story that she would be telling us.

'My father didn't have any children from his first two wives,' Māl would share with us, 'so he married a third one for this purpose. Luckily, I was born, and was brought up by my three mothers.'

Before she would finish her sentence, the children would interrupt her.

'Why did your father marry for the fourth time then?' the children, still not fully conversant with the ways of the adults, asked the question innocently.

'To get a son, a brother for me,' Māl would reply, matter-of-factly.

The children would get even more curious. 'Did you get a brother then?'

'No, never! That didn't happen, which is why I was a very precious child to my father and my four mothers.'

Shiv Narain and Dr Gwasha Lal too were like sons to Māl. She considered them her own and showered lots of affection and love on both of them. Their homes were akin to our own home as well. As kids, my cousins and I spent our holidays in these 'extended homes' quite frequently. In Dr Gwasha Lal's home there was the added attraction of being able to play with the Kaul children, who were our age. I have fond memories of having a lot of fun, playing the sitar, singing and having a ball with Nanaji, Dr Kaul's son, and his lovely sister Nancy.

But in the home of Shiv Narain, whom we would lovingly call Bhaijān ji, there were no children of our age. He had only one son, who was older to me and a contemporary of my eldest brother. The young man was quite serious-minded and wouldn't give much importance to children who were younger than him. Every time we visited Bhaijān ji's home, it would invariably be that my cousin (sister) Shyama and I would go together to keep each other company. Since there were no children of our age in the Fotedar household we were always welcomed as very special guests and pampered a lot, something that we would really enjoy. We would have the best things to eat, get cared for and fussed about, and the household always succeeded in keeping us happy for as long as we stayed in their home. Because the Dhar household was a large one, no one really bothered about our eating or other activities. It was not possible for anyone to pay individual attention to any child in a family of nearly fifty to sixty people. But in Bhaijān ji's home we got a lot of attention, and even a lot of freedom to do what we liked. I think we were being spoilt and pampered! But we'd feel like princesses in Pandit Shiv Narain's home.

Padmavati, Bhaijān ji's loving mother, was affectionately known as Benijigri and she too would ensure that we'd be thoroughly entertained. She had a wonderful way of telling beautiful stories and it was from her that I first heard some of the famous folk tales that we all love to this day. It was Benijigri who shared the famous tale of *Gul-e-Bakavali*, the Kashmiri tales of Noshlab, Sone-kisri, Heemal Nagraj, and so many others. Benijigri, by virtue of her own education and upbringing, was a treasure house of knowledge about religions, mysticism, history, literature, and poetry.

Shiv Narain's wife was called Jigri, a Kashmiri term meaning 'one's life'. She was from a noble family of Kashmiri Pandits who had been living in the town of Poonch for many generations. Apart from owning farmland, Jigri's family may also have been into some form of business. In fact, Jigri was quite a business-minded lady and would always think of new ways of turning a profit.

While Bhaijān ji was very handsome, tall, and fair-complexioned, Jigri was the absolute opposite of her husband. She was plain-looking and had very short legs, making her walk a little slow and ungainly. She would spend much of her time sitting on her elevated seat from where she'd order the house-help staff to do the many chores that she would oversee.

Jigri's nature, however, was sweet, and every time we visited her home she, along with her mother-in-law, Benijigri, would make us feel loved, cared for, and pampered.

I think she had a dream to set up an enterprise of women for which she wanted money from her husband. So whenever we were there, she would always send me to Bhaijān ji, her husband, who would be sitting in another room attending to the many problems that a host of petitioners would bring to his notice, to request and have him give Jigri some more money for her plans. I would willingly obey Jigri's orders like a good girl, and would waste no time to persuade Shiv Narain to give more money to his wife.

I recall the conversation as if it happened yesterday.

Shiv Narain: 'Hasn't Jigri told you that last week, and the week before that she has already taken a tidy sum of money from me? In fact, dear Khema, on one occasion you took the money from me to give it to her. Do you remember?'

Me, insistent: 'She wants more. You'll have to agree, please.'

'What has she done with the money I've given her? I have paid her more than hundred rupees,' Bhaijān ji said, shaking his head with genuine concern.

I must have been stubborn, probably to please Jigri, so I didn't move from Bhaijān ji's presence. He was irritated with my behaviour and must have thought that Jigri had brainwashed me so well that I wouldn't move without the money. Shiv Narain paused a while, and said, 'Ask her what she has done with the money I gave her last week.'

This was a legitimate query, I must have thought, and so I jumped up from the seat in front of Bhaijān ji and went to ask Jigri the question.

'Why does he want to know?' Jigri answered quite surprised that her husband was curious about what she had done with the money. Then, in a matter-of-fact manner, she guided me.

'Tell him that I'm running my business.'

I ran back to Bhaijān ji to convey the new information I had.

When he heard me, he almost jumped from his padded seat on the carpeted floor.

'Business?! What kind of business? With whom is she doing this business?' Bhaijān ji reacted sharply.

On this occasion, and during this conversation, I was able to extract only ten rupees for Jigri. She was very happy and contented to see the ten rupees. But her secret was out. Shiv Narain now knew that she was knitting sweaters out of the wool she bought with the money he had been giving her. Jigri would sell these elegant sweaters in the market with the help of their trustworthy house help, Nabha.

When details of the business finally trickled out, it was also known that if the cost of the sweater was ten rupees it would often be sold for just five rupees to someone who was poor or could not afford the full price. This would bring Jigri a tremendous amount of satisfaction and the gracious lady would therefore continue with her project—profit or no profit. I remember seeing Jigri ever-busy with her knitting project, which not only kept her engrossed but also deeply fulfilled at being able to serve those who were less privileged.

For much of the time till the mid-1940s, relations between husbands and wives were very formal. They would never talk to each other in front of their elders. Not only that, in the presence of their elders they would actually behave as if they were strangers to one another. There were so many incompatible couples who would be diametrically opposite in temperament, looks, and even education from their respective spouses. Yet, many such couples would carry on together for their entire lifetimes with just the pressure of society keeping the relationship in place.

At that time there were also no laws for divorce within Kashmiri Hindu society. In fact, annulling a marriage or separating from one's spouse, legally or otherwise, was considered a big blot and a stigma was attached to any such event that was suggestive of a couple being unable to gel with one another. In such conditions, and a number of couples having many discordant differences, it was not unusual for men and women to have extramarital relations—albeit these were carried on surreptitiously. Though accepted at some level, these matters were always spoken about in hushed tones, if at all.

To the southeast of Srinagar, in the beautiful Breng valley that falls beyond Achabal, lies the picturesque Kokernag spring. The name 'Kokernag' has been attributed to the spring (nāg) because of the gushing, ice-cold waters emerging from the deep aquifers spread out in three distinct streams, much like the claw foot of a chicken—*koker* in Kashmiri. This happens to be the largest freshwater spring in the Kashmir Valley, and Nunde-rishi, the mystic disciple of Lalleshwari, is believed to have uttered these words in Kashmiri in the fourteenth century:

'Kokernāg Breng chu Sonė-sund Preng.'

Meaning, the Kokernag spring near the village of Breng is a golden crown.

Kashmiris, who love outings and picnics, especially near beautiful brooks, springs, and in the dense and alluring pine forests, have always enjoyed visiting Kokernag for the lovely spring waters and the elegant garden that was laid out adjacent to the spring.

I must have been about twelve when Shyama, my sister, and I accompanied my father, Nir-kāk, and Bhaijān ji for a month-long holiday to Kokernag during the summer vacations. Bhaijān ji had taken a big house on rent for the holiday, and even when a few other cousins and relatives of ours turned up at Kokernag they were all accommodated happily in the house. In fact, the joy seemed to be greater as more members came together for fun and merrymaking.

Jigri had a close relation who was married to the son of a big landowner from a village not far from Srinagar. Jigri's relative was very beautiful and vivacious and used to visit the Fotedar household in Srinagar often. We would meet her each time we went visiting and to us young girls she seemed like an angel as she would dash around and up and down Jigri's and Bhaijān ji's house, running simple errands and making herself useful.

Her husband, the landowner's son, on the other hand, was ugly and a complete contrast to his angelic wife. His face had the pockmark scars of a smallpox infection that he must have survived as a child. It must have been a morganatic marriage for the rich landowner as despite his wealth he would not have got a bride of the same social status as himself because of his deficient looks. It is my guess that Jigri's relative, who would have been of modest means, would have given their beautiful daughter in lieu of a hefty dowry and probably some land that the landowner would have proffered.

Jigri's relative also accompanied us to the tourist resort of Kokernag that summer, ostensibly to give company to the newly married bride, Dullari Bhabi, who was married to Bhaijān ji's son. In one's childhood one does not notice too many things, but looking back, one can understand the behaviour of adults, their actions, and even the impishly playful things that they did.

Both my father, Nir-kāk, and Shiv Narain were handsome and would have been in their late thirties around the time we had the holiday. I'm sure they must both have been infatuated with the pretty lady and flirted with her. On her part, she too would have reciprocated the warmth and the attention she was getting and would have been gracious to them with her actions and behaviour. I remember her giggling a lot too. Her giggles were really infectious!

Part III
Innocent People, Simple Lives

7

Säd Makkārs

Throughout history, there have been people who preyed on the gullibility and the ingenuousness of others to make quick money or defraud the credulous public for personal gain. The same was the case in Kashmir.

In Srinagar, such a group is known, in Kashmiri, as *säd makkārs*, or charlatans, from the fact that they are sādhu (*säd*) pretenders (*makkār*). These people, who preferred to be called 'fortune tellers', wandered from one locality to the other trying to make a quick buck. Some of the more seasoned members would often assign labels such as 'God's messengers' or 'God's friends' to themselves, and much like other mountebanks would try to dupe the simple and guileless Kashmiris with their tricks.

These people would go to people's homes in groups of two or three at a time. They would then loudly proclaim their presence and start to suggest things from an interpretation of the stars that would bring joy to the householders. Nothing of course was beyond their divination and foretelling, and they would cover every aspect of life—right from the birth of children to their education, their marriage, and the time and place where their children would be born in turn! They would even divine if the baby, who would be still to be born in a few months from a visibly pregnant and a recently married daughter-in-law, would be a boy or a girl, and whether the child would look like the mother or the father (or any of the grandparents if they happened to be within earshot).

The kind of questions the *säd makkārs* would attempt to answer were typical and common at that time. People had minimal requirements and life was relatively simple and uncomplicated. Not that there weren't any problems—health and finances were constant concerns as was the birth of healthy children who could survive till adulthood. Jobs were not common but people would manage, living in large joint families where the earnings of just a few, often only one or at best two adults in the entire family, would support all the others and their progeny.

The *säd makkārs* were therefore ever ready to answer queries and engage with common householders. Sometimes they would gather the information about the home that they intended to visit from neighbours, to impress the people of the household with their knowledge of their affairs, which they would 'divine' there and then. Sometimes an advance party would spread the word in the locality about the power and reputation of a group of 'God's messengers' and sing paeans of their clairvoyance.

It is said that some people can be fooled sometimes, but not everybody can be fooled all the time. Which is why even the people of Srinagar had determined a system of classification for the *makkārs* based on their merits. The better the reputation, the more the money that would pour into their pockets. People would then wilfully seek their goodwill and blessings. Rich *makkārs* would go to the homes of the rich. They would also dress differently and more opulently than the ordinary *makkārs* and were therefore easily distinguishable from them. Typically, they wore neat clothes, with a pheran as a covering, and draped a big white woollen *cādar* (pronounced tsā-der) on their shoulders—a sign of their genuine spirituality and authentic approach to their work.

There is no denying that like in the rest of the subcontinent there was an amazing degree of acceptance of all kinds of people and professions. Some *säd makkārs* were really respected and much attention was paid to their insights, divinations, and commonsensical advice.

At the Dhar household, as soon as they entered the main door and it was announced that the *makkārs* had come for a visit, the grand dame of the house, Māl, would welcome them. They were then respectfully seated on the carpeted floor, where she sat too. The leader of the group would sit a little further up on the carpet while his *chelas* would sit deferentially a few paces behind him.

'How are you, Lassa Joo? It's been a long time since you've come this side. I hope all is well with you and your family?'

Before he could answer, the help in the house would also be asked to bring in refreshments for the visitor.

'Please send some tea and *phulkas* for Lassa Joo.'

Lassa Joo was a regular visitor to Rishi Vihar. Hearing his name, followed by the warm welcome, brought a contented smile on his face. He settled himself comfortably on the floor, leaning happily on the large white bolster by the wall, in anticipation of the tea that was about to be served to him.

The room was quite large. Big round bolsters were kept around the room, close to the walls, to provide support to anyone sitting there. Like all *säd makkārs*, even Lassa Joo was carrying a big bag with a number of gadgets and knick-knacks, and a thick, flexible metal chain that was nearly three feet long with links that were an inch or so in diameter. Much of the stuff in the bag was meant to amaze and frighten people who took a peek at his wares; and much of it was a mishmash of modern gadgets or parts of radios, cameras, medallions, amulets, beads, and incense.

After having tea and after sharing the latest gossip, Lassa Joo was ready to open his 'bag of tricks'. By this time all the children, womenfolk, and male elders who were not at school or at work, had assembled around him. Even kids and women from the neighbourhood would come in as word went around that Lassa Joo was visiting Māl at Rishi Vihar.

By now, everyone was watching him with curiosity, wondering how he was going to play with and rely on the flexible metal chain for divination this time. Lassa Joo was a performer par excellence. He took the chain out of his bag and began whirling it around his shoulders, round and round for some time till it got some momentum. While whirling the chain in this manner, it seemed to make a big, grey circle around his head. This was also accompanied by a strange humming sound, much like the sound of 'Om' that emanated from the chain links, making the ambience all the more mysterious.

All the ladies of the household, the neighbourhood folks, the house help staff, and children would wonder with curiosity to see how this mysterious metal chain was emanating such a loud sound. Meanwhile, Lassa Joo, with his gestures and the swift movements of his hands would vary the sounds to a crescendo, in a way that it seemed like he too was reaching a level of 'heightened divinity' and precognition.

After whirling the chain twelve or fifteen times, he threw it on the floor with a bang, and then looking closely at the random pattern created by the serpent-like chain, uttered these words in Kashmiri, in a sing-song, yet authoritative, tone:

'I'm now in the power of the All-Knowing! I'm getting His commands! He has commanded to share that very soon some sort of festivity and celebration is going to occur in this household! I'm ordained to tell you all that some good news is around the corner!'

The chain would writhe like a live serpent, as he would say these words, making the situation seem prophetic.

I am sure none of the spectators would really know what Lassa Joo was alluding to. Each one interpreted the prophecy in the way that suited them! Hearing good things about their future, all the persons present were glad that happy times had been predicted. Children, adults, ladies, and the men present there would all revel in the thought that Lassa Joo—speaking with the authority of the All-Knowing, no less—had given them precise answers to the queries that they had in their minds.

One of Māl's granddaughters was called Pichru. She was Māl's daughter's daughter and would often visit her grandparents. However, if she had vacations she would happily spend her holidays with her cousins, uncles, and aunts at Rishi Vihar.

As a young teenager, Pichru was full of humour and wit, and was a master at repartee. She was beautiful and had a plump countenance that endeared her to one and all. She composed poems about events, people, and conditions on her feet and displayed extraordinary creativity. Pichru was the darling of everyone. Everyone in her family and her mother's family adored her, showered love upon her, and always expressed joy at being in her company. Whenever she talked or shared a joke or a humorous poem, she would see to it that whatever she said would bring cheer to the family.

Her younger sister, Nani, and she had devised a language, a novel language that only the two of them spoke and understood. If there were secrets to be kept between the two and they didn't want their brothers or cousins to find out they would quickly lapse into their unique tongue and rattle of what seemed like gibberish to us! She was also excellent at mimicry. No one ever felt that she was doing something unusual, because she made mimicking look so easy. Her skill was truly phenomenal.

Once, while in the presence of her extended family, she was mimicking the way a lady from the neighbourhood spoke and conducted herself. The whole room was in splits, rollicking with laughter at the way Pichru was speaking and mimicking the lady with the unusual style. Even as everyone was enjoying the fun, all of a sudden, the lady's daughter entered the room. Even as the laughter was immediately suppressed, the young woman began to enquire about her mother.

'Is my mother here? I heard her speaking to someone just now.'

The situation was so awkward that nobody uttered a word. When she repeated the question, one of the ladies in the room, keeping her presence of mind, told her that her mother, who had indeed been there a little while ago, had already left!

When Pichru was in her teens, her grandmother, Māl, would have been in her seventies. Yet as the grand dame of the household she exuded great charm and grace and looked beautiful. No one would ever be able to guess her real age.

Māl and her husband Ram Chandra Dhar had five sons and three daughters. All had good government jobs. The three daughters were married into good KP families that had a rich background. All of Māl's children were fond of their mother and would spend considerable time with one another too. The daughters would visit their mother often, and many of the grand dame's traits and mannerisms were carried through them to their families as well.

During the day everyone in the family would be busy with their respective professions and work, but the evenings, after everyone was back home, would be spent in their own unique 'club life' where all would assemble in the big hall to enjoy the gossip of the day, share jokes, and have a relaxed time in the company of loved ones.

Pichru and her younger cousin, Surender, who was affectionately called Sardar, were the key stars of the family and would entertain the entire clan with their mimicry, humour, and ready wit. Everyone would laugh to their tune. Sometimes the laughter would continue for so long that some people would have tears in their eyes and some would even have rolled on the floor laughing, in a state of uninhibited glee.

For this unique family in the heart of Srinagar, living and celebrating and enjoying together created a beautiful sense of oneness and serenity despite the fact that life for its members was not entirely without problems. The world looked beautiful, peaceful, and wonderful. Everything was in a state of joy and no worries were allowed to play on the minds of the members. The affection for one another and the ritual of sharing, celebrating festivals and achievements, playing games, cracking jokes, mimicking and making queer fish of others, and generally adding spice to their lives—all in the relaxing ambience of the family club—created a haven that seemed a world away from the hustle and bustle of the outside world.

It was Sunday, offices and schools were shut, and all the members of the family were therefore in no hurry to go anywhere.

A leisurely community breakfast was another Sunday ritual that everyone looked forward to. On Sundays, Māl was very keen to have something special prepared—a treat that would be difficult to serve on days when the elders and the children were in a hurry to leave home for work and school. Corn breads with honey or thin rice 'sputters' (*chēre-çot*) served with kehva tea that everyone adored were made every other week.

Tikaram, the chief cook, along with other helpers would always intimidate the children into obedience by threatening that he would not make their share of the goodies if they wouldn't obey his orders. The children, in turn, would entreat him to order them and assign them whatever work he wanted them to do. Tikaram enjoyed this very much. Both Tikaram and the children knew that it was all for the sake of fun and enjoyment, and yet everyone played along and made Sundays even more fun.

All were busy having a nice sumptuous breakfast when all of a sudden, a big group of people entered the hall. Seeing Lassa Joo enter along with his team of three *makkārs*, the children automatically made space for them by moving to other corners of the large carpeted hall. The children were all very disciplined and well mannered and needed no instructions to give the entourage of *säd makkārs* the respect that they deserved. As the men began to be seated, Lassa Joo sniffed, took a deep breath.

'That's a wonderful aroma coming from the kitchen,' he said, sniffing audibly in true *säd makkār* style, even as he was demonstrating that he knew what was cooking at that hour.

'Well, you are a bit too late to have today's delicacy, but you will have kehva instead,' grandmother Māl said quickly. 'Just be comfortable and the tea will be on its way.' Māl was very considerate not to overburden the cooks.

A visit by Lassa Joo and his team always meant that he would open his bag soon after the kehva was enjoyed and the spectators too had settled down.

As all the attention was on the *säd makkārs* no one noticed Pichru quietly leaving the room and heading upstairs.

Lassa Joo and his troupe were by now in full form. They were answering questions, making predictions while in a trance, and eliciting guidance from the All-knowing spirit.

It was nearly half an hour later that Pichru made her entry into the hall. It was no ordinary entry, because even her own family members just could not believe it was she. She had washed her long hair, which was still quite wet, and left it open, letting it spread like long slender serpents across her shoulders. She had worn a big white robe, which was long and covered her feet. In her right hand she held a big iron pitchfork, taken from the kitchen where it was used to remove burning, red-hot cinder from the wood stove upon which the food was cooked. In the other hand she held a big iron chain to match that of the *makkār's*. As she entered the hall, she began to shout out words of gibberish so loudly that nobody could utter a word. Everyone was dumbfounded. Nobody knew who this person was, including Lassa Joo and his frightened helpers.

'How dare you enter my domain, you *makkār*, don't you know who I am?' she said out loud, looking Lassa Joo straight in the eye, even as she kept shaking her head in a circular fashion so that her black, wet and full-length hair spun around, making an unusual *swoosh* sound. Her right hand, with the pitchfork, was bobbing up and down, making a thud on the floor as she completed one circuit of her head. Then some more gibberish and phrases were used that all *säd makkārs* were familiar with.

Pichru, in her current avatar, was in command.

'I warn you,' she continued, her tone ferocious, 'do not dare to fool the people around here. Now tell me, will you leave on your own, or should I have the spirits expel you unceremoniously? I want your answer; the spirits are getting impatient!'

Saying this she slammed the forked side of the pitchfork on a raised edge of the floor, making the spongs vibrate with an eerie *ooohn* sound.

The scene was so swift, so sudden, and abrupt that there was no time to ask Pichru to stop this gimmick, even if she was recognized by her family. Her grandmother—discerning woman that she was—quickly realized who the young, long-haired lady-*makkār* was, but thought it prudent to keep mum, lest the cat be out of the bag, which might bring opprobrium on the family for forcing Lassa Joo out of the house.

Sensing the gravity of the situation Lassa Joo and his boys began to collect their things hurriedly, to beat a hasty retreat from the terrifying scene. He may also have been keen to prevent further ridicule of himself in front of all the spectators and especially his own young chelas. He was sure that the newcomer had entered his domain recently. Because of Pichru's gestures he did not for a moment doubt her authenticity as a *säd makkār*.

By now Pichru was in a frenzy. Her gyrating had reached a swift pace and she was uttering unintelligible words.

'Haven't you heard me? I am going to take you to task!' she shouted at no one in particular, her voice shrill and loud. While uttering these words she hit the pitchfork on the ground again, as her whirling head gained speed.

Before anyone could stop the group of *säd makkārs*, they all hastily ran away and out of the hall without exchanging the customary salaam and namaskar with the householders. They were in such a hurry that they even forgot to wear their shoes properly, hurriedly picking them up and running out barefoot.

When the *makkārs* had all left the home, Pichru abruptly threw away her robe, and settled her dishevelled hair with her hands. That's when everyone let out a collective gasp. It was their own darling Pichru who had frightened poor Lassa Joo and his associate *makkārs* away!

―⚭―

Māl was a little upset that their regular *säd makkār*, Lassa Joo, had been unceremoniously sent away by her very own granddaughter, Pichru. In her defence, Pichru insisted that the *säd makkārs* were crooks and quacks, and if they truly had any powers then they wouldn't have run away at the sight of a witch.

Māl wasn't amused.

'I know these are not your words, but those of your father, who does not believe in these things' she said, annoyed. 'But who asked you to ridicule them in this way? The poor man Lassa Joo and his group have left our home in a huff. Don't you do such a thing again!' The grandmother was visibly annoyed with the cheap joke. Pichru too was upset about her granny's reaction and began to weep loudly.

Pichru was a darling of all the family members and nobody wanted her to be upset and thus spoil the beautiful Sunday mood that morning. All her uncles got up and began to coax the girl not to feel bad, even as they complimented her on her remarkable acting skills and creativity. Pichru smiled and she was happy once more.

That morning it was also collectively resolved that nobody would ever speak a word about the manner in which Lassa Joo and his *säd makkārs* beat a hasty retreat from Rishi Vihar.

8

Van Buḍini

Benji would always say, 'Khalila, see even today he doesn't want to have his dinner. Ask him how is he going to be strong if he doesn't eat properly?'

'He should eat properly,' Khalila would reply. Khalila would help around the house and was entrusted with the care of Surender, Benji's son, who was affectionately known as Sardar or Sardara. Khalila loved Sardar dearly and made sure that he was with him at all times.

'If he is weak or meek,' Khalila said to Benji, 'who will call him Sardar, the strong man?' Surender, at that time a little boy, would hear the conversation with rapt attention.

'I don't like this food! I don't want to have it!' Surender would say loudly, eager to leave the plate full of rice and delicacies to go out to play with his cousins.

'All right, then you may have to call the genie,' Benji would say. 'Khalila, tell him that Sardara neither listens to anyone, nor does he want to eat anything.'

As Surender heard this conversation he would resume eating some morsels from his plate, while his mother Benji would help him. This was a bit of a routine at supper time.

'I know it's not true. There is no genie! I am not afraid of genies.' Surender would say defiantly, although we all knew that he was afraid of whatever he thought a genie was and about whom he'd heard a lot of stories from his mother. Benji was rather emphatic in her descriptions of what genies were capable of and she would dwell on the parts that were most frightening.

'The genie takes away children who don't listen to their mother and don't eat their food properly,' she would say gleefully. But the same story repeated to Surender for months together was fast becoming a tall tale. Khalila could sense that young Sardar was no longer in awe of the genie and decided to do something practical about it—if for nothing else than to make it easier for Benji to feed Surender and to have some fun with his little ward as well.

Khalila, despite being a helper in the household, was treated as a member of the family. He lived at Rishi Vihar, away from his village, and would do all sorts of work during the day, apart from looking after his wards—Surender and a few other young cousins of his. In the evening, however, Khalila would also prove to be a pretty creative entertainer to the children and the adults alike.

At the time of children's meals, he would coin all sorts of fables based on animals, jinns, kings and queens, empires, fairy tales, and the great Sinbad the Sailor. He had the knack of weaving these fascinating stories together to impress the ladies of the household, who were even keener to hear the stories than were their hungry children.

Khalila was often at his creative best on these occasions. If he had been born in these times he would have been a great actor of this era. There was no match to his mimicry. He had even collected a variety of odd clothes for the specific roles that he played as part of his evening entertainment and fun. In fact he had collected a number of pumpkin and melon shells for making them into masks for the different roles. It used to take him months to dry these shells to give them a proper shape, after which he would meticulously carve the opening for the eyes and make long, fierce-looking teeth. Most of his leisure time was spent in these things, which I think were dear to his heart. This kind of art was making him special amongst the members of the family, who loved him for his creative genius.

For his acting, all the ladies of this household would lend him any help that he would ask for. Sometimes he would demand even the best clothes from Ram Chandra's wardrobe, since the role required it!

One sunny morning, around noon, while Benji was feeding Surender, Khalila suddenly vanished from the scene. Surinder was in an especially irascible mood and was being disobedient, and just did not want to touch his food despite Benji's loving entreaties and threats. This little drama of life was going on in one corner of the big hall. On the other side of the hall, Surender's grandmother, Māl, was explaining something to the family carpenter and the mason—both of whom were respected craftsmen and regular visitors to the family. They had both made considerable improvements in the house over the years. Both of them were sitting in front of the grandmother. The carpenter had a long pencil on his ear, which he would use to mark wood and explain his solutions using diagrams.

Grandmother, the mason, and the carpenter were so engrossed in their conversation that they were oblivious to what was going on in another corner of the carpeted hall. Helpers were coming in and going out, doing their work. The menfolk were all at their respective jobs outside the home. Everything that day looked peaceful and all was well in the world.

All of a sudden, a hideous-looking thing entered the hall, with the loud jangling of *ghungroos* and of trinkets. Everyone in the hall turned their necks towards the door and saw a large, ugly creature entering the hall. Grandmother, all the children, the carpenter, mason, and the ladies of the household were frightened out of their wits. The carpenter and the mason quickly jumped out of the window nearby and landed on the paved walkway adjacent to the large garden. The creature settled itself on the big seat next to the wall that was placed towards the centre, segregating the hall into two parts. One part of the hall was where the men would sit, and the other one was for the ladies.

Grandmother, though momentarily shaken, did not utter a word, not knowing how to react to the unusual situation. Sensing the gravity of the moment but amused and surprised that his disguise had actually frightened people out of the hall, Khalila in the attire of a crazed, ugly witch wearing a mask with sharp, long teeth and long black hair, turned towards Grandmother and whispered, 'You need not be afraid, Mother.'

Recognizing his voice, Māl was relieved!

'You rascal!' she hissed, partly in anger. 'What made you play such a trick? All the children, Surender, and his cousins were so frightened!'

As soon as the mason and the carpenter saw what they thought was a terrible-looking jinn, and jumped out of the window, they began to shout and wail deliriously, truly mortified by the horrible sight they had just seen.

'Ḍän hā! Ḍän hā! Çelivo! Çelivo!' they shouted in Kashmiri, announcing that a ferocious witch (ḍän) had entered the home of the Dhar family, and all that needed to be done was to flee (çeliv). (Pronunciation guide: the sound symbolized by the uppercase and lower case letters, Ḍ and ḍ, are hard, palatal 'D' sounds, as in the English word 'day'. Without the dot beneath them, the D sound is akin to the sound of 'TH' in the words 'the' or 'they'. The letter C has the sound 'ch', as in the word 'China'. But with the cedilla symbol beneath it, Ç the sound transforms to 'zz' as in the word 'pizza'.)

The two men—their simple leather sandals in hand—were in a frightened daze as they ran out to the street shouting, bringing fear and anxiety to all those whom they encountered or who heard their loud wailing. They must have had quite an impact on those who saw them, barefeet and delirious.

Kashmiris are intrinsically curious people and enjoy anything that is entertaining. It doesn't matter what the event may be as long as it's novel and provides grist to the gossip mill, which in itself is stimulating. While the carpenter and the mason were both running towards their respective homes, many people ran with them, asking them to clarify what had frightened them so. Soon there was a large group of people in pherans, all running with the original bearers of the awful news and adding novel and bizarre features from their own imagination to the, by now, phantasmagorical story of the dän.

Soon the people who'd encountered the fleeing duo spread the word that nobody should venture towards the Dhar haveli (big house) since a hideous, giant witch had visited it and she had plans to stay. The mason and the carpenter too did their bit to set the record straight. They confirmed that indeed a giant witch, ugly as death, had entered the hall of the Dhar haveli right in front of their eyes.

'The ḍän would be there even now!' the carpenter announced emphatically. 'I saw her enter with her face all terrible and contorted! She has no plans of leaving. We don't know what might have happened to poor Grandmother and the rest of the family.' This news spread like wildfire in the mohalla around the Nalla Mar area. People in the vicinity of Rishi Vihar were extremely concerned about the welfare of the Dhar family, which they considered a big shield against misfortune and calamity—not just for their area but for the entire city.

Soon a crowd had assembled in a big square near the haveli. Scouts were placed at key points to keep an eye for the beast lest she should come their way to scuttle the meeting. The local butchers got their slaughtering knives with them for added security.

The people present in the square were scared, fearing that the ugly dän might make their locality her permanent home, thereby disrupting business and may even demand food in the form of livestock and chickens, adding a further burden on the meagre incomes within the community. It took the crowd considerable time, and much heated debate, to come to the conclusion that the beast had somehow to be shunted out of the city. The witch, from all the for them descriptions obtained thus far, seemed to be too fierce for them to even consider the option of killing her. However, the crowd acknowledged that the immediate problem was also to determine how best to mitigate the fact that the dän had already made its residence in the Dhar household. Everyone was unanimous that no time could be wasted in setting their plan into motion, so that the dän should not do any harm to the members of the family. It was also decided that someone would have to immediately inform the male members of the Dhar family about the calamity that had befallen them.

Soon it was evening. The crowd in the square had become a procession that had by now lined the road all the way to the front gate of the Dhar home. When Shambhu Nath returned on his tonga from his office at the court, he was alarmed to see so many people lining the main street. He would normally take the family tonga to work and back, and as he got closer home, some concerned seniors from the community stepped on to the road and blocked his way.

'Baiji *banvāz* (a shortened form of *Bandā-navāz*—respected sir) we cannot allow you to go towards the haveli,' they shouted almost in unison. 'A huge, ugly, and hefty dän has entered your house!'

As the crowd eagerly moved in around the tonga, another concerned and genuinely frightened neighbour shouted to Baiji.

'We are anxious about the well-being of all the members of the family who are all stranded inside. Nobody has been able to escape from within except for the mason and the carpenter! They've both had a narrow escape and have had to run for their lives after jumping from the window,' the man concluded, crying bitterly.

'Run for their lives?' Baiji said with great shock, as he grew pale from the terrible tidings that he had just received. 'Are the members of my family all inside still? What exactly happened?' he enquired, looking truly dazed and confused with the news that had been shared with him. He was puzzled to hear about the situation. He was an erudite man and knew that the story of the dän was too far-fetched. Yet, the people around him were genuinely afraid and in shock. He knew it couldn't all be one man's imagination.

Baiji was determined to enter his home and assess for himself what was really happening. But nobody allowed him to move towards his home. All the people made a human barricade to prevent further his movement.

'Baiji, we won't allow you to go to your home, it's very risky! We request you to please stay at Haji sahab's house till we safely extract the other members of your family,' one of the senior community members suggested.

It was a very tricky situation. Baiji was keen to find out for himself what was going on but the crowd just wouldn't relent.

All of a sudden, Baiji caught sight of Khalila, looking his ordinary self again, and standing somewhat away from the main gathering. He seemed to be shouting something and was even waving his arms, but due to the din of people nobody heard him or paid much attention to what he was trying to convey. Baiji, however, raised his arm and beckoned Khalila to come to him. Khalila ran towards the tonga and soon everyone saw him trying to move closer to Baiji, endeavouring to share something with him.

All the people who had been speaking with Baiji, who was seated in the front of the horse carriage, encircled Khalila, and started to extract the latest news about the worrisome episode.

People were heard yelling at him in fear and with trepidation.

'Pray tell us, is the witch still there? How did you manage to come out? What about dear Grandmother, the other ladies and the children? Are they all right?' Now all the attention was on Khalila as heads turned towards him and many more queries started.

By now Khalila was next to Baiji. That's when Baiji sensed that something didn't quite fit. He could feel that Khalila looked neither frightened of the witch nor was he perturbed by the whole episode. That's when Baiji decided to use his skills as an attorney to question him directly.

'Were you there at that time?' he asked Khalila sternly.

Sensing the gravity of the situation, Khalila's innermost actor popped out again and he started off by making a sad face.

'Sir, please sir, I beg forgiveness! I was verily there when the dän made a sudden appearance. But sir, she isn't a ḍän she's a *van buḍini* (an old hag with magical powers living in the forests [*van*]),' Khalila said, looking down, ensuring that his eyes didn't meet Baiji's. His monologue, however, was far from over, and he continued speaking, as he sensed that everyone in earshot was listening to him with rapt attention. With his best histrionic skills he started pleading for the hag.

'Sir, please, save the situation in the haveli. She won't leave our place, until, until …' he trailed off, not finishing his sentence as he simultaneously burst into tears. By now Khalila had fallen at Baiji's feet.

'Until what, Khalila!? What does the van buḍini want?' Baiji asked Khalila as he picked up the tearful man by his shoulders. 'What does she want, and why aren't you talking? Tell me everything, now!' Baiji was really concerned and getting increasingly impatient and angry.

Baiji's body language must have revealed that he wasn't entirely convinced that an old hag with demoniac powers had entered his house. Many people in the crowd sensed this and piped in.

'Sir, he is telling you the truth! Even *vosta* Razāq and *vosta* Sullā (*vosta* is a Kashmiri term used for the word *Ustād*) both saw the jinn, the van buḍini. They mentioned that the horrible-looking creature is holding Grandmother, the other ladies and the children hostage in the home.' Many others were adding their own little perspectives to this tale as if they were witnesses to the entire scene.

'How come you've been spared and allowed to leave the house,' Baiji asked Khalila, as the man stood up and wiped his wet eyes with the sleeve of his pheran. Baiji had probably guessed by now that someone was playing mischief but wasn't sure, and so he turned towards the only person from inside the haveli.

'Sir, I left the house as the van buḍini ordered me to communicate her demands to you. She was sitting very close to our beloved grandmother, and I had no option but to quickly come to you,' Khalila said, his eyes still looking down. 'She has made it clear that she won't leave the house till her demands are met.'

'What does she want?' Baiji asked impatiently. Many others exclaimed loudly as well. 'What are the demands of the wicked dän?'

'Sir, the hag is demanding the meat of a healthy male goat today,' Khalila said seriously, 'and has promised to leave our haveli after ten days only if that condition is fulfilled by sundown today.'

There was a collective gasp from the people who were within earshot.

'Ten days! That too after eating a full goat!' someone exclaimed.

'Why can't the horrible witch leave after she has stuffed herself?' another elderly man enquired.

Khalila was obviously not done yet.

'Kind sir, that isn't all,' he said, looking at the elderly man. 'From tomorrow, she has ordered that she be served four square meals, with adequate amounts of meat and chicken to go with the large quantities of rice that we expect her to eat. And if we disobey her, she will curse the entire city. This is the terrible message that she wanted me to convey to you all, and that's the only reason why I'm alive and before you all.' Khalila was in his theatrical element and in full control of the situation.

By this time Baiji, who knew Khalila well, knew that it was none other than their very own talented actor who was behind the mischief. But he knew that tempers were high and if the people gathered around him at that time were to find out that this was but a hoax, they would be very annoyed and angry, and might harm Khalila. So Baiji kept quiet and didn't dig for any more answers.

'Why didn't you tell us about this earlier, Khalila? We could have done something about it before dear Baiji got back from work,' a few elderly and concerned people from the crowd said.

'I was shouting for quite some time trying to give you the message, but no one paid heed or listened to me,' Khalila said.

'So what now?' someone asked, voicing the collective mind of most of the people in the crowd.

'She is awaiting the meat of a goat to be brought to her. I suspect if this is not done in time, she may venture out of the haveli and come on to the street, and might pick up anything that catches her fancy.' Khalila's words injected a chill in people's minds and now it was apparent that fear had truly gripped them. Now the time had come to take action and mitigate the risk to their own lives and those of their loved ones.

'What are we waiting for? Let's get a goat for the horrible van buḍini,' one of the local leaders in the group shouted, galvanizing the crowd into action.

Baiji and Khalila were requested to wait until the arrangements were complete.

In about an hour, all preparations for the meat were done. The meat of a freshly killed male goat of medium size was arranged in a big wicker basket and handed over to Khalila. It was now clear that Khalila would carry the meat to the van buḍini and secure further instructions about Baiji and allowing his entry into the haveli.

'We are sure the hag will be happy to get this,' the people who had actually obtained the meat were telling Khalila and Baiji.

Some elderly persons came forward and offered:

'If she wants to have something else, ask her, and we'll arrange for that too.'

No one, however, volunteered to accompany Khalila inside. Instead they bucked him up, boosted his morale, and egged him to go into the house, the wicker basket neatly balanced on his head.

'Do inform us when she accepts the meat. We will all stay here with Baiji banvāz till then,' some elderly people from the crowd shouted to Khalila as he started to head towards the house, after crossing the Mär canal on the little footbridge.

'I will surely come back with any news I have,' Khalila said, making a long, fearful face. He also feigned trembling, as if he was very reluctant to go inside, but was doing so only because the community elders wanted him to go in, and he was unwilling to obey them. He took hold of the basket on his head and reluctantly moved on, carrying himself slowly.

Now Baiji and the other people settled down for the wait. Khalila had promised to get them news regarding the van budini. As they waited, each minute seemed like a long time and it wasn't long before some people got restless and waited on the road.

―――∽∞∾―――

As soon as he reached home, Khalila—breathless but elated—headed for the kitchen. Here the head cook, Tikaram, was preparing the evening meals on the earthen cooking space, called *dān*. Two other helpers were also in the kitchen. One was washing utensils and the other chopping vegetables. All three of them saw Khalila at the kitchen door holding a basket in his hand. They must have noticed something in his body language that made them curious. They left their respective jobs and went towards Khalila, curiously cautious.

'What's this new trick that you're planning, Khalila?' Tikaram asked with amusement. 'And what new masks are you carrying in your basket?'

The other two tried to yank the basket away from Khalila's hands, but he resisted.

'Don't touch the basket!' Khalila said loudly to the two kitchen helpers. 'Inside this is my treat for all of you. Today the haveli will feast on my account,' he continued, feeling smug as he said this. 'But there's one important condition: till dinnertime, no one other than the four of us should know what I have brought in this basket. You get it? Nobody must know, not even Mother.'

Tikaram looked at Khalila seriously. 'Show me what's inside and then I'll decide,' he said.

Khalila opened the lid of the wicker basket and showed the three men the large chunks of fresh goat meat that he had brought in. The meat was so fresh it was steaming.

'It's a deal then?' Khalila asked, looking at Tikaram.

'Wow! That's a lot of meat! Where have you got that from, Khalila?' Tikaram asked.

Khalila put his hand on his moustache and began to twirl it upwards. In a confident tone he answered Tikaram's query.

'Only I can do this! It is only my brains and skills by which I make miracles and defeat even wise men, like Haji sahab.' He then narrated the entire saga and the drama that had happened on the roadside, in Baiji's presence.

All three men listening to Khalila were awestruck. For the first time they admitted his superiority.

'Hari Om!' Tikaram said. 'You are a masterful deceiver! But this game is going to stretch long. What's up your sleeve now, Khalila? You are a real actor and you also love to play with embers and red-hot chillies.' They were praising his skills and pointing to the high-stakes game of risk that he had undertaken.

Khalila was on top of the world. His friends and colleagues were praising him, and that meant a lot to him.

When he was leaving, Tikaram told him mockingly, 'Don't forget to bring the van buḍini a little early. I'll keep her share separate from the meat that'll be cooked for the others.' He winked at Khalila, and all the four men laughed heartily.

The retainers who worked in the household had a world of their own. In the absence of proper entertainment, they would perform all sorts of musical operas and plays of well-known Kashmiri poets whenever they had the time. Usually this was done late at night with proper music and props, and the tamasha would go on till the early hours of the morning. Like Khalila there were a couple of other domestic helps too who were gifted, and either had marvellous voices or were good at playing musical instruments such as the *surnai* or the *rabab*. Sarvanand and Mahadev Ram were both good singers. They were also versed with the latest trends of that era. They would perform in the style of laḍishah, sing folk songs, and sing the *vaks* of Lalleshwari, the fourteenth-century Kashmiri mystic. Laḍishah lyrics are meant to be full of satire and make queer fish of the government about the ills of society, about the business class, shopkeepers, and almost anyone who showed disregard for the values of selflessness and honesty. This also provided an inoffensive way of conveying one's grievance to one's superiors, who, by virtue of being shamed through song, would always endeavour to get pending irritants dealt with and commit to the work that was to be done.

It was evening now. After what had seemed like an interminable wait, Khalila had returned to the crowd on the road and announced—again with the appropriate body language that came from being a good actor—that the old hag from the forest had very happily accepted the gift of meat and was pleased to have it. The crowd burst into spontaneous applause. As the crowd dispersed for the evening, Baiji was brought home.

That evening, the haveli witnessed a gala time! In the kitchen all the helpers were helping each other. There was also a lot of commotion there. While cooking, all of them were discussing the van buḍini, her appearance, and Khalila's acting and other skills. Khalila had become their hero overnight!

By the time all of Baiji's younger brothers had returned from their respective jobs, they noticed the heightened activity and the commotion in the kitchen, and details about the van buḍini and how she had 'appeared' were known to everyone in Rishi Vihar. On their way home, they had also heard how Baiji banvāz had almost rid the haveli of the van buḍini, but that something more had to be done to appease the horrible, greedy ḍän.

Although the people were scared of the van buḍini, her presence in a respectable family in the neighbourhood was equally a source of great entertainment for the people. The rumour mill was spinning vigorously, and even hearing and spreading the gossip was entertaining!

Within the haveli too there were mixed feelings. The smaller children, whose mothers had frightened them with stories about the hag from the woods, were horrified that one of them had actually come to be in their own home. The older children, who knew that it was Khalila who had played the part of the van buḍini to perfection, became his allies and did all they could to make the actor play his part with increasing sophistication. Then, of course, there was meat for dinner that evening, which was a source of joy for all the children!

While there was an overall sense of fun and amusement within the haveli, Baiji, his brothers, and Māl were concerned. The whole affair of the van budini, which was to have been a family joke, had become a public matter now. They had gotten wind that many people in the neighbourhood were holding meetings to determine how best to rid the community of the menace, the old witch!

By the morning of the next day, the whole city of Srinagar was agog with the rumour that a witch had entered the Dhar household. People from afar who may have had some work in the neighbourhood would tarry a while longer just to get a glimpse of the van budini. There was tremendous curiosity to see the hag since over the past twenty-four hours she had become a veritable monster of fierce demeanour!

From this day onwards, the haveli also started to receive baskets of fresh meat and chicken. Many others sent goats' legs, some brought goats' heads with the brains in place (goat brains are a delicacy in Kashmir) as also other inner parts of the goat such as the liver, heart, and stomach. People had this belief that more offerings would make the witch happy and she would vacate the city sooner than expected.

As the offerings for the van budini started to come in, curiosity around the hag grew as well.

'What does this awful creature look like? What is she wearing? What and how much is she eating? How is she behaving with the family? Aren't they scared of her?'

As people began to pour into the haveli to satisfy their curiosity, it was the work of Khalila and his children accomplices to answer any questions and send people away satisfied.

By the third day the problem was creating ripples everywhere. At work, Baiji was confronted by a group of advocates enquiring about the well-being of his entire family and asking probing questions about the old hag who had chosen to come to their haveli.

That evening, Baiji, his mother, and all his brothers sat together to resolve the menace of the mythical van buḍini, which had been created by Khalila with the help of the older boys of the family.

'We have to end this problem,' Baiji said emphatically. 'At my office everyone was asking me about it today. All sorts of questions are being posed, and I'm not happy to be a part of this charade.'

'When they asked you questions, what did you say?' one of the brothers asked.

'I was really fumbling for an answer. I told them truthfully that I hadn't seen the van buḍini myself, but I knew that she was within the haveli and being well looked after,' Baiji said, smiling.

The other brothers too had had similar experiences. Srinagar was curious, and everyone was asking the residents of the haveli a lot of questions. It was therefore decided that the matter had to be brought to an appropriate end.

Khalila and the older boys of the family were called to attend the meeting. They were told that the joke had boomeranged and had ceased to be a playful gag any more because it involved the whole city, and there was genuine and understandable concern about public safety. The ruse of the van buḍini had to be stopped forthwith.

Everyone was unanimous that Khalila had displayed great theatrical genius not only on the first day, when he frightened the younger kids as well as Razāq and Sullā (the carpenter and the mason), but even that afternoon in the presence of Baiji and Haji sahab when he showed considerable skill in dealing with the crowd. Khalila was praised profusely, and he was also told that he would be the one to bring the hoax to an appropriate end. Khalila the actor was given an appropriate script and when he was satisfied with his part the meeting ended.

The next day Khalila put on nice, shimmering clothes, applied a lot of fragrant oil in his hair and combed it with a middle parting that was suggestive of his going for a party. He then left for the market, taking a few of the younger children of the household along, who were also suitably dressed in festive clothes. By this time all the little children were being unusually obedient, since they knew that it was Khalila who somehow controlled the van buḍini, whom they still feared.

When Khalila and the kids crossed the street and reached the market, everyone's eyes turned towards him. People gathered around him and the children and began to enquire about the welfare of people in the haveli. They were also keen to know why he was in such a good mood and how he was attired so nattily and where he was going with the kids.

'Are you going somewhere for a party?' many people asked. But instead of answering their question, Khalila began to congratulate them all one by one, saying loudly 'Mubārakh! Mubārakh, it's our victory, it's your victory!'

'Mubārakh for what?' Many people asked him simultaneously.

Khalila was in form and at his eloquent best.

'The ḍän has left the haveli and she has gone for good! This is our victory!'

'You mean the van buḍini? Has she really left?'

'Yes, the van buḍini, who else? She has blessed all of you. She is very pleased with the people of Navakadal, Safakadal, and Zainakadal especially, and your hospitality has paid off,' Khalil said in one breath, exuding happiness.

'Mubārakh, Mubārakh, this is great news,' the people gathered around him said in unison. They all hugged each other and exchanged happy greetings.

Within no time the message spread like wildfire. 'The horrible evil witch has left the Dhar household, and has done so happily. She has blessed us all and has assured the householders that nothing evil will befall the people of this area.' This became the talk of the town.

People circled around Khalila and the kids, enquiring curiously, 'Tell us, how did she leave? Did she demand anything more before leaving? To whom did she declare her decision?'

Khalila was ready and quipped. 'It was Mother, of course, to whom she announced her departure. She was very happy with Mother, because she has shown tremendous respect and reverence to her, besides serving her nicely. She told Mother that she would now return to the forest to be with her kin.'

'Mother's wisdom has saved us all,' an elderly man said loudly. 'May she and her family be blessed!'

Khalila and the children spent hours answering questions. He was invited to the homes of a few neighbours, and served tea and sweet breads for bringing the good news.

People were rejoicing. Now there was no reason to fear. It was certain that the beast would never venture towards the city of Srinagar again.

For almost a week thereafter, people kept pouring in to congratulate Māl, her eldest son Baiji, and all the other members of the family for having dealt with the horrible van buḍini with grace and aplomb and thereby saving the city from calamity. People came with packets of almonds, candy, and cardamoms to show their gratitude.

For Khalila and his accomplices, this was a vindication of his theatrical genius!

9

Architects of Change

The Dhars of Rishi Vihar were a rather big joint family.
The van *Buḍini* episode had raised Māl's cachet even further.

People would now say—even more emphatically—that she was a beauty with brains. Attired in her beautiful maroon pheran and wearing a *kalpush* and *targa* on her head—as traditional KP women at that time would (before taking to the sari)—she looked regal as she moved around overseeing activities and supervising the work of the many helpers in the house.

Ram Chandra had, upon his return to Srinagar from Lucknow, become the first local graduate in the Maharaja's territory of Jammu and Kashmir. His appointment to a good position in the Maharaja's education department, with a relatively good salary at the start of the twentieth century, placed him as one of the higher paid government employees in the state. Understandably, he had clout within the community and, being helpful, he was respected and revered by all.

Māl was no less than her husband in terms of her vision and broad-mindedness on social issues. Though not educated in the modern ways, she had had a traditional education within Kashmir. As Ram Chandra's wife she was always ready and by his side, willing to stand by him and do things that would be considered 'modern' even by today's norms. For instance, both Ram Chandra and Māl were at the forefront of installing a 'gymnastic centre' within the home—with parallel bars fixed between two walls and a *malkhamb*—for all the children, including the girls. In this household all the girls were sent to school (rather than being homeschooled, as was the norm in Māl's generation and earlier) and they were even taught music, for which a music teacher was appointed who would come home.

During the thirteenth century CE when Islam entered Kashmir and many Kashmiri Hindus got converted, most of the freedoms that Hindu women had enjoyed till then—even those of the other classes—were gradually whittled down and curtailed. This happened gradually as Muslim kings imposed restrictions and caveats on the general population. This crimped the liberal ethos and erudition of men and women for which Kashmir was renowned. Matters got progressively worse at times of internal turmoil when invasions of marauding armies became frequent. By the time the Afghans were in control of Kashmir from around 1750 through 1839 CE, the cruel and barbaric atrocities that the people of Kashmir had to suffer had peaked. Women and children were abducted, raped, tortured, and killed with a wantonness that Kashmir had never witnessed before. Women began to be hidden from the Afghans, their faces blackened with soot and cinders, and their hair left unwashed, unkempt, and matted so that they would look unattractive and unlikely to elicit the attention of Afghan soldiers or mercenaries.

Understandably, with over eight decades of unprecedented cruelty, the lives of the people of Kashmir, and especially those of women, changed forever. The entire focus was on surviving and using every trick that was humanly possible to stay alive and ensure the well-being of one's loved ones and immediate family.

It was therefore no longer customary in Kashmiri homes to teach girls to sing or play musical instruments as an art. The earlier traditions of having women learn the arts, and be erudite were all overwhelmed by the tragic events of the prior centuries.

By the start of the twentieth century it was considered to be below the dignity and status of well-bred women to learn music or to sing and dance. Ram Chandra, who knew the tragic reasons for the general aversion towards music, was determined to change the perceptions of society by changing the mindsets of people, which he knew had been formed and become hardwired through centuries of pain and tragedy.

He was therefore in the forefront of bringing in whatever changes he could. He encouraged his grandsons to learn to swim, which was another personal skill that had been neglected by the well-to-do in Kashmir partly because of the fear of drowning and the concern of catching the flu by swimming in cold water. He was appreciative of creative endeavours undertaken by members of his family and if the initiative to do something new or novel was taken by his own sons and daughters or grandchildren, he would feel very proud and happy. Ram Chandra was known to reward his grandchildren handsomely if they succeeded in making something novel and creative on their own. He knew that some of his grandchildren were very talented and he would spend time with them, interacting and guiding them towards the things that they enjoyed. Being an educationist, he never tired of sharing with them new ideas and information from around the world as well as things and new ways. He would even discuss world history, the rise and fall of civilizations, and the role that ordinary people and leaders had played in the unfurling of history.

He was impatient to see India become independent before he quit the world.

Unfortunately, he left for his heavenly abode sometime in 1945 and therefore could not witness the tricolour being unfurled on the ramparts of the Red Fort on 15 August 1947. He was barely sixty-five.

10

A Dussehra to Remember

Among all of Ram Chandra's grandchildren, it was Rajinder Nath—affectionately called Rajṭoṭh by all (the word *ṭoṭh* in Kashmiri means 'dear one')—who was very creative and skilled at making artefacts, models, and an array of charming toys.

Rajṭoṭh was also quite inventive and scientifically oriented. One day he made a strange device that functioned like a telephone but was made of small clay pots. He would make large and small toys, stuffed animals out of straw and cloth, and papier mâché mannequins that looked like miniature people.

One day Rajṭoṭh made a big toy 'East Indiaman', a ship modelled after those used by the British East India Company for trade with China and the British Isles. This model, with beautiful sails and a polished hull, looked authentic, with immense attention to the minutest of details. This ship, which was meant to be a floating model, was placed in a little pond not far from home, where it would move like a real ship with its sails puffing up in even a mild breeze.

From a distance it looked so real that it had a lasting impact on adults and children alike.

Another day he made a fluffy squirrel climbing the wall, all elegantly painted in the natural colours of the little animal. Its tail was made of dried paddy grass, with the long seed-laden hay hanging behind the creature, giving it the look of a real, restless rodent. Later, the squirrel became a decoration piece in the drawing room of the house.

Every member of the family would praise Rajinder's talent and appreciate his skills. Ram Chandra too was very happy and admired Rajtoth's creative bent of mind.

The festival of Dussehra was round the corner. It was understood that the boys would do something to make the occasion a unique one. So they put their heads together and decided to make big effigies of Ravan and his brothers Kumbhakaran and Meghnad.

However, Rajtoth was busy making a huge airplane, with cardboard, nails, and thin shiny paper. The wheels of this plane were made out of thread reels. Assembling this model plane took quite some time. His cousins too were helping him, and the room where they were working looked like a small factory, with tools, scissors, paper, gum, bamboo sticks, and the big sheets of shiny paper strewn around the floor.

Whatever the boys were doing was supposed to be a surprise for Dussehra. The effigy-making couldn't be kept a secret but the plane was the element that was consciously not divulged.

The adults in the household and the children were excited about the coming festival. All started to ask one another about the progress of whatever was being planned. Even grandfather didn't know what kind of surprise entertainment was planned for Dussehra. He was confident that the boys would not disappoint, especially since they had also collected a hefty kitty from him and other elder members of the family to defray the costs of their endeavour.

Dussehra finally dawned. The entertainment was planned for sundown. By now almost everything for the show was in place. Rajtoth and the other older boys locked the doors of their workshop room and nobody was allowed entry for the rest of the day. Only a small 'core group' of the boys were there to give last-minute touches to the models and the artefacts to be used that evening. The younger children were curious as to what was happening, and were doing their best to peep into the room through a few cracks in the door. However, none of them could make out what was actually going on inside the room.

By evening the big boys emerged from the room carrying big balls of string. They then fixed both ends of a parallel string-track to two high points on the roof of the house that was directly opposite the place where the three effigies—of Ravan and his brothers Kumbhakaran and Meghnad—had been erected. The other ends of the string-track, running downwards towards the effigies in a gradual slope, were tied to two limbs of a bamboo pole fixed in front of the effigy of Ravan. While all this was being done, the younger children followed the older boys, making a lot of excited noises.

Seating for the evening was also arranged in front of the effigies, albeit a little distance away. Since guests from the locality were expected for the show that evening, a special line of chairs was arranged for them as well, and a large rug was also spread on the ground. The atmosphere was crackling with expectation.

Just before sundown, the ladies, men, children, helpers, Grandfather, and Grandmother were told to dress up nicely and be ready to witness the grand show scheduled for a little later that evening. Children and adults from the neighbourhood—all of whom were also dressed in elegant clothes—started to trickle in for the show. The whole ground was full of people. Everyone from the nearby locality and even those from beyond Navakadal and Safakadal had come and all were eager for the show to begin. Everyone was wondering what kind of surprise would be displayed this year.

Soon, Grandfather, Grandmother, and all the members of the family were seated in the rows of chairs, along with the elderly people of the entire mohalla. The children of the family and the neighbourhood were all seated on the rugs on the ground.

At the appointed hour, everyone was asked to settle down. All of a sudden a few loud crackers burst somewhere near the highest point of the building behind the audience. The noise drew everyone's attention towards the big window next to where the string-tracks had been fixed.

As soon as the smoke of the crackers wafted away, a large model airplane, suitably perched on the string-track and gradually accelerating towards the effigies, became visible. The plane was dazzling from little light bulbs placed along its wings that shimmered with the shiny coloured paper. Its nose was emanating sparks that made the whole spectacle really impressive.

As the airplane began to gain speed, it even made a shrill noise not too different from that of a real aircraft. Everyone in the audience was awed. A sudden hush descended on the spectators and a few shouted, spontaneously and excitedly, '*Aleiy! Havei-jahāz hā!*'

By now the plane was thundering down rapidly towards the big, main effigy and as it drew closer one could see a sparkler at the nose burning bright and emanating a trail of smoke in its wake. As soon as the plane crashed into the big effigy of Ravan, it burst into flames and set ablaze the other effigies as well and the crackers burst loudly and rockets started to fly skywards.

The loud bursting of the crackers and the effigies going up in flames drew spontaneous applause from the audience, especially the children, who were watching the great show with utmost attention. The entertainment, however, wasn't only for the children. Even the elders, including visitors from nearby localities, were deriving great pleasure from the grand show. Everyone was clapping with joy each time a new set of firecrackers was ignited. Rockets went whizzing up in the air, adding to the thrill of the evening spectacle.

As the effigies were reduced to ashes, the other items of entertainment that had been planned for the evening commenced. The children, arranged in groups according to their ages, were brought in front of the spectators to do their little acts of singing, dancing, and making fun of the times through the satirical laḍishah style of poetry. The evening entertainment had the audience laughing with joy. They were so excited that they just did not want the show to finish. Grandfather, Grandmother, and all the members of the family were proud of the boys and girls who had made the entertainment so special.

After the show was over, all the children and the organizers came forward, bowed their heads, folded their hands, and thanked the audience for their encouragement. The spectators burst into spontaneous applause.

A big basket of sweets was distributed to the children of the entire mohalla. The special show and entertainment that had been arranged for Dussehra was talked about for a long time afterwards.

11

Drama in the Kitchen

It was quite a chaotic situation when Tikaram, the cook, had to go to his village for his annual one-month leave. He was the head cook and the master of the kitchen of the large family of nearly sixty people. On any given day, he was helped by at least three and sometimes even four assistants. Without him, the helpers were good for nothing.

It would be a problem deciding who would take charge of the kitchen in the absence of Tikaram. He was aware of his importance and position in the family, and would blackmail the ladies by pretending that he had to go to his home to attend to some urgent tasks. He would never assign complete charge to any of his assistants lest the assistant usurp his position and fill the vacancy arising from his absence. So even the assistants had become overly dependent on him and much like Pavlov's dog would only respond to his instructions and orders. Without his instructions they would do no work at all. So it was clear that while Tikaram was away, a good cook—and someone who could get the helpers going—was needed in the kitchen.

In the Dhar household there were five daughters-in-law. One was away with her husband in Calcutta. The elder two daughters-in-law, Sati and Benji, didn't know how to cook. Whenever they entered the kitchen for even minor work, they would be like bulls in a china shop, clumsily getting in the way of the staff and unclear of what to do.

The other two ladies, Benigashi and Dulabhabi, were quite smart in this respect. They knew their job well and could manage the kitchen adroitly with the help of the assistants. Both of them were lean and thin and relatively younger than the other two, so their actions were quite swift and precise when it came to doing things in the kitchen. Their mother-in-law, Māl, who was also called *Bǣd Mǣj* (big mother) was full of praise for both of them, and would repeat that they were truly assets to the family, especially when there was a 'cook crisis' in the house.

I do remember observing as a child that Benigashi's son, and my cousin, Gyantoth was always wearing the neatest and the cleanest pheran amongst all the children. Gyantoth's pheran had a clean and crisp inner cotton *poots*, which was like a removable inner lining to the garment. Its sleeves were turned upside down to give the pheran the perfect look of a dress. The pherans of the other children used to be clean too, but they were never sparkling white. This may have been another reason why Māl was appreciative of Benigashi.

When Tikaram's leave was cleared, Benigashi was therefore automatically assigned the position of the master of the kitchen. But there was a little wrinkle to this arrangement. Kantha Ram, who was Tikaram's oldest assistant, always thought of himself as being as good as Tikaram, if not better, in the skill of cooking and managing other helpers. Yet, despite his capabilities, he had a flaw in his personality—he had no control over his temper and would rarely take responsibility for the things he was supposed to do.

So, for even the smallest of errors he'd throw a fit. If by chance he himself made an error, he would pretend that someone else had done it. If an associate confronted him and tried to suggest that he was needlessly blaming others for his own lapses, Kantha Ram would flare up and do something unusual to compound the issue and leave things worse than they were originally.

The celebration of Maha Shivratri, or Herath as it is known in Kashmir, is one of the most important celebrations of the year amongst Kashmiri Pandits. Thirteen days of preparations and festivities culminate in prayers and feasting on the fourteenth and fifteenth days, respectively. On the fifteenth day, also known as salaam (peace), non-Hindu friends, neighbours, and colleagues from work visit their KP friends—usually with gifts to offer—and partake of nuts and kehva and the other sweetmeats offered.

Herath is celebrated during the fourth moonless night in the dark half of the lunar month of *phālgun*, and falls soon after the dark days of winter give way to the life-affirming season of spring. Understandably, it's also a time to have one's homes thoroughly cleaned and decorated in time for the biggest festival for Kashmiri Pandits. All rooms, staircases, the kitchen, and halls are cleaned with a fervour that needs to be seen! Herath cleaning was also an annual ritual and helped clear out the muck and soot of winter, and spruce up the entire house for happy and sunny days for the rest of the year. The children especially had to dust their books and satchels. Even the married daughters of the family would come home to be with their parents. After chipping in with the preparations for Herath and staying over for a few days, they'd return to the homes of their respective husbands, carrying loads of presents for their in-laws. One essential part of the 'hamper' of gifts was a *kāngri*, the traditional Kashmiri firepot, which was a functional present that was used by all to keep warm, but also represented 'life' and the element of fire, '*agni*', and its ability to transform that which is base to something pure. Every daughter, whether rich or poor, would get this present on Herath. All sorts of colourful *kāngris* were made by craftsmen, and these were available in large numbers in the market around Herath.

During the winter months the rugs in the rooms, the namdahs, and the straw matting beneath them would all get damp and dusty. In preparation for Herath new rugs and straw mats (*vaguv*) were bought and laid in the rooms that were being spruced up. Everything that would bring people out of the winter mood into the joy of the coming seasons was done. People would also bathe and wear fresh, new clothes for Herath.

For each of the thirteen days preceding Maha Shivratri, special dishes were prepared in the kitchen. All the seasonal vegetables and fruits (*nadru*, walnuts, and water chestnuts) were served as delicacies to go with the general enthusiasm in the run-up to Herath.

In the meantime, the men, women, and children would try their hand at playing with cowrie shells. To give the play a sense of competition each cowrie was valued at five or ten paise. The winners would then trade their shells for some well-deserved cash! Snacky treats were served to the players with hot kehva while the main dishes were served with dinner at night.

Some of the more enthusiastic adults would even play poker and 'flash', using two or three decks of playing cards and that too with high stakes. The gambling sessions would continue every afternoon and continue till late in the evening of the entire fortnight, and would make for great entertainment and enjoyment.

In the run-up to the festival of Herath, Māl, her daughters-in-law, and the visiting daughters of the household would ensure that there was a lot of fun to be had, even as the cleaning and preparations for the big festival were under way. Within the kitchen there was a big copper boiler, called *maṭṭ* in Kashmiri, which was designed to hold water that would get heated by the hot effluent gases from the wood fires of the kitchen hearth. This ensured that even before the advent of electricity and cooking gas in Kashmir, there was—at least in the richer households—a ready source of hot water throughout the day during the winter months. But because the maṭṭ had a finite capacity, it required some prior planning to ensure that there would be enough hot water available for all the ladies—young and old—who were to have their ritual, pre-Herath head-bath! Usually, the little girls and boys would be bathed first, and on the next day, the women would bathe, starting with Mother. Typically, one or two ladies would assist Māl with her bath in the washroom. She preferred one of her daughters-in-law and one of her smarter granddaughters to assist her. After her, one by one, all the other women used to have their ritual bath and then, wearing nice, clean, warm clothes, they would greet each other and wish all a happy Herath.

On such days, there was always a lot of excitement. The occasions also gave the women a chance to bond with one another and have a little 'special' fun of their own. So when all the male members left for their respective jobs, the whole field was open to the ladies to plan the day the way they liked and to make merry.

Savouring the right foods was an important part of the enjoyment. Women would suggest—to those among them who were skilled in the kitchen—to prepare a few unique Kashmiri dishes that they would all like. These were foods that were unique, seasonal or special, because like *hogād* (dehydrated fish), for instance, they were difficult to make on a regular basis. Difficult, because preparing them required a lot of effort, apart from oil, spices, and special dry condiments to bring out the flavours. The task of preparing something special was always entrusted to Dulabhabi, who would happily oblige.

Mealtime on this day was a fun affair. Not only was the menu special, it was also mandatory to top it up with the traditional

Kashmiri salted tea, sheerchai. There was also a lot of laughter, sharing of jokes, and all kinds of friendly and engaging interactions on these occasions.

At lunchtime, Māl would taste the dishes first and share her views.

'Dulari, the dried fish tastes delicious. I know how difficult it is to cook hogād. You've really cooked it with immense care and love.' Dulabhabi would smile, blushing because of the praise.

'She is a master in these things,' Sati would add.

By now the food was laid out and the women would be happily enjoying the meal of rice, fish, and brinjals cooked with *soçal* greens.

'The soçal is equally tasty,' Benji, the other daughter-in-law, would say.

'What about Kantha Ram? Did he allow you to make these things freely and without hindrance?' Didā asked, knowing how petulant the head assistant cook could be.

'We don't need his permission to do what we please in our kitchen, do we?' Benigashi said this with some irritation.

'He is a bit of a disdainful fellow, a real *shoda*. One doesn't know when he'll do what,' Didā clarified.

'When is Tikaram returning? He's been away for more than a month already' Benji asked.

'He was expected yesterday. I'm sure he'll be on the way back to this place. He always returns in time. Besides, it is Herath time and he knows he has to be here, isn't it?' Mother said reassuringly.

―⦿―

It was the sixth day leading to Herath. Tikaram had still not returned from his annual leave. Rishi Vihar was looking all cleaned up and beautiful—ready for the big festival ahead. The new matting, the embroidered rugs and curtains in the sitting room and the other rooms that were used by the ladies looked dazzling and everything looked spick and span. From this day onwards a thick, large and beautiful Kashmiri carpet was spread in the main sitting room, transforming the room into an opulent one, which gave the new furnishing a royal feel. Carpets were occasionally used on festivals, but were otherwise rolled and packed safely. It felt good to bring out the best for Maha Shivratri.

In the evening the house would come alive with the excited sounds, laughter, and chattering of young and old family members playing cowries or poker together. All the new and relatively younger daughters-in-law too were encouraged to play all the games and participate in the enjoyable pastime.

In the kitchen, some dishes were being cooked under the guidance and firm control of Benigashi and Dulabhabi. The other, older daughters-in-law, Benji and Sati, were also trying to be helpful. Benigashi was assessing the taste of the dishes that had been prepared by Kantha Ram in order to ascertain which spice may still be needed to give the dish its perfect taste. When she took a spoonful of the big pot of fish, which was boiling on the fireplace, she found that the salt in the preparation was less.

Benigashi looked at Kantha Ram and asked— 'Haven't you added salt to the fish yet? There's no salt in this. Have you forgotten to put it in?'

This was enough to provoke Kantha Ram. By the time Benigashi was looking for the salt container, Kantha Ram—in a huff—took the boiling pot of fish off the fireplace and put it outside of the clean and 'purified' kitchen space. In utter disregard for the ritual norms of hygiene, he deliberately placed the pot on the floor, in the space that was meant for keeping one's shoes.

All the ladies, the few children around, and the helpers who were witnessing this scene were aghast and shocked at Kantha Ram's behaviour. One of the ladies shouted, 'What has happened to you, Kantha Ram? Oh! Oh! The fish has now gotten *chyot* [impure]!'

Sati was pale with concern.

'Oh! Oh oh, the food has become impure, çhyoṭ! What are we going to serve the family? What will they eat tonight.' Sati sounded genuinely frightened, and was angry at the wilful and grave error committed by Kantha Ram.

'He is shoda and a fool! He doesn't even know what he's done.' Benji was shouting at Kantha Ram too, scolding him.

Benigashi and Dulabhabi were giving vocal explanations to their elder sisters-in-law that they had said nothing out of the norm that would have provoked him so. By now the other helpers in the house had gravitated to the kitchen. Sidha, Sarva, and Prema got there to witness the unwonted scene. While the women were beating their chests in despair, Prema quickly got hold of a big kitchen twill that was meant to pick up hot and heavy vessels, and in a swift move, picked up the large fish pot and brought it back into the kitchen. He then took out a wide-mouthed, but shallow, earthen vessel, which contained a mixture of fine whitish-brown clay (usually procured from sacred hills and sold by vendors) which had been soaked with water. A small wet rag, dunked in the smooth clayey mass was also handy. This clayey mixture was used to smoothen the surfaces of the clay fireplace in the kitchen at the end of the day, when the cooking was over. The process served the dual purpose of keeping the clay cooking place (dān in Kashmiri) clean, and making it look shiny white and flush the next morning.

Prema's presence of mind was evident that eventful evening. Before Mother or any other member of the family could come to know the drama in the kitchen, he took the rag from the shallow vessel and scooped liberal amounts of the wet, gooyey clay from it. Then as swiftly as he had brought the fish pot back into the kitchen, he applied the wet clay on the outside of the hot vessel that had the cooked fish in it, and declared emphatically that the pot had been purified and was as clean as ever before.

Drama in the Kitchen

The concept of 'purity' and the performance of purity-related rituals amongst Kashmiri Pandits have been important customs for the community. In this day and age many of the concepts related to *shroçar* or *cheçar* (purity and defilement) might seem unscientific, but there was a time when the ideas were considered a vital aspect of being a Pandit. The concept was extended to foods and even animals, sometimes in ways that were downright hilarious. So if a pet dog entered the kitchen, the place would have to be purified by cleaning it with holy water and using the white clay mixture to smoothen the clay floor and the cooking hearth. However, if a stray kitten got into the kitchen and helped itself to some foods, that was fine and the kitchen was not defiled!

Prema's presence of mind, and the trick of using the purifying mud appropriately, seemed to cool everyone's tempers. But Sati, Benji, and some of the other helpers were still extremely annoyed. Pointing to Prema, Sati asked—'Do you want to fool everyone? How has the fish become pure after having been placed outside?'

'If he hadn't done what he did,' Dulabhabi piped in, 'what would we have served for dinner tonight? It will take us another day to clean and cook the fish. Not to mention the wrath of Mother.'

Dulabhabi's perspective set the two older ladies thinking.

'But I cannot kill my conscience. At least I won't have it,' Sati said with a grin on her face.

'You want to save your dharma, Sati, but what about the others?' Benji asked, irritated.

The conversation about the pot of fish continued for a while longer between the children, the ladies, and the staff that had assembled in the kitchen. Most of the children had no clue as to what had happened. At the same time they were smart enough to guess that something was amiss, and that fish may not be on the menu that evening.

My younger brother, Sardar, being the youngest of the children who were in the kitchen at the time of the event, went into the sitting room where Mother and other members of the family were having a conversation.

Very innocently he looked to his grandmother, Māl, and shared with her that his mother Benji and Sati would not be having fish for dinner that night.

Māl, thinking that Sardar was joking, was amused.

'And why aren't they going to have fish?' Mother asked Sardar lovingly. 'Of course they too will have fish, as will we all because these are the days of Herath. Nobody can say "no" to anything good these days.'

While Mother was having a conversation with Sardar, Sati came running to the room lest Sardar, in his innocence, spill the beans before all the others.

'I was just joking with Prema,' Sati said, panting. 'The fish was of a good quality and it's been cooked well.' Sati was doing her utmost to divert Mother's attention from Sardar's innocent prattle.

'Jan Mohamed, our vendor, said that the fish was a *mahseer* and the best quality in this season. It must be really sweet and tasty.'

Mother's words were reassuring. She obviously had not heeded the child's words. Sati breathed a sigh of relief.

When she left the room, she and Benji called all the children together and exhorted them not to tell anyone what had happened in the kitchen. Benji gave an eight anna coin to Sardar and said, 'Don't divulge what happened to anyone. We have to keep this a secret between ourselves.'

Sardar had no clue about this episode. But since Benji had bribed her son, the other children too began to blackmail their mothers.

'We'll tell everyone about this secret if you don't give us some money too.' The poor mothers gave in lest the children reveal all to Māl. So, reluctantly, they all began to give two, three annas to all of them.

At dinnertime that evening, when all the members began to eat, all the children were conspicuously watching their elders relishing the fish. Not knowing what had actually happened, all they knew was that it had to do with the fish that had been cooked.

The body language and the behaviour of the kids must have been odd, because Mother noticed something.

Looking at us all, she said loudly, 'What's the matter with you all? Why aren't you having your dinner?'

The elders, and especially the mothers of the children, glowered at the kids. This was all that was needed. Without further ado, all the children began their dinner and relished the fish.

The story didn't end there though. Sidha, Razāq, and Sarva also began to gently extract their pound of flesh, milking the so-called scandal.

'Oh, oh! Why did you make our dear mother and elders eat the impure fish?' they would ask the women who knew about the incident. 'You know it's a sin to offer impure foods. If Mother get to know about it there will be a catastrophe in the home. *Tobah! Tobah!*'

Fortunately, the women didn't fall into the blackmailing trap.

Benigashi was the most vocal.

'Yes, if Prema hadn't purified the pot, you would have enjoyed fish for days together, eh?' she told them sarcastically.

'Prema has done a great favour to all of you. You should reward him for his presence of mind and wisdom.' Sidha said this in a way so as to suggest to the ladies that there was an expectation of a hefty reward for them all.

'Why are you pleading Prema's case?' Dulabhabi asked Sidha angrily.

After being pestered in this fashion for a few weeks, and considering that it was Herath time, I'm told that the women did finally relent. Some token money was given to all the helpers in the kitchen and to the other help within the house. But while the secret was safe, deep down the ladies were feeling a little guilty to have agreed to serve fish to the family that was technically not kosher!

A positive outcome of the event was that Kantha Ram was extremely embarrassed by his action and was full of remorse for what he had done. He seemed to sober down after this incident and was far more obedient to Tikaram, besides being far more committed to his work as a helper in the kitchen.

12

A Windfall on Diwali

It was the month of October, in the year 1946. Our father, Bubji—as he was affectionately called—was posted in Jammu city as the income tax officer for the entire Jammu province. In those days officers of the government had tremendous powers because they were fewer in number, were accountable, and by and large were dedicated to their work and were honest. They commanded respect from the people and most officers were also helpful to them, thus easing their lives and being of assistance in many ways.

The festival of Diwali that followed the Navratris was the main festival of the month. Our friends from the neighbourhood came to our home and told my brother Sardar and me about their plans for the special day.

'We're going to get lots of crackers from the market today. We plan to buy the latest and the loudest crackers for the evening. Will you come with us?'

They were all enthusiastic about their plans.

'How much money have you taken with you?' I asked them.

'Bhushan has four annas, Kanta has two annas, and Vindri has four, so all together we have ten annas.'

'What about Ravinder? Hasn't he got some money for the crackers?' Sardar asked, intrigued.

'He too has some money, but not sure how much. Now you too should get some money for the patakas, so that we can go to the market together.'

My brother and I were convinced that we should go to buy our share of crackers with our friends. We then went to look for our mother who was busy doing some work in one of the rooms in the house.

'Benji, give us some money to buy crackers for tonight. All the children are going to the market to buy them,' we requested her.

'You can't go out on your own,' she said firmly. 'I'll send Shamlal to buy patakas for you.'

Benji was clear—she didn't want us to go shopping for crackers with our friends.

My brother would take none of this. He was insistent.

'No, Mother! Give us some money. Everyone has got money for crackers.'

It took us quite some time to plead for the money. Our friends, who had waited patiently at the door so far, got fidgety since we were taking time to return, and decided to head for the market without us.

After much cajoling and pleading, Benji gave me an eight-anna coin.

'This is enough for crackers,' she said emphatically.

'You have given eight annas to Khema! I also need money!' Sardar said petulantly. He was persistent and adamant.

Benji was forced to give Sardar some money too. The coin looked similar to what my mother had given me, so Sardar was satisfied. He looked at me, and said, 'Let's go now.'

'Don't go alone, children,' Mother insisted. 'I'll send Shamlal with you.' She began to look for Shamlal.

We had other plans, however. While she was busy looking for him, we both gave her the slip and quietly crossed the road to reach the bustling Paccadanga bazaar, which was busy with kids and adults shopping for the festival.

Holding hands, Sardar and I looked for our friends. They were nowhere to be seen. It was difficult to manage ourselves in the rush of the pedestrians, who it seemed were oblivious of us. Everyone was rushing from shop to shop picking up candles, earthen lamps, crackers, and sweetmeats for the celebrations in the evening.

We were in a fix about which shop to go to. We were also unclear about where we ought to buy the crackers from, now that we couldn't find our friends. We found that there was a tremendous rush at one of the shops. So many children were in front of the shop, waiting for their turn to come. So we decided to wait there for the crackers.

'Keep your coin ready, Sardar. This is the shop that seems to have all the right kinds of crackers,' I suggested. Sardar, who was my younger sibling, would obey me most of the time. He began to search in the pocket for the coin.

'I can't find the coin!' he said, his voice tremulous, as he pulled out the pockets of his knickers, inside out.

'It must be in your shirt pocket,' I suggested. 'Search properly.' I too was getting a little panicky and joined Sardar in searching all his pockets.

'Where did you keep it? In which pocket did you put the coin?' I chided him.

'I kept it properly, but I don't know how it's lost,' he said as tears welled up in his eyes.

'I told you to give me the coin,' I shouted angrily. 'I would've kept it safely. But you didn't listen to me.'

Sardar was now desperate. He started searching in his knicker pockets again. He again turned them inside out, and shook them hard. And lo and behold, the missing coin fell out, got tossed on to the road, and rolled into the open drain that was below the steps of the shop.

We were shocked and horrified to see the coin roll into the gutter. Sardar began to weep loudly. I too couldn't stop weeping. Both of us just didn't know what to do.

Hearing children weeping beside the shop on Diwali day drew the attention of the assembled people there.

'What is the matter? Why are you weeping?' some people asked us. Others too joined in. 'Are you alone? Where are your parents?'

There were so many concerned questions from the people at the shop that we truly didn't know whom to answer first. Suddenly, a person from the crowd who seemed to recognize us stepped forward and with a surprised look said, 'What are you both doing here?'

'Masterji,' I said, recognizing him as the tailor master who taught our mother, 'I've lost my money. It was an athanni.' 'Athanni' was a colloquial term used for an eight-anna coin.

'Where did you lose it?'

'Here in the gutter, that's where the coin went,' Sardar said, pointing to where the coin had rolled into the drain.

―――∞―――

Masterji was a tailor master who was teaching our mother how to stitch. His actual name was Allahditta and he was very skilled. Despite his best efforts and the time Benji invested into the craft, however, she never became proficient at it. But to impress members of the entire family, she would volunteer to stitch torn pyjamas or shirts of those in the family. When Masterji came to teach her at our home, both Sardar and I were ever curious to observe what he would teach her. Benji was quite excited about learning how to stitch. We too were therefore equally excited to see what Masterji would teach her. Whenever Masterji came, he was received graciously. He was offered sweets, biscuits and tea before he started his work.

In one of the earliest classes, he asked Benji to get two toothpicks to start the first lesson. Then he instructed her to pretend that these two toothpicks were stitching needles, and that she must first place them in the palm of her hand. Benji opened her hand, as a good student would, as Masterji gave her further guidance.

'Pick up one needle and take it straight to your right ear. Then bring it back, drop it. Now pick up the other one, and take it to the right ear. This exercise is very important because everyone holds their needles the wrong way, which is the cause for many stitching errors later.'

While Benji was following this exercise, Sardar and I found it funny and began to giggle loudly, which embarrassed Benji. She wanted to shoo us away, but we were determined to see this funny way of teaching. Masterji kept his cool, to show that ustāds are always calm and not easily ruffled. In order to encourage his pupil, he said, 'Children are always like this. This is the time when they should have fun. Later, they'll have so many pressures, with studies, sports, and what not. They must enjoy.'

He was quite friendly and would get toffees for us sometimes. In fact, Masterji was a hefty man in his middle years, who was not only an accomplished tailor master but was also very helpful to people in need. He would go out of the way to help people, including those whom he didn't even know. He applied henna on his hair to give it a reddish tint, not only to keep his head cool but to look young and smart as well. He was also known to be a man with a humorous side, capable of making people laugh.

Due to these pleasing qualities Allahditta was also known widely in the city of Jammu.

His first lesson involving the toothpicks lasted for days together, till he was compelled by Benji to move ahead.

When Bubji, our father, asked Benji what she'd learned in the day's lesson, Sardar and I were ever ready to answer his queries amidst giggles. 'Masterji is still on the two toothpicks.'

'What? Still on the needle exercise?' Father would exclaim, amused. 'I think he should move ahead. Now that he's been coming here for nearly ten days.' He was also poking fun at his wife and Masterji to please both of us. With a pause he began to say again, 'You should insist that he teach you something more.'

Bubji knew that Benji wouldn't insist that the teacher speed up the lessons—because she was very traditional and would never speak up to her teacher and offend him by saying anything directly about his teaching ability. She would consider it to be most rude and indecent. Since Bubji was after her, however, she reluctantly mustered the courage to have a word with Masterji about the pace at which she was learning the skills of tailoring.

My mother had very strong notions about her lineage, and the traditions and customs of the KP community. She was especially proud of her heritage, and would quite often say that she belonged to Rishi Datatreya's clan of Kauls, who were also rulers of Kashmir once. She would always emphasize and talk about her grandmother, who belonged to a noble family, and was the only daughter of her parents. She was called Zap Khan. Since she was a precious child and the only daughter to her parents, she was given the pseudonym 'Khan'. I guess this was due to the Pathan influence in the Valley.

Zap Khan was married into the Kaul family and inherited all the property of her family. Benji would further add that at the time of her grandmother's marriage, two maids were sent with Zap Khan to her husband's home to help her. In her in-laws place she was made to do all sorts of odd jobs. While doing her chores, her pheran—which was studded with elegant pearls—would get snagged in corners, and many of the pearls would be ripped off. These would get scattered all over the places where Zap Khan was working.

While hearing this story, I would feel sad for my great-grandmother and retort, 'She had two maids with her, why didn't they help her in the work?'

'Because no one dared to question her mother-in-law,' Benji would say, adding, 'it wasn't possible to break the custom.'

Benji would say this in a matter-of-fact way. Then with a pause she would say again, 'Besides, doing chores was also a way to teach Zap Khan to be self-sufficient in the tasks at home so that later on she would feel at ease.'

Masterji went out of the way to help us retrieve the coin from the drain. He was even willing to get the coin from the gutter himself. While he was rolling up his sleeves to put his arm in the drain, some people asked him, 'Why are you doing it yourself? Give one anna to a sweeper, he will do the job nicely.'

'Don't you see the children are weeping?' he said to the onlookers, indicating the urgency.

'Do you know the children?' one person from the crowd asked.

'They are the children of the Income Tax Officer.' Without waiting, Masterji had begun his work to get the coin from the running drain.

'Which IT officer?' some people asked together.

'Dhar sahab, who else?' Bubji was by that time a fairly well-known person and familiar with the business class due to his work in the income tax department. As soon as the people heard that we were Dhar sahab's children, so many people came out of their shops and began to search for the lost coin. Now there were a number of teenage boys and elderly people all searching for the money.

As people cleared the drain with their bare hands and pulled out whatever they could—along with the gooey mud—we were surprised that so much change was brought out. Everyone seemed to manage to pull out many coins—two-anna coins, four-anna coins, one-anna coins and more! But the eight-anna coin was not to be seen anywhere.

The helpful people gave Masterji all the change that they had scooped out of the gutter, after washing off the mud. It added up to much more than eight annas! But Sardar was still adamant to get his own eight-anna coin, which was new and shining.

All were eagerly showing us how much work they were doing to get our lost money from the drain. They were indeed toiling to please us. By this time even Masterji had become a bit of an organizer, and was directing people towards the lower part of the drain, where he believed the coin may have settled due to the force of the water. His logic proved to be correct. A person did indeed find the eight-anna coin from where Masterji had suggested.

'I think I got your coin,' the man shouted excitedly, showing the muddy coin to Sardar. Someone from the back got a tumbler of water saying, 'Let's first wash it to see if it is the same coin that belongs to Kākāji.'

When the coin was washed, it was the lost coin. Seeing this, Sardar jumped up, excited and thrilled.

'This is my coin, this is my coin!' he shouted gleefully. Everyone heaved a sigh of relief. Now the people, along with Masterji, began to count the coins that Sardar and Masterji himself had. All together it was more than five rupees (about eighty annas), which was a big amount in those days. All the change was kept with Masterji who, it was agreed by all, would help the children with the shopping for the celebrations that evening.

Most of the people accompanied Masterji and the two of us to the shop from where the things for the fest were to be purchased. It looked like a small, albeit joyous, procession. Soon, everyone began to direct the shopkeeper to keep all the best types of crackers, sweets, and earthen lamps for us. It seemed as if they were shopping for their own home. I had always wanted a doll of clay, which used to have a bobbing head, thus making it lifelike. Even that was ordered. Sardar got himself a bat and ball. Lots of things were purchased, so Masterji ordered a big round bamboo basket to put all of them into it. One boy was then paid to carry this basket, which was now full to the brim, up to our home.

While going towards our home, almost everyone wished Allahditta and asked him about the small band of people that was following him. He offered a witty reply and kept everyone amused. The procession kept growing as we approached our home. Many people were keen to show their faces to our parents, to let them know how helpful they had been.

At long last we reached our home.

Our parents were looking around for Sardar and me frantically. They had no clue where we had been, and why we were away for so long. Our friends from the neighbourhood had returned from the market long back. They too didn't know of our whereabouts. When our parents saw Masterji along with so many people with us, they were relieved. Forgetting everything, they hugged us and welcomed Masterji and the other people. Masterji gave them a complete and vivid picture of everything that had happened, how he found the lost money and more, and how they'd all bought the things for Diwali. Those who didn't know of how the drain had yielded such a bounty were delighted to hear about it. On Diwali day, it sure seemed like a good omen.

Our parents were indeed very happy to see us with goodies, sweets, lamps, toys, and other things. They thought it was very propitious to get so many gifts on this auspicious day. Everyone was given gifts and sweets. Masterji was praised in front of the assembled people and rewarded handsomely for the help he had rendered to us.

That day, our house was the best decorated and illuminated one of all the houses in the entire area. This was one of the most memorable Diwali festivals that we'd celebrated till then. We were truly celebrating the abundance of existence and the grace of Goddess Lakshmi, which had come to us on its own.

13

Beejān

I must have been in class one or two at the most when the incident concerning Beejān occurred.

Though my grandfather, Ram Chandra, was quite modern and progressive according to the norms of his times and encouraged his daughters to go to school, yet in many other ways he too was tradition-bound. So while education of girls was in order, at the same time he was very strict not to allow girls and boys of the family to play or mingle with children of those from lower stratas of society. Ram Chandra thought it was beneath him and his family to be overzealous in interacting with common people.

In our household, therefore, any interaction with people or children from other families was usually supervised by our elders. Typically, the children would rarely venture out of home, which was like a veritable fortress except while going to school with designated chaperones. Besides, there was no need to go out because being a joint family there were so many members to interact with and children to play with. All the brothers, their spouses and children, along with relatives and some cousins were living under one roof and were self-sufficient amongst themselves. Rishi Vihar was their world and apart from considerable fellowship and enjoyment within the family there was a conscious effort to make the evenings special through song, entertainment, and jokes.

There was rarely any need to go outside for any sort of social interaction or 'clubbing'. In fact, the level of entertainment was pretty impressive, with the children and adults all rehearsing regularly to sing all sorts of film songs, share poems, read poetry, narrate jokes, and mimic one another. The talent and the entertainment skills of the children were unanimously appreciated and encouraged by the elders of the family. On days when there were entertainment competitions, prizes were liberally distributed to encourage the young artists.

In spite of the restrictions placed on free interaction of the children with one and all, some untoward things would occur and this would irritate the elders in the family due to their rigid attitude.

I must have been seven or eight when I once visited a neighbour's house—to meet my friend Ratni. My cousin (sister) Nani and I—who was almost my age—had a lovely chemistry with our friend Ratni, and we three enjoyed one another's company. That was the reason why we would be together to play with our collection of dolls for hours together.

Invariably it was Ratni who'd come to our place and we'd all have fun in the lawns of our home. But once in a while, Nani and I would go to Ratni's home to play with her toys, which were made of clay and fascinated me. She also had a nice toy kitchenette, which would draw us to her home.

It had been a few days since Nani had returned to her home. I must have felt lonely and so—probably with my mother's permission—I went to meet Ratni in her home. As I entered, I saw Ratni and her sister Kishni having a chat with their uncle, who was called Beejān by them.

'Are you going to give us a ride in your vehicle? You have been promising us for a long time now.'

'Tomorrow *pakka*. I will take all of you,' Beejān said, making a sign towards me. He had obviously noticed as I'd entered the room.

Both the girls were overjoyed and were sort of ecstatic to extract a promise for a ride from their uncle.

'We're all going to have a ride on Beejān's *gāḍī*.'

I had no clue as to why both the girls were so excited, and where they were to go with their uncle.

'Tell me,' I asked Kishni, 'where are you both going?'

I was obviously very curious. Before Kishni could respond, Ratni held my hand and dragged me out of the room as if to convey something very important. Then in hushed tones she said—

'You know, today for the first time Beejān has agreed to take us on his gāḍī.'

'On his gāḍī? Has he his own vehicle?' I enquired curiously.

Ratni ignored my question and instead continued to speak excitedly.

'Thank God, Beejān has at long last agreed to give us a ride on his big gāḍī. He has invited you too, so that means you can also have a ride with us. Don't you think it'll be great fun to go in his gāḍī? It is not just an ordinary bus, or van.'

By now I was really curious. 'It isn't a bus or a van? Really? What is it then?'

'Please, please tell me, what is this special gāḍī?' I pleaded. 'Is it his own vehicle? I've never seen any gāḍī at your door before!'

'Haven't you ever seen that big gāḍī that has very, very big wheels and moves slowly along the road while pressing the road flat?' Ratni said excitedly. 'That's Beejān's vehicle, and he drives it!'

'Really, you mean your uncle really drives that huge thing?' I must have been very impressed.

I was happy to know about Beejān's gāḍī and began to fantasize about having a ride on an unusual vehicle.

'You know, it is open from all sides. You can see everyone and have great fun besides getting a nice cool breeze.'

'But there are no seats to sit on, where are we going to sit?'

'It will be like a royal ride, where princes and princesses stand on their chariot,' Ratni said with a flourish. She must have recently read some fairy tales that were still vivid in her mind.

That night I couldn't sleep. For most of the night I visualized the ride on the roadroller. I imagined that I'd touch the stars after riding the chariot of some strange land. In my thoughts, all the girls of my school looked like fairies, prancing around the beautiful land I'd reached on my chariot. One of the girls in my school was a bit nasty and prone to bullying the other girls in class. She became the witch in my imagination. So in my thoughts I threw her from my chariot, something that I wouldn't dare do in reality.

The next day, I waited patiently to choose the right moment to sneak out to Ratni's home and take a ride on the roadroller. When everybody at home got busy with their respective routines and schedules, I found it opportune to leave home for an exciting and important adventure.

When I reached Ratni's home, Beejān was already there and both the girls and their mother were terribly excited, almost as if they were going on an airplane ride for the first time! Ratni's mother was very proud of her brother Beejān, who was the driver of the roadroller. When they saw me, they all began to dance around me to show their excitement.

Beejān was a hefty man with a large moustache, which suited him and befitted his profession. He was also quite tall and fair and ready-witted too. His hairstyle was akin to that of the reigning film star of that time, Dev Anand. He had worn a new multicoloured muffler around his neck and carried a 'tired' baggy coat with matching pants. He was quite delighted that his nieces and I would be riding with him that day. He even suggested that he had worn that new muffler for this special occasion. All of us were appreciative of his 'carriage'!

'Are you ready, girls?' he asked us when he was ready to leave. 'Let's go now.'

With this he got up and signalled us to follow him. Like little robots all three of us girls went with him on to the main road, where the roadroller was standing. We were very keen to climb on to the top of the heavy machine, but that was not possible on our own. Beejān came forward and picked us one by one and put us on the top the roadroller in the little space next to the driver's seat. We were so excited with this expedition of our lifetime!

As soon as Beejān began to start the machine, two of his friends came from somewhere, along with two small children.

'Beejānā, take them along as well,' they pleaded, and even before he could say anything, they put the two other children on the roller. We hardly had any space to move. With these intruders we felt squeezed, but kept quiet lest Beejān feel offended. By the time the machine started to move forward, many children from everywhere collected behind the roadroller, making it a small, albeit a noisy procession. All the kids wanted to have a ride on the roadroller and shouted—

'Please sir, please give us also a ride! Please! Sir! Pleeeaaase.'

The commotion drew even more children from the neighbourhood on to the street, as also their mothers; some running out with their toddlers in arms, thus making the procession even larger. We felt so privileged to be on the roller. All the kids were staring at us from the road.

Many of the mothers started pleading as well.

'Please, Beejānā, let these children also have a ride on your marvellous roadroller.' Some mothers were prodding their kids to shout louder to get Beejān's attention and to ensure a ride for themselves. Beejān was feeling very important even as he kept the roller trundling forward. All those on the road were grasping their chins—as an earnest sign of supplication in true Kashmiri style—imploring 'dear Beejānā' for a ride. At one stage the kids were so numerous that a few inadvertently started to go ahead of the slow and shuddering roller. Now Beejān was also shouting and telling the people, especially the kids in the front, to stay away from the front of the roller, lest they get hurt.

'Be careful! Mind your steps, get out of the way!' he said, gesticulating wildly even as one hand grasped a lever sticking out of a freewheeling steering wheel. It seemed to us that with his gestures he was controlling both the machine as well as the mob. There were some rowdy boys too who wanted to climb on to the machine while it was rolling back and forth. At this point, Beejān stopped the roller, came down from his seat and went straight to the boy who was frolicking around a bit too much. He caught him by his collar and slapped the boy hard on his face, and shouted—

'Do you want to die, you scoundrel? Get lost! You cheap mischief-maker! Go away, now!'

Beejān was really angry and wanted that the mob obey him. His scolding the boy did the trick; the mob began to make space for the roller to move. Beejān was quite satisfied with this gesture of the people and then with an air of magnanimity he indicated that he wasn't so bad after all.

'By turns all of you will have a ride on my roller,' he said, triumphantly. 'You have to be patient.'

As soon as he declared this, there was a ripple of approbation from the crowd. He had succeeded in mending his relations with the crowd.

The roadroller kept moving forward and backward, and all the children who were on the roller were so happy and thrilled. I was on top of the world. This was a unique experience of my life. In my mind I was thinking that I was on an expedition to conquer the world. I was very keen that someone from my home should see me on this fascinating trip to fairyland.

I was still in my reverie when lo and behold one of our helpers was returning from some errands in the market, not far from where the roadroller was making its short and slow jaunts back and forth on the road. I saw him, but realized that he hadn't noticed me or any of the other children on the roadroller. He was intent on watching the crowd, which was following the roller. But I was keen that he see me on this gigantic roller and tell my family members about the thrilling experience I was having. So I began to call out to him.

'Sidha, Sidha, see, I'm here.' My voice got drowned in the roar of the engine and the commotion around us, and Sidha hardly noticed anything. But I didn't give up, and I shouted repeatedly, trying to draw his attention. In this task, the other children on the roller also chipped in and we shouted in unison.

'Sidha, Sidha, look here, we are here!' When Sidha heard his name, he turned towards us. He must have been shocked to see me on the roller. He came running towards me, and told me to come down.

'What are you doing here? Beejānā, please stop your crate for a while. I'll get her down.'

'No, I don't want to come down,' I said defiantly. 'We are having a nice time here. See Kishni and Ratni are also here with me.' I was determined not to leave my perch on the roadroller.

'We are not alone here. This is Beejān's roller.' Kishni was pointing towards the driver. 'He's my uncle.' She was the eldest amongst the three of us, but her words did not influence Sidha. He was protective of me and was determined to take me home. But I was not at all willing to go home with him. I behaved like a stubborn child and shooed him away from the place. Kishni and Ratni, and the other two children on the roadroller, also helped me by pleading with Sidha to let me stay for a while. Sidha didn't want to look like a fool, so he left the place quietly.

I was now feeling relaxed. It was fun to see the sea of children following the roller. We were getting hysterical with each movement of the roller, forward and then backward, the jerky movements giving us such joy! We were laughing with delight and having great fun. I had forgotten everything about myself, my home, my surroundings, and the world around me.

Then all of a sudden, I saw two familiar persons coming towards me. It was Sidha again, but this time he'd brought Sarvanand—our seniormost help from home—with him. I knew they'd come to take me home. They both went straight to Beejān and told him to stop the roller. He obeyed in a jiffy, and stopped the roller.

Before I could understand what was happening, one of the persons caught hold of me, and took me home. I was miffed at the sudden end to my reverie, and shouted, 'What are you doing? Where am I going? Where are you taking me? I want to be with Ratni and Kishni. Leave me alone!' I was whining, kicking, and crying all the way till we reached home.

'Here you are! If we hadn't got her down by force, she would have stayed on that huge machine for the whole day.' Both Sidha and Sarvanand were speaking to those gathered as they put me down on the floor in the main *ravak* (porch) outside one of the large rooms.

When I looked around, I was shocked to see all my family members—my parents, my grandmother, uncles, aunts, cousins—and all the helpers assembled there. The room was big, and yet seemed crowded and packed with them all.

My grandmother was sitting on the floor in her usual place, on the beautiful embroidered woollen rug. In front of her was a nice walnut-wood box, which was carved with beautiful motifs. In this box she used to keep money for her daily spending. She would also keep lots of almonds and cardamoms for kehva tea, which were used only when there were special guests.

My father and all my uncles were seated in their respective places. They looked like a jury in session. My grandmother looked very much like a judge, stern and stiff, and was looking at me with visible contempt. I found myself standing in front of her—much like a criminal who'd committed gruesome crimes! Everyone assembled there was gazing at me, and I was scared, but unsure about my fault. That's when my mother suddenly appeared from nowhere and slapped me hard on my face. I was bewildered, not knowing why she was behaving like this. Then I heard her speak.

'She has acquired this bad habit of going to meet Kishni and Ratni quite often because from there she's free to mingle with the urchins on the street. She doesn't know what she is doing.' My mother spoke with annoyance in her voice.

'Leave her now. I know how to handle her.'

My grandmother was speaking to my mother authoritatively. My mother immediately stood back, like a good, obedient daughter-in-law. While my grandmother was about to pronounce her verdict and the punishment that was to be meted out to me, one of the members of the jury, my eldest uncle, Baiji, interrupted the conversation. Looking at his mother he said, 'Mother, while I agree that sneaking out without permission is an offence, this being her first mistake, we can forgive her this time.'

Then he looked towards me, asking me gently, 'How did you get on the roadroller?'

Baiji's kind look and tone were reassuring, which encouraged me to speak. I was collecting my thoughts and wanted to say something, but was still feeling a little afraid of all the elders in the room. I was also looking towards my cousins, those who were my age, for some help. They were equally interested to know about the fascinating roller ride of mine, and how I got on it in the first place.

'Baiji has asked you something, are you not listening?' Lalaji, another uncle, said to me loudly, forcing me to concentrate.

'Who took you there?' Ṭāṭhāji, my other uncle, enquired.

'Beejān gave a ride to us on his roller.' My voice was so feeble that it seemed that they hadn't heard me at all, so I repeated the sentence once again. I was shivering with fear but somehow gathered some courage, and said, 'Beejān took us on his roller.'

'Beejān? Who is this Beejān?' my grandmother said loudly in a sarcastic tone, so that all those who were present wouldn't miss what she was trying to convey.

'Who is Beejān?' others also enquired. I wasn't sure how they'd react when I'd tell them who he was.

'He is Ratni's *māmā* [maternal uncle].' I was very nervous as I spoke, and was still expecting some sort of punishment for this big lapse of mine.

'So that's how! I was wondering how she managed to be there at all. I will definitely give Ratni's mother a piece of my mind, and warn her not to allow her children to roam around like street dogs. They are spoiling our name, and that of our children. It doesn't behove them to do all kinds of cheap tricks and gimmicks.' My grandmother's attention was diverted from me, and now she was focusing on our neighbour's derelict attitudes and deeds. Thanks to Grandmother's attention going to our neighbour, everyone forgot about me and got engrossed in conversations regarding the prestige of our family, our status, and the family name and honour, which they thought was getting besmirched by rash acts such as mine. I was still standing there, not knowing what to do.

As the conversation progressed and conclusions were drawn, members of our family started to leave the scene. All my cousins, however, waited for me behind the door of the room. I winked at them, hinting that I would soon be with them. Nobody noticed when I sneaked out from there to join my cousins. All were happy to see me and to share the exciting experience I had had on the roller.

'Yes, it was fun, great fun!' I could feel from the look on my cousins' faces that they were envious of me. In their minds, they seemed to be thinking, 'The scolding and the slap were well worth the experience she's had on the roller.'

I couldn't agree more!

Part IV
Mystics and Mysticism

14

Nandė Lāl Bab: The Clairvoyant Mystic

Nandė Lāl was the name of an eccentric Kashmiri mystic who lived in the village of Nunner, near Ganderbal. Born in 1896, Nandė Lāl ji, Nandė Lāl Bab or Nandė Bab, as he was lovingly known after he showed signs of mysticism, was a saint, a spiritual guide and clairvoyant, revered by Hindus and Muslims alike across the length and breadth of the Valley of Kashmir. The term 'Bab' in Kashmiri means 'father' or 'venerable elder', and Nandė Lāl ji was given this honorific fairly early in his life as word of his understanding of the Truth and the way he helped the people of Kashmir spread far and wide.

He was an eccentric mystic for a number of reasons. In his youth, and even later in life, he would dress up in European clothes, wear a hat with a few pom-poms hanging on the side, and often tie a rope around his waist. Dressed thus, he would roam the streets of Srinagar, glad-handing people and scaring off others by giving them a glowering look or snarling nasty words and curses at them!

If not in European clothes, he would dress in other odd attire. A classic shirt with shorts and an old overcoat, like those of the Allied Forces in World War II, was his other sartorial innovation. On some days he'd wear a traditional Kashmiri pheran, with a hat or a woollen monkey cap. Because he was tall and lanky he could carry all kinds of clothes, however bizarre, with unusual grace. While walking the busy streets of Srinagar, he was always accompanied by a bunch of his disciples who were at his beck and call. They held his 'precious possessions' in their hands in case he needed them at any time of the day. Usually, his possessions comprised an umbrella, a few odd-shaped tin boxes that held his bric-a-brac, and a duffel bag in which there were all sorts of paper pads, pens, marbles, small papier mâché boxes, and bundles of paper with something written on them.

Whenever Nandė Bab would walk on the road, people made space for him to move freely. Sometimes he'd halt suddenly to go to a random shop and make gestures indicating that something good was to happen to the shopkeeper. He would say this in such a way that only his disciples could understand the language. The shopkeeper along with his staff would stand with folded hands to show reverence to the saint. Shopkeepers would offer lots of almonds, dates, cashew nuts, and other dry fruits to him, which his disciples would gladly accept. The rumour was that if Nandė Bab stepped into a shop, then business would reach new heights. So shopkeepers would request and coax him to enter their shops, but he would not oblige them all.

Because he was a clairvoyant and able to see the future, his renown grew and people were eager to be with him and hear him. However, since he spoke in a garbled manner, his disciples would write his comments on small pieces of paper that were given to the eager devotees to help them understand what he said. Many others were wary of him because they'd be afraid that he might say something about them or their loved ones, which they'd be unable to stomach.

Nandė Bab was also unpredictably spontaneous. He would be quietly smoking his hookah or puffing a cigarette at his humble home in Nunner in the presence of a few of his ardent devotees, and all of a sudden he'd direct them to take him to the home of someone in Srinagar, or Dehradun or Delhi! He wouldn't even give any time for preparations. The devotees would hurriedly arrange transportation and take him wherever he wished to go.

Whenever he entered anybody's home—usually unannounced and even at odd hours—nobody had the guts to stop him. People were in complete awe of him and while they had mixed feelings about him, one thing was clear—no one wanted to incur his wrath. His predictions were so true and accurate that people would be wary. In fact one day he entered the home of a well-to-do family and there he performed the last rite rituals of someone there to indicate that someone in the family was going to die soon.

In the Indian mystical traditions, there are three categories of mystical saints and hermits. One has absolute control of himself and his outward behaviour is like that of any other normal human being's. He shows evidence of tremendous spiritual wisdom, is poised, has a sober nature, and freely mingles with people as he guides them on their journey of discovery. The second type of mystic appears to be semi-mad, has eccentricities but is also clairvoyant. Whatever is likely to occur in the future, he can foresee, and out of compassion for the people around him, he gives them a hint or a glimpse of what might occur. The third type is the person who wants to be away from the humdrum of the world. Such saints usually live in secluded places, in faraway forests in the deeper regions of the Himalayas or other mountain ranges.

Nandė Bab belonged to the second type. To those who may not have known him closely, he too would appear mad. Which is also why he was called Nandė Bab *Mastāna*—implying that he was a carefree mystic, entirely immersed in the Divine. Despite his quirky behaviour, his clairvoyance drew more and more people to him.

Ten days prior to when Sheikh Abdullah—prime minister of the state of Jammu and Kashmir from 1948 to 1953—was about to be arrested in August 1953, Nandė Bab had gone to the secretariat. He went straight to the first floor and beat a big tin with his wooden stick, making a loud racket. When the government officials, who were working in their rooms at the secretariat, heard the noise, they came out to see what was going on. No one dared to stop him lest he curse them.

People who knew of Nandė Bab interpreted the event and understood that some grave misfortune was about to befall the people of Kashmir and the Sheikh's government. Exactly after two weeks, Abdullah was arrested by the Government of India and sent to jail. Many knew that Nandė Bab had tremendous spiritual powers and could avert any misfortune. Some of the people at the secretariat hoped that he would do what was right to protect his people from suffering. Others were happy that at least they had been forewarned and could deal with whatever might happen in the future.

Another incident linked to Nandė Bab's clairvoyance concerned one of his ardent Muslim devotees. Noor-ud-din, who was the vice chancellor of the University of Kashmir in the early 1970s, was a great believer in the mystic and a well-known devotee of his. During his tenure, word went around that an educationist close to the chief minister—a lady called Miss Mehmooda Ali Shah—would summarily replace him. Apparently, even the orders for the change had been prepared by the government.

Obviously, when Noor-ud-din heard about this he was devastated, and to bring solace to himself and his family he visited the ashram at Nunner village. Noor-ud-din and his family sat quietly before the mystic, along with the many other visitors present there. Nandė Bab, who had his eyes shut, seemed to be in a trance. Then, all of a sudden, he opened his eyes and picked up a half-burnt cigarette butt from a nearby ashtray and threw it at Noor-ud-din. He also looked at him fiercely.

'Who is that nasty woman? How dare she even think that she can take your position,' he thundered. 'I have given you your position! Nobody dare dislodge you!'

Everyone in the room knew that Nandė Bab had blessed Noor-ud-din, who too was grateful and left with a spring in his step. As predicted, a day later the government order in favour of Miss Mehmooda was not only withdrawn but Noor-ud-din's tenure as vice chancellor also remained unaffected by the winds of change.

Some of the KP families in town were Nandė Bab's favourites, and he visited them often or even stayed with them for months together at times. People would get and prepare all sorts of delicacies for him, which he would relish. After eating any meal, he would give away the leftovers to those he was close to in his flock, and by and large they would graciously accept his offerings as 'prasad' and eat them heartily. Many of his Muslim disciples were also happy to share what he offered although Nandė Bab intuitively knew if anyone from another faith was likely to resist any of his rituals. Such people were also welcome but would not be called out for sharing food or anointing of tilak.

Amongst the few families that Nandė Bab was fond of visiting were the Thussus and the Dhars. Not just my side of the family, but even other branches that were related to Ram Chandra, and an even more distant branch who owned large orchards in different parts of the Kashmir Valley. All the families that he preferred to stay with were quite well-to-do and were either professionally renowned or excelled in business. In his early years Nandė Lal ji remained a frequent visitor to the chosen families and would be happy to interact with all the members of the household. But later he stayed put in one of the secluded rooms, spending most of his time meditating, and engrossed in his own world. In fact, in the home of the Dhars, who owned orchards, Nandė Bab would often pitch his own tent in their spacious gardens in Karan Nagar. The mystic would be assisted in his daily routine by a bunch of assistants and devotees, who would rarely interact with members of the host family. That's how Nandė Bab would get the kind of seclusion so essential for his meditative practices.

Yet, in spite of this, many people would visit him during the day and stay for hours in his presence. On days when he would allow visitors he would order tea for fifty people at a time, which had to be served. There was no scope for refusal. For that matter, one of the helps from the host household was also dedicated to assist Bab's aides, and to do anything specific that Nandė Bab wanted him to do.

Sometimes Nandė Bab would order anyone and everyone to do very odd and strange things. For instance, one spring day he ordered everyone to pluck all the weeds from the lawn outside and present their 'collection' to him. Everyone present, and even those who may have joined later, willingly did as they were told, not knowing the meaning of the act but certain that the mystic was doing it for their own good. Yet nobody dared ask him why he wanted the weeds to be collected. When not in the presence of people or interacting with his disciples, he would keep himself busy writing down all his utterances. On the face of it, the utterances were all garbled sentences and were in a strange, mysterious language that had no meaning apparently. However, a few out of the many little pieces of paper with the mystical sentences would have one or two sentences which would carry a lot of meaning to a specific person. Nandė Bab would pass on that piece of paper to the man either when he would be summoned or more likely when he would make a sudden, spontaneous appearance. The man would receive the paper gratefully in front of the other people present and would prostrate himself before Nandė Bab ji.

Most of the time Nandė Bab's predictions were precise and relevant. Such was his reputation that no one doubted that his predictions would materialize. In one KP family, their nubile daughter had already been engaged three times but each time, for one reason or another, the engagement would be terminated. The family got very concerned for the poor girl since the breakups were affecting her mind, and they were therefore, desperate and in anguish. They had lost all hope in this regard. One day suddenly, Nandė Bab entered their home unannounced and opened the door of one of their rooms. He made himself and his all disciples sit down comfortably on the carpeted floor of the room. And then, he and his disciples began to sing the beautiful Kashmiri marriage songs known as *vanėvun*. He ordered the householder to bring a kāngri (an earthen pot to hold burning charcoal embers which is decorated with elegant wicker-work; used extensively in Kashmir to keep oneself warm in the winter months. It's also used for rituals such as the burning of frankincense, fragrant *isband* seeds and gum on its embers) and told the lady of the house to bring the isband. The symbolism of the vanėvun, the ordering of a kāngri, and the demand for isband was not lost on anyone since they are only used for happy occasions. When all the people who were living around the area heard songs of marriage, they came rushing to witness what Bab was doing there.

By the time a crowd had assembled, Nandė Bab was in ecstasy—dancing and singing. People had no doubt that good news would be round the corner regarding the daughter's marriage. Everybody was elated.

A few days later a boy from the USA, from a good KP family, indicated that he was keen to return to America only after he had found himself a good woman to be his wife. Apparently, he had seen the girl—the daughter of the household that Nandė Bab had visited just a few days prior—at a nearby temple, and had liked her. He therefore suggested that his parents initiate the process of connecting with the girl's family. As expected, Nandė Bab's predictions came true. The girl liked the boy too and was happily married in the following week, after which she flew joyously to America with her husband!

Not surprisingly, therefore, if there was some problem in the lives of people, they would go to Bab for guidance or a solution to their travails. In this process they would sometimes spend days together, waiting for a benign glance from Nandė Bab or the handing out of a paper slip with a sentence or two that would give them a clue of a way out of their afflicted minds.

One evening, the mastāna mystic was in a very good mood when he entered the private side of the house of the Dhar family, where he had been staying for a while. This was rare and created a stir. He seated himself comfortably in the middle of the large room, where everyone would assemble in the evenings. All the family members were surprised to see Nandė Bab in their midst and soon everyone else collected there to see why he had come to the inner side of the house.

Nandė Bab was laughing heartily even as he sat down and glanced around the room to see who all from the family were there. He began to sing a very sweet song, usually sung in families when someone in the family is pregnant. He then began to say '*shokh tė panzun*', which in Kashmiri is a mantra to ward off the evil eye on a newborn baby.

There were so many eligible mothers in the family at that time, but while singing this prayer Nandė Bab gazed at me continuously, much to my concern and making me conscious. In fact he just did not take his gaze away from me. Instead, he sung even more songs associated with the birth of babies, indicating that someone in the family was expecting one. Everyone in the family was obviously quite surprised since there had been no formal announcement of any of the daughters or daughters-in-law expecting. Understandably, the guesswork began. Which lady in the family could it be? While the guesswork was on, Nandė Bab called out to me to sit closer to him. I was very reluctant to be near him because I did not want him to openly indicate to others that it was I who was pregnant, for all to know. He was insisting that I come closer to him. When I didn't get up for a while, my grandmother ordered me to get up and obey Bab's request. I got up hesitantly and went towards Bab. He asked me to sit on his lap. Like a child I did as he suggested. As if I was a child, he put his hand on my head and stroked my back, my head, and shoulders very gently, carefully, and tenderly. Singing the relevant song for the occasion, he took some sweets from the plate that was in front of him and offered them to me to eat. There were four-five plates of delicacies in front of him. Instead of eating something himself, he was making me eat almonds and sweets. I was terribly embarrassed by his actions.

The lyrics of the song he was singing were,

'Whatever you want, it will be sent to you.
If you want even the rarest of things to eat, they will be kept ready for you.
You the unborn, who is very special to me, are to come to the world.
The world's best things will be kept ready for you.'

Singing thus, he kept feeding me nuts and sweets continuously. I was perspiring and wanted to get up from there, but he was not allowing me to get up. My mother, grandmother, and the rest of the family members were telling me to be patient and do as he was suggesting. By this time, the truth had been declared by him and the family knew my secret.

Everyone now knew—without a shadow of doubt—that the baby to be born would be a baby boy. This was evident from Bab's gestures and body language. He kept congratulating everyone in the family through appropriately chosen songs that were associated with the coming of a new member in the family.

A little under nine months from then, a baby boy was born to me as had been predicted by Nandé Bab. This boy, my firstborn, also had a chance to meet the great mystic on a few occasions as a teenager.

I also recall that a few years later, as my dear grandmother Māl was about to leave her body, he visited the Dhar household again, and spent a few days interacting with the family. Just a day or two before my grandmother moved on, he kept changing his clothes and reappearing in the garden where all were seated, in new sets of clothes as the old ones were actually discarded in a way that all could see.

His message was clear—the body, after its work was done, had to be discarded like old clothes. The soul, however, was everlasting and would take a new form upon its reincarnation.

15

Graṭė Bub and the Miracle

Kashmir has for aeons spawned and attracted all kinds of mystics—rishis, masters who would never speak, munis, saints of all faiths and denominations, and peers and godly persons on their own personal quest to discover the One Truth. Because the Dhars were relatively well-to-do and treated seekers with utmost respect and care, many such wandering mystics would come to our home in Rishi Vihar and spend days, if not weeks, staying there and interacting with the members of the household.

These people were drawn to visit our family quite often because they were treated fondly and with utmost reverence. There was not a single well-known saint—those who were contemporaries of either Ram Chandra initially or his sons later on—who hadn't visited this home. It was a matter of satisfaction to the members of the Dhar family that saints visited them of their own volition. Some of the frequent visitors—some before my time but whose names I recall—were Krishna Joo Razdan, Kushok Bakula Rinpoche, Ahad Bub,

Sona Bub, Sultan Sæb, Nandė Bab, the seer of Manigam, Kashkāk, as well as Gratė Bub, Sati Dæd and her daughter Dekė Dæd. These were the regular mystics who would come to spend time with the family. Their presence would bring a lot of cheer and happiness to all and would also keep everyone engrossed.

Most of the saints and mystics would be accompanied by many of their followers and devotees who would also stay as long as the saint was in residence. The presence of additional people would increase the workload on the householders and the house staff, since it was certain that they would demand not just a lot of attention, but would also request a steady stream of refreshments and snacks throughout the day.

The house help was ever ready to serve them in order to secure the blessings of the holy men and women, and thereby improve their lot in life.

Looking back, I realize that all the members of Rishi Vihar were truly believers in all faiths. Their outlook was broad and all-embracing. Everyone, it seemed, accepted the diversity and variations in the paths taken by different mystical seekers as being akin to the profusion of rivers in the world, which though different would all ultimately merge with the waters of the interconnected oceans. There were no religious biases or hatred for any religion. In fact Baiji—the eldest son of Ram Chandra, who became the head of the family after his father's demise—had tremendous faith in Buddhism and meditated regularly. Because of him, there was also a strong influence of Buddhism and many in the family were initiated into the practice of chanting and silent meditation. Yet, all holy people—both men and women—were treated respectfully, with equal special treatment being given to the Hindu, Muslim, Sufi, or Buddhist saints. They were all welcomed and served with affectionate devotion.

Within the extensive house library, there were, in fact, a large number of books on all kinds of spiritual and edifying subjects. Our grandmother, Māl, who was well versed in spoken Persian, would recite the verses of Jalaluddin Rumi and Omar Khayyam with an ease and fluency that gave no hint to anyone—scholars included—that she didn't really know how to read and write. Māl quoted Persian couplets in the course of her day-to-day conversations and used them very appropriately to make a point.

One morning in the month of September, sometime in the early 1950s, it so happened that Graṭė Bub along with his disciples visited the Dhar family. He went straight to Māl's room, and settled himself comfortably. He and his devotees were welcomed respectfully, and served throughout the day. He conversed with grandmother, and answered some of the questions that a few ladies asked him. Everyone was of the view that by sundown he would leave.

But as the day wore on, there was no movement either by Graṭė Bub or by any of his devotees. They seemed to be happy where they were. Naturally, dinner too was served to them. Yet there was no sign of them leaving.

It was customary to have mystics and saints stay at the house of a householder for as long as they wished. No one therefore even dared to ask the saint or any of his followers about their intentions. After dinner, therefore, in order to accommodate the saint and his devotees, Grandmother had to shift to another room. No one knew how long they were going to stay and that seemed fine. It did require the assigning of an attendant, however, who would look after all of Graṭė Bub's needs.

There's a reason why people in Kashmir called this unique mystic Graṭė Bub. In the Kashmiri language *graṭė* (pronounced *grah-tah*) is a stone-grinding wheel that's used in pairs—one atop the other—for grinding grains. Legend had it that as a young man, Graṭė Bub had slept on a grinding wheel for twelve years, after which he had attained enlightenment and the power of *siddhas*. No one knew his real name and no one cared any more. One thing about him, however, was established. Over the years—as a seeker—he had attained extraordinary powers but he would rarely use them.

Baiji and Sati had five children, and Shyama was their only daughter. Shyama had been married into the Wazir family a few years ago, and had recently delivered a bonny baby girl. Since the infant was the first grandchild in the family, she was very special and precious. Everyone loved her, and since Shyama had come to her parents' home after her delivery, everyone had had a chance to be with the baby and cuddle her. Everyone adored the little baby girl who was treated not as the grandchild of just Baiji and Sati, but as the darling infant of the entire Dhar family. She was lovingly named baby Nimoo and was affectionately also called 'Nimlāl'—dearest Nimoo Jewel—by all in the family.

Nimlāl must have been about a year old and had just started to walk and run when one day, while playing in the garden at her maternal grandparent's home, she got hurt. While walking around happily, she stumbled and struck against the wooden fence when a partially embedded nail in that fence hurt her forehead.

The wound on her forehead was deep and little Nimoo was bleeding profusely. Seeing her bleeding, the whole family was shocked and panicky. Ṭāṭhāji, Shyama's uncle, who was at home at that hour, rushed to Nimlāl upon hearing her cries and shouts of other concerned women, and swiftly took her in his lap with the intention of rushing her to a nearby dispensary. He didn't even wait for the horse-driven tonga to be brought out. He just ran towards the nearby clinic.

A number of women and most of the house help were running behind Ṭāṭhāji. No one was sure where he was headed, but presumed that since he was carrying a child who was hurt, the nearest doctor's clinic would be the destination. The women with Ṭāṭhāji were beating their chests and crying out loud.

'Our dear Nimlāl has gotten hurt. She's bleeding.'

On the road, those who recognized the anguished party went with them up to the hospital—making it quite a crowd by the time they got there.

There are many remarkable qualities that Kashmiris possess, but in my view the one quality that stands out is their eagerness to help those in need. Throughout my life I've seen ordinary people, simple folk, going out of their way to help another person in need.

So when the party reached the hospital, many amongst them rushed to the doctors on emergency duty, and pleaded with them to attend to the little girl immediately. In this process they also determined the family doctors' background and quickly established that one or the other doctor was related to one of them. With this additional 'connect' they would urge good treatment from him.

Fortunately, Ṭāṭhāji kept his cool as he waited patiently for the family physician to arrive. He took a quick look at the little girl, suggested the procedures to stop the bleeding and the whole thing was sorted out without a fuss. Baby Nimlāl got a few stitches and a tetanus toxoid shot, and was soon back to her normal self. The Dhar family, however, was upset that their darling baby had got stitches and because the news of this went around quickly, streams of relatives came to see darling Nimlāl, even as she was recovering.

Many months went by, and once again, Graṭè Bub—accompanied by a number of his devotees and his staff—arrived at Rishi Vihar. As always, he was treated respectfully and ushered into his favourite room.

All the ladies of the house would visit saint Graṭè Bub in his room whenever they got time from their household duties. Sati,

Benji, and the others would go and sit in his presence, seeking the saint's blessings.

Shyama, accompanied by her daughter Nimlāl, too would often time her visits to her parents' place to coincide with some happy event or function within the family. So when it became known that Graṭė Bub was at Rishi Vihar, she too came to be with her parents and spend a few days with them.

Nimlāl, ever the favourite with all, was soon whisked away by the ladies and taken to be with them. Soon she found herself in the room where Graṭė Bub was interacting with his devotees and family members. She was placed on the carpeted floor where she cheerfully played with the things that the saint had kept on the floor.

Next day, Grātė Bub's room was filled with visitors who had come to pay their respects to the saint. A singer was melodiously chanting verses from Lalded's *vākhs* and from Nunde-rishi's verses, while playing a harmonium alongside. Everyone was in a state of joyous ecstacy and was clapping and swaying with the music and the chanting. Some men and women were repeating the verses and the whole room was filled with an uplifting spiritual mood.

All the ladies of the Dhar family were also there. Nimlāl by now was in Sati's lap and everyone was relaxed and blissful. While this was going on, Prema entered the room with a big *samovar*, which was filled with boiling kehva tea, and a basketful of bronze *khāsus*—the traditional gripless metal cups—in which the kehva was to be served.

Prema couldn't have chosen a worse time to enter the crowded room with a samovar full of hot tea. Not only was it difficult for him to navigate the gaps between the people seated on the floor, serving tea to the guests was even more so. But before anyone would direct him to stop offering tea and wait till the chanting was over, the handle of the samovar broke off, and much of the boiling hot tea from the vessel spilled on the floor of the room, scalding many people present there. Some of the tea also fell on poor Nimlāl who had also gotten off her grandmother's lap and was now on the floor.

The little child let out a shriek as the hot tea burned her skin, and her loud shrill cries of agony stopped all the chanting and singing. Everyone was panicky. The little child's legs, her body, neck, and arms were badly scalded. Her clothes were taken off but she was in pain and was crying continuously.

Amidst all the commotion, as Nimlāl was still weeping bitterly, Sati took her grandchild in her arms and put her in front of the saint saying, 'Now you have to make her all right! I won't leave you alone till she is fully well!'

Someone in the room suggested that the child be taken to the hospital. But as this suggestion was being debated, Sati, her daughter Shyama, and many other ladies from the Dhar family began to plead with the saint.

'Please Bub, you have to make our dear child all right. Otherwise her family members (the Wazir family) will curse us for this calamity.'

There was considerable commotion in the room. Yet Graṭē Bub was sitting through all the tumult with a peaceful look on his face—almost as if nothing untoward was happening at all in the room! He was, of course, looking towards the child, Nimlāl, who was still crying with pain. Next to her the ladies were weeping and sobbing, feeling helpless.

After a while the benign saint looked towards Sati and said, 'You don't want to send the child to Uma Devi, do you?'

Sati was aghast.

'What are you talking about? Who is Uma Devi? Don't you hear our child's shrill cries of pain?' Sati was weeping bitterly.

Shyama, who was also wailing, added, 'My daughter is in a bad shape, do make her well again, please Bub!'

Sati continued.

'Her in-laws will curse all of us, Bub, please save her. She is precious to all of us. Please do something.'

All the ladies in the room, along with the visitors, began to plead and request the saint, their hands folded in submission.

'So you want to keep her?' Graṭė Bub asked them all innocently, without being unduly ruffled. His equanimity was in stark contrast to the utter despair on everyone else's faces.

Graṭė Bub directed one of the devotees from his group. 'Sona, go down and get a few leaves from the cherry trees in the garden.' Sona was up on his feet and quickly ran down to the garden. He wasted no time in getting the leaves and handed them to the saint. Grātė Bub took the cherry leaves and began to clean them with the sleeves of his pheran. By now the room had quietened down. Nimlāl was still sobbing but she was being rocked in someone's lap.

The saint now put the leaves on Nimlāl's tiny body, covering all the red and inflamed scalds with them. He was chanting mantras quietly as he was placing the leaves on the child's body. Gradually, Nimlāl's crying and sobbing subsided, and it was evident that the leaves had had a soothing effect on her body. The people in the room dried their tears as well, and a few people prostrated themselves at the saint's feet, expressing gratitude and speaking words of praise.

All the attention was now on the revered saint, who was continuing to apply the tender cherry leaves on Nimlāl's body with full devotion and concentration.

This action of his took nearly fifteen to twenty minutes. As soon as he was done, Nimlāl wanted to go to her mother and showed signs of restlessness. Seeing her so, the saint began to look at the child in her face and asked her lovingly.

'Do you want to go to your mother?'

The little girl nodded, and she began to get up. She got up briskly, in a way as if nothing had happened in between, and ran towards her mother. Her mother, Shyama, hugged her and put her hand all over her body to see if the scalds were still there. There was not a trace of redness on Nimlāl's little body. It was unblemished! Not an iota of either swelling or redness or blisters! The spectators, and the many more who had assembled in the room, were astonished and stunned to see a veritable miracle.

All the people present there, with their hands still folded, began to sing devotional songs of praises to Lord Shiva, who was Graṭé Bub's favourite deity. The saint too was in ecstasy and all around him were full of gratitude and were experiencing an uplifting, divine presence in the room.

Part V
Marriages, Love, Neighbours, and Brides

16

The Marriages of Rajṭoṭh and Sondhlal

Rajṭoṭh, the firstborn of my parents, was quite young at the time of his marriage. He had just started college when it was presumed that he was now 'ready for a bride'! In those days—and this was around the mid-1940s—marriages were an important feature in one's life and had to be performed sooner than later. Besides, Sondhlal, my cousin, who was a couple of years older than Rajṭoṭh, was also getting married, and having a joint wedding for both the boys made a lot of economic sense. It was a fairly common practice in joint families to perform the marriages of eligible, similarly aged children together to avoid having to spend extra money for the wedding, and to avail of the benefits of pooling the family resources as also doing away with the hassle of planning and executing multiple big events as typical marriages used to have.

Since Rajṭoṭh was the eldest child of my parents, I can imagine that they would've been quite keen to have a daughter-in-law in their family, ever since he turned fifteen or sixteen.

I'm told that when my mother, Benji, would see a good-looking KP girl anywhere, she would immediately think of her as the most eligible wife for her son! Poor Rajṭoṭh!

Fortunately for him, the search for a suitable and accomplished girl who would become his bride took the better part of four years to settle and finalize. By then, Sondhlal was already engaged to a girl from a well-to-do, respectable family. So, no sooner was a suitable girl found for Rajṭoth, he too was formally betrothed to her, and the parents of the two boys started to plan for their joint wedding.

The criteria for choosing the 'right' girls to become brides, in those days, hinged on a number of social and economic factors. First, the girl's family had to have visible evidence of economic stability for at least three to four generations, and if the family had been prosperous for even longer, so much the better. Second, the family had to be an 'honourable' one, the kind that could be considered '*khāndānī*'. Thirdly, although not the most important, the girl had to be fairly good-looking and accomplished in housework. If the girl was of a good nature and was well mannered and polite, that was even better.

Boys and girls—typically sixteen- and seventeen-year-olds—would be quite excited to get married, largely because they didn't really understand what they were going in for. Getting married was a custom, so everyone followed it without asking too many questions.

Because mortality rates—even among teens—were high, marriages were an important milestone in one's life. Parents used to feel relieved to see their sons and daughters married. They would feel that with the marriage of their children, the burden of caring for them and the responsibility towards their welfare would now be shared by the *families* that would be involved. This also explains why—more than the looks of a boy or a girl—it was the economic and social standing of the families that mattered.

Having a big joint family, with many adult members and many more children meant that there was always a crunch for space.

Children would sleep in large rooms on a few mattresses spread on the ground over namdahs and carpets, while the married adults would have rooms of their own. Every time a young man in the family became a benedict, the head of the family had no option but to add a few more rooms within the basic structure of the main house, according to the necessity of the space. This was done to ensure that the newly married couple had some privacy and a little space to call their own.

At Rishi Vihar, the addition of rooms had been going on for some time before Rajtoth's marriage (to accommodate the needs of our older cousins who were already married by the time Rajtoth became eligible). Two huge buildings got erected in addition to the existing two buildings, to make it four. These new houses were huge, and looked somewhat like squat castles. The houses were interconnected to enable members of the family to move freely from one house to another without having to step out. With so many entrances and interconnected corridors, these connected houses were wonderful play places for all the children, who would love to play hide-and-seek. It would take them hours to find the ones who were hidden, because there were innumerable hiding places and little cave-like rooms in the basements of the houses. Three of the four houses had shingle roofs. The older one, which was also a big house, had a traditional Kashmiri roof. These roofs, which had been in vogue in Kashmir since the earliest times, were made of wooden planks that were placed on beams that were usually hewn from the trunks of straight deodar trees from the nearby forests. On top of the planks, by way of waterproofing, sheets of birch bark were neatly placed layer after layer so that even if some moisture was to leak through, the birch bark would protect the rooms beneath the roof. The next layer that was put on top of the birch bark sheets comprised soft clay, and even this layer was covered with yet another layer of birch tree sheets. Finally, the roof was topped with locally available clay, creating a layer that was anywhere between ten to fourteen inches thick. The roof, of course, always had a good slope to ensure that rain and snow would quickly run off the roof. Difficulties would arise in winters though—especially if there was heavy snowfall—which would add a heavy burden to the mud roof. Many Kashmiri houses were known to have their roofs cave in when the snowfall was excessive and it would fall when everyone was asleep. If it snowed during the day, when people were aware, all hands—including other adults from the mohalla—would be enlisted, given wooden paddles, and urged to get on to the roof and clear off the snow.

Because the roofs had a layer of mud on top that was always moist and exposed to the sun, people used to sow bulbs of common Kashmiri flowers during the autumn season. So in springtime, many houses would look stunningly beautiful with abundant flowers—daffodils, narcissi, red tulips, and even wild flowers that would grow on their own—on the rooftops, giving an entire locality a lovely spring look. It used to be a breathtaking sight, especially on sunny days, with houses in an entire mohalla looking pretty with tulips blooming on the roofs in abundance!

Another fascinating aspect of these houses was that during the winter months, after the snow had fallen, and even after most of it had been removed from the roofs, there was still considerable snow on the roof and a lot of water contained in the mud. During the day, when it was warm, the snow would melt and there would be a constant pitter-patter of water droplets falling to the ground from the high roofs. However, when it was night-time, the temperature would fall and often plummet below zero. This sudden drop in the temperature would create big and long icicles along the edge of the roof. Not just icicles that looked like slender stalactites, there were even ice sheets that were formed during the nights making them look like beautiful, crystal-glass curtains. The houses looked really pretty. Many brave children would venture to reach the icicles hanging from the roof, and pluck them to make ice lollies!

On many occasions, if the temperature stayed on minus seven or eight degrees Celsius for a week or so, even the top of the Dal Lake would get frozen. That used to be a delightful time for children who would slide and slip on the surface much to their amusement. The children would use rudimentary planks of wood or folded woollen blankets as sleighs, with some of the older children pulling the younger ones on the blanket. Despite the absence of sophisticated gear for sledging, the children would have such a lot of fun.

Marriages were an occasion for celebrations within the families involved, and since there were not too many such occasions to celebrate, it was customary to have many small and big events around marriages that would go on for weeks and sometimes for months together.

Because there was a lot of work involved in arranging a wedding—from hosting and feeding relatives to ensuring that all the appropriate rituals were done as per the requirements of the scriptures and traditions—all the near and dear relatives, and even those who were distant cousins of the parents of those getting married, would assemble at the home where the wedding was to take place. This would happen weeks before the actual date of the wedding, so the festive mood would be created long before the actual celebrations. Even children, who would ordinarily live in their own homes and go to school from there, would bring their books and satchels along and would attend school from the 'celebration home'. It used to be a merry time for all the family members as well as for the children of the family.

The pace of life was slow. There were few, if any, worries about the future, and there was no competition or a desire to 'outdo others'. Life flowed like a river—mostly smooth and placid, but not without an occasional problem or two, some of which could be quite disruptive.

And so, sometime in 1948, Sondhlal and Rajṭoṭh finally got married. Sondhlal went through the marriage ritual with his bride a couple of days before Rajtoth. The dates had been decided in consultation with the family's guru ji, who was known by his name followed by the reverential term *boi* in Kashmiri, which means 'brother'. This tradition of calling the priests of the KP community boi had emerged in the seventeenth century, when the community decided that in order to survive and remain economically afloat, the Pandits had to take up work other than the traditional work of Brahmins. Yet, since following the rituals that were required in everyday life and at times of celebrations and death was ordained in the scriptures, these could not be ignored. Hence every KP family decided that the firstborn male or the eldest brother would become the guru for all the others in the samaj, and carry on the traditional, spiritual learning, and the dharma of the community. All others from the family were, thereafter, free to work for the ruling elite and use their erudition and skills for the welfare of all. These Kashmiri Pandits were called *kārkuns*. The gurus were known as *gor* in Kashmiri, but were called brother (boi*)* so-and-so, because they were after all brothers of the kārkun families.

The elders in the KP community took this very significant call about the 'bifurcation' of the community primarily for economic reasons. After the advent of Islam, the Pandits were reduced to utter penury. Many people, including the forefathers of Pandit Motilal Nehru, fled from Kashmir at this point in history. Life was proving to be difficult, mortality had increased, and all families were suffering terribly. The economic hardships were excessive because many of the temples, which would have been a source of income to the Pandits, were broken or replaced with mosques, since much of the erstwhile Hindu samaj in Kashmir had been converted to Islam and no longer patronized traditional priests and gurus.

A week after Sondhlal got married, it was time for Rajtoth to get married. I was a little girl then, and remember vividly going to Sondhlal's in-laws' place—a few days later—with other elders in the family for our first formal feast at their house. They had a huge old-fashioned house, but the decor within it was modern and tastefully done. It made quite an impression on me as a little girl.

I was especially impressed with the unique and elegant curtains that every door that connected two rooms had. These curtains, which were strung together from what looked like pearls and slender glass-pipe beads, sparkled and shone brightly. My other siblings and cousins were also fascinated by the tinkling sound the beads made each time the curtains were touched.

In contrast, the house of Rajtoth's in-laws was quite modern. The outer structure was relatively new and it had a different look and feel therefore. In addition to this, they were living in the Civil Lines area where all the senior government officers lived. Compared to the old city of Srinagar, it was in an exclusive area.

Rajtoth's wife, Jaya, had no brothers. Her parents had only begotten daughters. Jaya was the eldest of them all, and the first daughter to get married in the family. Therefore, her marriage with Rajtoth was a very special event in her family.

A fortnight after his marriage, Rajtoth was invited to his in-laws' home for a dinner party. In order to get to know the family members better, it was customary for the respective families to host a dinner in honour of the other family members. All the elders were invited and even children, including the kid brothers and sisters and cousins of the groom, would accompany the benedict, who was considered the chief guest.

So with a big battery of kids in tow, Rajtoth, his parents, and uncles and aunts went to his in-laws' home. All the guests, including the children and the groom, were received regally. They were welcomed into the lovely home and sumptuous varieties of delicacies were offered. In between lots of dryfruits and cups of kehva came the appetizers. Then the entrées arrived along with all the elements of a delicious and hearty Kashmiri Pandit meal.

After dinner, the bride's father and mother requested my father that they would like their daughter and their new son-in-law to stay the night with them. They even suggested that all the children—those who were old enough to stay away from their parents—were most welcome to stay as well.

His in-laws had obviously arranged for a proper night-suit for Rajtoṭh, in anticipation of his staying back. However, since a large number of his little siblings and cousins were also staying overnight, the problem was, how could all the children be allowed to sleep with their best dresses and pants on? For the girls amongst the children, there was no problem, because they easily fitted into the nice dresses provided by the bride's sisters. The dresses of the little boys were a concern!

When the problem was being discussed in front of the members of the family, the bride's grandfather spoke in a very reassuring and polite tone—'You've made a mountain of a molehill. It hardly matters what kind of clothes they wear during the night, isn't it? In any case, in the morning they are going to wear their own clothes.'

Jaya's grandfather was a tall robust man with elegant white hair, and a white moustache. He was wearing a long, clean white pheran, which suited his entire personality. His word therefore wasn't just a suggestion; it was a command.

Nobody dared to disagree. Besides, Grandfather had offered a wonderful and practical solution. The issue now veered to the question; whose clothes would fit whom?

So all the girls of the family were brought into the main hall where the entire band of guests and the members of the host family were sitting. The bride's father took a look at the little guests who'd be staying overnight. Then his gaze went towards the girls of the family, who had just entered the room.

'Sheila, your clothes will fit Gyanji. You take him and give him his clothes,' he ordered.

'Kaki, your clothes will fit Bulla and Sardar nicely, so will you please take them along?'

The Marriages of Rajṭoth and Sondhlal

'Rani's or Nichi's clothes will fit this boy. What's his name, please?' one of Jaya's uncles said, pointing towards one of the little boys who was sitting there.

'His name is Kagga,' Rajṭoth said, introducing the boy to them.

'Now the problem of the boys' clothes is over. All the girls—Shyama, Khema, Pichru, Nani, will have no problem at all. They can borrow clothes from our girls.'

This amusing process ensured that everyone was satisfied. The children (unlike many youngsters today) were quite excited to be wearing the clothers of the host's daughters, and even the boys were fine with the idea that they'd be wearing girls' clothes for the night!

All the girls and boys from both the families left the main room to change into their nightdresses, and to continue the fun into the night. In this process all the children became friendly with each other. With the clothes having been changed, they all returned to the big room. The boys were in girls' clothes, which made them a little hesitant and awkward for a while. But Jaya's grandfather was a wise person, and sensing the delicate situation, he was quick to comment.

'Aren't all the lovely children looking so nice and beautiful in these dresses? It suits them all so well! It's almost as if the dresses were made for them. They fit them just like their own clothes.'

Grandfather's remarks were reassuring. The children smiled, and made light of the awkward situation.

Once everyone had settled down, Grandpa noticed that Gyanji—who was one of the older boys in the group—was reluctant to go to the washroom, and chose to be seated. He was hesitant even to stand up. Sensing that there could be a bladder boo-boo if Gyanji didn't go to the loo, he said to him, 'Young man, in Glasgow, as in all of Scotland, the men wear skirts, called kilts, when they have to go to formal occasions and when they play the bagpipes.'

'You mean the *men* wear skirts and play their bagpipes?' an uncle of the bride asked empathically, to keep the conversation going. By now the interest of the kids, including Gyanji, had waxed and they were paying attention to the conversation.

'Baiji, have you ever seen them playing?' another gentleman enquired. 'I too love bagpipes. Watching lairds arrange for a bagpipe performance around their properties is a fun thing to do.'

The conversation took all present there to a fascinating part of the world, and everyone was engrossed. The benedict, Rajtoth, chipped in with his understanding of the way the people of Scotland lived, and many others from the bride's side followed thereafter, sharing their views and ideas. I suspect many were motivated just to make a good impression on the groom. What had started as a distraction for Gyanji had by now acquired a dynamic of its own, and was gaining more energy and was engaging everyone.

Quite understandably, the children soon forgot about the clothes they were wearing, and were listening to the scintillating conversation with rapt attention. Nobody knows when Gyanji, Sardar, Bulla, and Kagga went to the washroom, quietly and without any fuss, and hurried back to be a part of the conversation.

17

Nav-sheen Mubārakh

Being an educationist, Ram Chandra was keen to propagate a modern, beneficial education system for all in the entire Kashmir region, which for historical reasons had remained steeped in an outdated approach to education. Ram Chandra was so committed to his mission that he travelled across the length and breadth of the state, meeting teachers and headmasters and inspiring them and their students to adopt new and modern methods of teaching and textbooks that broadened the horizons of youngsters.

Ram Chandra was also keen to help and facilitate the education of promising young men of poor means. He was also helpful to many of his poor, distant relatives—especially those who were living in far-flung areas and who didn't therefore have access to proper schools—and actively sought them during his tours.

Whenever he found a promising, bright relative who could benefit from a proper education, he would insist that the youngster be sent to Srinagar to stay at Rishi Vihar and pursue his studies along with the other children in the household. At Rishi Vihar, all such children were treated as family, and apart from being given guidance to enable them to go through a proper education, they were housed and fed with all the others in the large household.

Being quite well-off, Ram Chandra's family had adopted a style of living that was slightly conservative on some matters but modern otherwise. It was a unique admixture of different worlds that would seem quite unusual to a visitor. In spite of the prevailing feudal system in society, the limited rights that women had on account of the many invasions, and the intimidation and coercion that Kashmir had been subjected to, Ram Chandra was emphatically supportive of women's education and their emancipation from many of the horrid social and religious impositions. These social impositions, such as the restrictions on widow remarriage, or women having to deliver babies in a secluded part of the house made the lives of women even more difficult as they were already burdened by the hazards of childbearing, limited medical facilities, and working and living in generally poor and insanitary neighbourhoods. He was also keen that the girls should learn music and be conversant with other arts and crafts as well.

Ram Chandra's wife, Sukhmāl, or Māl as she was lovingly known, was also supportive of Ram Chandra's efforts. In many respects both of them were far ahead of their times and appreciated the importance of modern education in changing times. Ram Chandra's contemporaries too held him in awe on account of his intelligence, his erudition, and his progressive world view. His friends and other people in the community would always endeavour to be in his presence and try to emulate him while learning the ways of the modern world.

During one of his visits to Gilgit, in the northern realms of Kashmir, Ram Chandra had a chance meeting with the British assistant resident of the state there. The conversation understandably veered to the way the Maharaja's government was establishing a modern system of education. Ram Chandra indicated that while progress was being made, the quality of textbooks was still not up to the mark and he probably singled out a textbook of geography to make his point.

Ram Chandra must have made quite an impression on the assistant resident, because a few weeks later the diwan of the state received a letter from the resident in Srinagar, suggesting that Ram Chandra Dhar was the ideal person to write a modern, updated text book on geography for schools in the state.

I'm told that the book was written by him and was used as a textbook in schools in the early decades of the twentieth century. Sadly, I've been unable to lay my hands on a copy of this book so far.

Ram Chandra and Sukhmāl were very keen that their youngest daughter Didā and their eldest grandson Gashā's marriage should be performed together. They were both eligible and almost of the same age. Gashā had also finished his studies recently. Gashā's parents had neither a say in fixing the marriages nor in making any of the preparations. Because the marriages of Didā and Gashā were now the concern of the entire family, Ram Chandra and Māl would take a decision on all related matters.

Since Gashā was the eldest grandson in the family and Didā the youngest of the patriarch's daughters, they were 'special' in many ways, and everyone who was even remotely associated with the family was therefore interested in the upcoming joint wedding. That the marriage ceremonies and associated festivities would be performed on a grand scale and in a way that was befitting to the status of the family had also reached keen ears. The speculation of how the marriages would be conducted added to the overall excitement.

It was obvious that the search for a suitable girl to be Gashā's bride, as also a suitable groom for Didā had started. In those days there used to be middlemen—usually Muslim men engaged in some vocation or the other—who would also trade in information on suitable boys and girls in the KP community. It is they who would be abreast of the many wonderful qualities of the young bachelors and the girls who were eligible for marriage. They would know the details of the families of the boys and girls (known as the *kulavali*), their status, and any other information of interest. These middlemen were quite well respected and had special privileges in all families, which included access to the key decision-makers in the household on matters related to matrimony and finances.

As the news of the search spread, all sorts of offers started pouring in through middlemen and relatives. The suggestions for brides and grooms that came in became a hot topic of discussion in the household after everyone was back from work.

As expected, after a search that took a few months, a suitable girl for Gashā and a handsome groom for Didā were identified. This was a matter of satisfaction for the family members since now the wedding preparartions could begin in earnest.

The marriage ceremonies were performed lavishly. Ram Chandra and Māl as well as all their loved ones were satisfied and happy. Didā was given a substantial dowry. Since Gashā's bride was the first bride brought into the family from within the grandchildren of Ram Chandra and Māl, she too received—by way of gifts from her new family—the choicest of gold ornaments that were a part of the heirloom collection. She was even presented a number of beautiful and opulent shawls and saris that left all the little children gaping in wonderment.

The bride received the gifts and the warm affection showered upon her with utmost graciousness. She was the epitome of beauty for her times; her deportment was graceful and her interactions with others were well mannered, cultured, and sophisticated. She was soft-spoken and soon became everyone's darling. Though she was the 'bhabi' (sister-in-law) of Gasha's siblings and cousins, interestingly, she was called by that name by everyone, young and old alike! Very quickly she got a hang of the way things worked within the Dhar family and was quick to anticipate and grasp everyone's expectations within the large family group. She was also good at being responsive. Whatever she did, she did lovingly and creatively and it was noticed by one and all.

One of the first things that she did was to knit sweaters, gloves, and a pair of socks each for all the adult male members of the family. That meant knitting dozens of pullovers along with knee-high socks and gloves for the men. She was obviously well versed with knitting and swift with her fingers. I still recall how amazed I'd be to watch her knitting with great mindfulness and agility, almost like a machine. Her hands would move rhythmically and smoothly, with the 'tic-tic' sound of the metal needles rubbing against each other as each new loop of wool was transferred to the other needle.

Bhabi had many other talents too and everyone appreciated them. Quite naturally, she also received praise liberally. Her talent seemed all the more special because she was educated, which added a lustre to her many skills and placed everyone in awe of her.

In my family, the women of my mother's generation were neither educated very much nor did they have any special skills or talents. They were loving and caring towards their husbands and respectful and devoted to their elders. But that's what they did, and that took up much of their time. I'm not sure why, but the kitchen was an area where these women would rarely enter, leaving the cooking to our cook, Pandit Tikaram, and his helpers. In my childhood I thought it was improper for girls to enter the kitchen! The result was that neither my mother nor my aunts (except the younger ones, like Benigashi and Dulariji) had any great culinary expertise!

When it was discovered that Bhabi was also an accomplished cook and could make a variety of delicious snacks and entrées, everyone was exultant! None of the women could even *imagine* how she could make the delicious things that she was purported to be good at.

One weekend, when everyone was home, Bhabi took the initiative to cook some delicacies for the family. Whatever she had made was lip-smacking tasty and there was much appreciation for her skill and the effort that she'd put in. All the ladies of the family were understandably speechless and observed how truly talented Bhabi was. She wasn't just a Jane of all trades, she was also a master of many.

Bhabi married in summer. It was now late December, and in the few months that she had been with the family, she had not only won everyone's affection, but she'd also endeared herself to one and all. Her caring and gentle nature was a great quality, and she received the blessings of all her elders liberally.

When everyone would prepare to retire post dinner, Bhabi used to go to Māl's room to see that her bed was done nicely and was warm enough for her grandmother-in-law to be comfortable in. She would ensure that the drinking water in the silver flask next to the bed had sufficient tepid water that Māl could drink during the night. She would also help Māl take off her thick warm clothes and change into her nightclothes. She'd also ensure that the kāngri—a small earthen pot, enclosed in a tightly woven willow mesh in which hot charcoal embers are placed to keep people warm in winters—was ready and full of charcoal, to last the night. She would also wait in the room, till Māl was asleep, in order to keep the kāngri away from the bedside, where it would be safe.

These were small tasks that Bhabi was attending to as a part of her role in the family. She was being the perfect daughter-in-law according to the norms of the time. After attending to Grandmother's needs she would go to the room of her mother-in-law to help her as well. This would take her quite some time and it would therefore be pretty late by the time she got to her own room. God knows whether she slept during the night at all, since she was also the first person to be up in the morning! Members of the family as well as the house helps would all praise her to the skies. Praise for her many virtues, her energy, and the myriad qualities that were in evidence.

Before Didā got married she would take care of the needs of the young and little girls of the house. She would comb their hair, help them change their clothes, and assist them to choose the fabric for their dresses as also the designs according to the fashion of the time. Didā was also considered a versatile and talented young lady by all her brothers and sisters. She also had a creative, artistic eye, just as Bhabi had. Quite naturally, with Didā moving to her husband's home, Bhabi took on the role of helping the children. Since the Dhar household—like all other KP joint families—didn't differentiate between siblings and cousins, Bhabi was truly the Bhabi of all of Gāsha's brothers and sisters, including the little ones. She was thus the sister-in-law to all the children big and small.

One morning, in December, Bhabi awoke with a feeling that it was unusually bright in the room. She opened the window and the scene outside was breathtaking. It had snowed the whole night and the entire lawn was covered in a blanket of pure, fresh, gleaming snow. The trees, the roofs of the houses in the neighbourhood as well as the flowering bushes and the paths were all covered in snow. It seemed as if the fairies had put a magic wand on the earth, and with their touch had covered everything in a sparkling blanket of white. No wonder everything was looking bright and beautiful.

Bhabi was really so happy to see this scene. She wasted no time to go downstairs, opened the house door and went to the open veranda, which was filled with heaps of snow. She took a big lump of snow in her hand and pressed it hard to make it into a ball. She was quick in her action, lest it melt before the surprise she was going to give to Grandmother. With this snowball she went straight to Grandmother's room and knocked on the door, knowing that Didā too had come to stay a few days with Mother and was sharing the room.

Knock, knock, knock! She rapped the door excitedly.

'Who's there?' Didā asked from within Māl's room.

'It's me. Mother had lost a key, which I found this morning. Have come to hand it over to her,' Bhabi said sweetly.

The door was opened and Bhabi was let in.

'I found it on the stairs,' Bhabi said briskly. She was alluding to the key that she had ostensibly found, showing her closed fist, which had become red with cold. Māl stretched out her hand from under the quilt to get the key. Before Bhabi could surprise her by placing the snowball in her plam, Māl muttered to herself, 'Shiva! I'm getting forgetful. Is it old age?'

That's when Bhabi put the snowball in her hand and shouted excitedly, 'Nav-sheen Mubārakh, dear Māl!'

With the snowball melting in her palm, Māl felt cold and said, 'Hey! You naughty girl! You surprised me! Has it really snowed? Obviously, it has! Let's open the window, let me have a look too.' Māl nudged Didā, who was lying on the bed by her side, asking her to open the window. Meanwhile, before they could say anything to her, Bhabi quickly left the room.

Didā got up and opened the first wooden covering of the window, which was called a *jalli-poat*—it was made of a carved, thin sheet of wood, where the carvings created an elegant 'net pattern' through which the world could be watched, but nobody from the outside could ever get a glimpse in! Besides, these jalli-panes used to not just add another covering over the window to keep the cold out, but they would also beautify the room.

The jalli-poat was a great device for those who wished to see what was happening in the neighbourhood, without anyone watching them! Quite naturally, those interested in gossip would spy on others through these panes.

A further set of windowpanes, made of solid wooden planks, and fixed (like the jalli-poat) on a couple of hinges, formed the outer covering of the window—the outer part of which would be exposed to the elements. These elegantly crafted wooden planks were very effective in keeping the cold winds out, especially during the harsh winters.

As soon as Didā opened all the four wooden panes, a gust of icy-cold air poured into the room. She let out a shout of delight! Both mother and daughter were excited to see the snow. Outside, the garden was absolutely pure and sparkling white! The trees, the roofs of the houses, the boundary wall, the hedges and the boughs of trees, were all laden with thick layers of snow. It was a strangely relaxing feeling for both Didā and her mother to see this enchanting scene, especially since just the previous evening it had all looked muddy, dark and dreary after the rain that had been pouring for a few hours.

They both took deep breaths, filling their lungs with the crispy air. They also began to look for Bhabi.

'Where has she gone?' Māl asked suddenly. 'This young lady has placed the burden of Nav-sheen on me. She is clever, she is. She pretended to have found some key of mine, eh?'

Didā smiled. 'You'll have to treat her to something big, dear Mother,' she reminded Māl, amused.

'Yes, of course! She has earned herself a big feast. I guess it'll have to be arranged for today itself.'

'You could give her a gift instead. Wouldn't that be all right?'

'No, not at all. Gifts can be given at any time. But don't foget that this is the first snowfall that our dear young girl is experiencing in our home, after her marriage. That makes the occasion special. Besides, she's also the first one to have wished me Nav-sheen. She definitely deserves a big feast!'

After wishing Māl in her bedroom, Bhabi lost no time and went straight to the room that her in-laws used, to play the very same Nav-sheen trick on her mother-in-law and her father-in-law. They too were taken by surprise, but were delighted that their smart and vivacious daughter-in-law had charmed them to a treat.

By now the whole household was up. There was excitement in the air. It had snowed after all! The children, without any preparation and unmindful of the cold dashed out into the garden, ignoring the cries and entreaties of their mothers.

Soon everyone knew that Bhabi had earned a double treat: one from Māl and another from Baiji and Sati. Bhabi's smarts, and the way she put the Nav-sheen tag on Mother and her in-laws were duly appreciated.

True to her word, Māl made preparations for a feast, which would be held in the evening on the same day. Sarvanand, who was also the tonga driver, got the horse and the hansom ready, shovelled the snow to enable the tonga to get out of the garage, and under the instructions of Māl, set out to invite relatives for the evening's dinner. It's difficult to imagine how Sarvanand managed to reach all the relatives, as snow, slush, and squelchy mud on some of the narrow roads would definitely have slowed his tonga down. Yet when he got back a few hours later he was beaming. All the relatives had been invited and were eager to come.

Dinners and lunches with close relatives were a delightful way to get people together—especially in the dark and dreary winter months—and foster social bonding and some fun. Life during winters was really tough, especially before the advent of electric lights. Falls on black ice in the *koochas* (narrow alleys between houses, especially in the congested parts of the city) were common, and people would rather stay indoors than risk a fall at night-time. Until the time that electricity was finally introduced in the Kashmir Valley sometime in the late 1920s, winters were a time when people would focus on completing their work during the few hours of daylight and then go to bed early. If it was imperative to visit someone, most people would walk between homes, except for those few families that had their own horse-drawn carriages. Walking made sense too, since everyone lived within the neighbourhoods around the Jhelum river and most of Srinagar was all 'contained' within the distance of the seven bridges on the Jhelum.

Feasts that were held in winters were incomplete without flying duck (called shikār or *pachhin* in Kashmiri) on the menu. Pachhin was typically cooked with red chilli powder and anise powder along with lotus roots (*nadru*). At Rishi Vihar a few dinners during the winter months were common, and this also gave the married daughters of the family an excuse to spend more time with their parents. It was obviously more fun being at one's childhood home than at the in-laws' place! If there were messengers sent from the in-laws asking the lady to return, bad weather or the danger of slipping on ice was often cited as the excuse for the lady choosing to stay with her parents longer!

The feast for Bhabi that Māl had promised was now under way. As the guests arrived, they all wished the family 'Nav-sheen Mubārakh!' Most had also got gifts for the new daughter-in-law of the house. All the guests were received graciously and seated on the thick carpets and rugs on the floor. They were given warm fur-lined blankets, to drape themselves, as well as a warm kangri to tuck under the blanket and to stay comfortable.

During the early part of the twentieth century, only a few large homes could afford to have a *hamām* (a hypocaust, which allows hot air from the kitchen fires to pass beneath thin slate stone slabs, called *patri* in Kashmiri, that formed the floor of a large room). Hamāms were created by having a narrow passageway under the room that would allow the hot air from the fires in the kitchen to flow, heating the stones, and thereby keeping the rugs warm and room cosy. Though the Dhar home had an elegant and spacious hamām it would need lots of firewood to be burned in the kitchen before any discernible impact of the heating was evident. Since social and other changes were also gripping the nation and times were uncertain, even the Dhar family had chosen to be austere and would therefore use the hamām only when it was absolutely necessary.

All the guests had now arrived. The ladies and menfolk were huddled together in the room to keep themselves warm. All the guests had worn thick woollen overcoats and pherans on top of their woollen sweaters, shawls, and coats. The overcoats were kept aside before the men were seated on the thick carpet comfortably, with their backs resting on the big huge bolsters against the wall.

Everyone was waiting for Bhabi to arrive, as if they were going to see her for the first time. Mother had given her a beautiful embroidered pashmina sari as a present, which she had to wear that evening, partly to show all the guests the kind of special gift she'd got from the eldest person of the household.

Finally, as soon as she entered the room, everyone shouted together:

'Nav-sheen Mubārakh! Nav-sheen Mubārakh.'

Poor Bhabi was feeling embarrassed and was blushing. She was obviously happy but also confused, not knowing how she was to behave. She sat demurely beside Mother, and while saying nothing she looked towards the assembled guests with a smiling face.

A fortnight after the Nav-sheen feast, another important Kashmiri festival, Shishur, was due to be celebrated. Shishur actually means 'the cold season' in Kashmiri, and falls during the coldest months of winter. Its significance comes from the fact that whenever there is a new addition in the family—a new bride is brought in or a baby is born in the family—prayers are to be held on this day and a celebration to be had to propitiate the spirits of the cold and ward off any evil that might be lurking in the dreary shadows of winter. On Shishur a new bride or the mother of a newborn would receive new clothes as a gift from her own parents as well as from her in-laws, along with specially decorated kāngris that would have a small silver tong attached to each one of them to handle the charcoal embers that would eventually be placed within the kāngri.

Often, a priest would give a new bride and any newborn baby a 'spiritually energized' charm (talisman), which would be attached to the cap of a newborn or the sweater of the lady. This was meant to keep off the malefic spirits triggered by someone's 'evil eye' on them.

Because of the recent feast and the appreciation of all for dear Bhabi, on Shishur she was given many lovely gifts, kāngris, and a few talismans for her long life and protection.

18

The Peers and Dhars

The Peers and the Dhars were neighbours. The two families lived so close to one another that only a common compound wall, and that too not a very high one, segregated their homes. Both the families were well-to-do and were well known in Srinagar.

The Peers too had a big family, much like the Dhars. As was common with large rich families, they had all their relatives (of the first circle, but distant ones too) living together as one big joint family. So there would be brothers and sisters, uncles and aunts, and many, many children all living together—happily and noisily—under one roof.

The Peers, being from the Muslim priestly class, were revered in the whole city. They were quite orthodox in so many things, but one thing that was common to both the Dhar and the Peer families was the fact that they gave immense importance to education.

The Peer girls and boys were also sent to school and to colleges for higher studies after their religious training from around 1940 onwards. They were quite content in their own style of living. Both the families were not allowed to mix very much with the common people of the mohalla, but were very friendly with one another. This friendship was based on the fact that both the families had lived together for a couple of generations. Their elders were friends and then their children and even the third generation also kept the connections alive.

It fascinated me very much to see the headdress of the elder Peer lady, who was called Appaji. This headdress was so high and magnificent that it used to give a very grand effect to Appaji's personality. We would take liberties with her and entreat her to show us her opulent *kasābe* (headdress), which she would gladly do to please us children. She would gingerly take it off to show it to us. It had so many small pushpins with colourful plastic heads to keep it fixed together. Some pins were plain, with round heads; many hundreds more were tacks with beautiful, nicely coloured plastic heads with wonderful motifs. These were all embedded in the headdress in such a way that it would give the effect of a perfect overall pattern. I often tried the kasābe on my head, till my aunt would find out and scold me for bothering Appaji.

'I am without my kasābe. If someone were to enter the room and find me without the headdress, that would not be good,' Appaji would say to us as she'd fix her gaze on the door, lest someone suddenly disturb her and the children as they were all enjoying the innocent conversations in their own little world.

Appaji's eldest daughter-in-law was also her sister's daughter. This lady was really adorable. She too had many lovely qualities and was a well-liked daughter-in-law. She was Appaji's favourite. Partly because she was her sister's daughter, whom she'd seen growing up since her infancy and also because she knew that she was a great addition to the Peer family.

Zaina too was fond of her aunt and mother-in-law. Affectionately she was called Zainlal by one and all. Her demeanour was endearing and I remember her as one who was always sweetly disposed, witty, and smiling.

Zainlal was very friendly with the Dhar girls of her age. My aunts—Gowri and Uma—who were affectionately called Behenji and Didā, and were my father's younger sisters, were almost as old as Zainlal and formed a wonderful group, soon after she came to the Peer household. My aunts also got married soon after Zainlal and whenever they would come to their parents' home (which was often) they would spend time interacting.

The friends bonded well and within months of getting to know one another, they became inseparable. This was the start of the second generation of friendships, which both the families looked upon appreciatively.

The girls used to meet each other quite often. In fact, a special wooden ladder to cross over the compound wall separating the two neighbours was erected so as to enable the young ladies to meet almost every day without having to leave their respective compounds. This way it was easy to avoid the long walk through the by-lanes to reach each other's homes and have to endure the gaze of the people on the road.

All three of them would spend a long time talking to each other. All of them were married. So, there must have been a lot of common topics between them. Mostly they would talk about their husbands, their mothers-in-law, sisters-in-law, and the atmosphere of their new homes.

'For you there is no newness in this home, right? After all, Appaji is your own dear aunt whom you've known from your childhood,' Behenji and Didā would tell her.

'Being an aunt is one thing, but when the same aunt becomes your mother-in-law, everything changes,' Zainlal would say, suggesting and emphasizing that all mothers-in-law are the same.

'At least you know how to handle her and her moods. In my case, my mother-in-law is quite a disciplinarian, being half Punjabi,' Didā would say.

'Thank God my mother in-law is very sweet and understanding. She is quite friendly with me,' Behenji would say proudly. Then after a little pause, she'd add, 'You may say anything, but it's wonderful to be married to a person whom you've known from your childhood. This way you know his strengths and weaknesses. It's easy to handle him,' Behenji would say that Zainlal had it easy, knowing her husband and cousin from before.

On this all three of them laughed heartily.

'Just to handle him?' Didā said with a glint in her eyes, as if to convey that marriages were not only for game playing but involved more than just handling one's spouse.

'If you had a system of marrying your cousins, then all the girls of your family would have been here in this mohalla forever. How wonderful it would have been,' Zainlal said.

'I wouldn't like to live in this mohalla for my whole life!' Didā said emphatically.

'That's why you're in Rajbagh!' her sister retorted.

They would go on chatting for hours in this manner, till someone would be sent to remind them about the time. Hours would pass by and they'd have no clue. Before saying their goodbyes they'd fix the time for their next meeting to catch up with one another and share news and gossip about the latest fashions, good patterns of knitting, and some interesting details and experiences of their respective married lives.

In this world of theirs, there was mutual trust, respect, affinity, and lots of love between them. They were like sisters enjoying each other's company and longing for the next meeting. Elders would also appreciate their friendship and encourage them.

It was soon after the first snowfall of the season in the month of January. Since every season in the Kashmir Valley brought forth its own distinct flavours and characteristics, the first snow was always special. Understandably, everyone was excited about it.

One Saturday morning, after all the male members of the Dhar family had left for their respective workplaces, the ladies of the family decided to walk around in the snow and have some fun. Sati, the eldest daughter-in-law of Māl and Ram Chandra, took the lead.

She put on her new, and as yet unused, fur shoe, which she covered with a rubber upper shoe to protect it from the snow and moisture. Her younger sisters-in-law, Benji and Benigashi, who were watching her, asked—'Where are you going, Sati?'

'Why?' Sati replied defiantly. 'To the garden, of course, to walk on the snow.'

Sati was looking a little more plump than usual because she had worn two hefty woollen sweaters underneath the thick and long woollen pheran. On her head she was wearing a big traditional KP *taraga* (the headdress). On top of the headdress was a long tail-like cloth, which was hanging up to her feet and was giving her personality a rather royal appearance.

Benji and Benigashi were also tempted to go into the garden to breathe the crisp, fresh, and icy air. They also had on attires that were similar to what Sati was wearing. They let Sati lead them into the garden.

The trio looked like well-padded astronauts in their thick clothes, walking gingerly in the thick snow, almost as if they were exploring a different planet! Their heavy clothes and the deep snow were hindering their steps and they made slow progress towards the baradari—a gazebo—in the middle of the garden.

When they reached the middle of the garden, Benigashi took a lump of snow in her hand and threw it on Sati. As soon as this act of hers was done, all hell broke loose! The three women scooped up snow and began to have a full-fledged snowball fight! All the children of the household also appeared suddenly, shouting and giggling, and began to put snow on to their mothers and upon one another.

The two parts of the garden that were segregated by the baradari in the middle soon looked like a battleground. The children—young and old—were running all over the place, hiding behind the gazebo, and suddenly surprising the 'enemy' with a well-aimed snowball!

The baradari was an integral part of the Dhar property. It was like a meeting place for the entire family. With its huge round plinth, simple roof, and elegantly carved side railings, it served as an ideal place for conversations and relaxation in every season. In the summers, the men would even meet their work associates in the gazebo. During the days the ladies would sit there with their friends enjoying their leisure time. For the children the place was always available for games and fun.

At one point in the heat of the battle, Sati took off her headdress and kept it on the railing of the baradari. Benji and Benigashi followed suit, and soon they too were without their headdresses. Without their headdresses, they all looked so different! Sati's chiselled features were more visible today. She was very fair and had black hair and looked sweet and graceful. The pure white background of fresh snow served to accentuate her grace. Benji on the other hand was more of a typical Kashmiri maiden with a fair complexion. She was taller than her sisters-in-law. Benigashi was the opposite of her older sisters-in-law. She was of medium height, with a wheatish complexion. Due to her lean and thin appearance she wasn't looking as plump as Sati and Benji, who were looking decidedly stocky with so many clothes on them.

Benigashi was quite fast at picking up snow and making projectiles out of it. She was quick to overpower Benji and Sati. Seeing her aggressive style, all the children came to the rescue of Sati from the snow battering she was taking. The 'astronaut' who was continuing to walk on the snow at a snail's pace was repeatedly falling and trying to get up again and again, even as she was being pummelled with flying snowballs. All those in the fray were having a lot of fun, and there was laughter and a lot of giggling and excited screaming to be heard. Everyone was in their best element.

The youngest of all the children, Sardar, would roll himself on the snow and quietly place small balls of snow down the necks and backs of everyone. People would shriek as the icy-cold ball would trickle down their backs. No one was bothered about the world outside. For once everyone forgot their respective roles. There were no inhibitions, no restrictions, no guilt, no fear—only pure unsullied fun. Young and old were in a frenzy playing with one another.

While this game was on, all of a sudden from across the wall some snowballs began to fly to our side. The intensity of the projectiles grew, and more and more snowballs began to pour on to the ladies and the children. The Peers also had come down into their courtyard to enjoy the snow and had decided to join the fun from across the wall!

In a jiffy on both sides of the wall, the ladies, children, girls as also the little and big boys were all arrayed in strategic positions—ready to defend their turf in the ensuing snow battle. The older boys—led by Brijtoth, Bapore, Gyantoth—and the younger boys were shouting loudly.

'This isn't kite flying, when Shareif-uddin and you would snatch our kites away. This is a real game of snowball fighting. Let's have a match and see who wins!'

'Do you think that you are going to win this game?' Qamar-uddin was provoking the boys of his age to play.

While the snowballs were flying across the walls, some of the first-floor windows of the houses, on both sides, opened. Appaji stretched her head out of one of the windows and said lovingly to the children on her side—'Where is the ladder?'

She was looking towards the young Dhar ladies who were not at all aware of her presence. While talking to her children, she ordered her daughter-in-law and her daughters to play in the garden too.

Everyone on both the sides got enthused by Appaji's words. In a jiffy the ladies and girls of the Peer household, along with their children, searched for the ladder. In no time it was found. Everyone was excited as the Peers climbed over, and were together in the garden where the Dhar women and children were having a good time.

Zainlal, her sister-in-law, Sidhlal, and the rest of the family members of the Peer household were playing like children, enjoying the fun of throwing snow at each other. The smaller children were busy rolling snow on the ground to make a snowman and a snowy fairyland while the older boys were having a snowball match between themselves.

It was an out-of-the-world scene and what a delightful situation to watch! Those who were not taking part in the game were watching from their windows to derive the utmost vicarious pleasure out of this unique panorama. In a matter of minutes, two or three snowmen were erected and the fight was over. Everyone was tired and cold, but so satisfied and thrilled at having had such fun and with everyone joining in the game. The whole garden had become a real battleground. There were mounds and heaps of snow all over. The ladies now wanted to rest and savour cups of hot kehva.

After the drama and the fun and excitement of the games wore off, the actors of the play wore their normal clothes once again, along with their headgears. Nobody could believe that just half an hour earlier all the Dhar ladies were having a snowball fight with the ladies of the neighbourhood—pummelling one another and their little boys and girls with fresh, watery snow.

In those days, it was a taboo for ladies to go out bare-headed. Playing with children was out of question, that too in an open garden! Māl, their mother-in-law, was unaware of this whole play. By the time she got up from her usual nap, all the ladies were their normal selves, pretending as if nothing unusual had happened. But one with a discerning eye—as Māl indeed had—could sense from their dazzling, joyous red faces that they had been up to something. The women were reassured that Appaji would never divulge their secret to Mother because they knew that she was a kind and a humane woman with a wise understanding of the need to channel the extra energy of young people into avenues of fun, especially during the long and cold days of winter in the Kashmir Valley.

19

Love, Life, and Death

It was a well-known fact that they were in love with each other. For years they had spent time in each other's company. Despite the fact that it was a taboo in Kashmiri society in the mid-1950s to admit that a girl was in love with a boy, the two young people didn't seem to care. Being in love was considered scandalous, especially if there was a display of love *before* one's marriage. If a young girl or a boy were known to be in love with each other, people would blow the affair out of proportion to malign the girl (not the boy as much) as well as the girl's parents. Under these circumstances, with the prying eyes of people and immense social pressure, couples in love would rarely show the courage and insist on getting married. Like in many Bollywood movies of that era, unrequited love was more common than not, largely because social norms were hard and difficult to bend and a variety of reasons were put forward as to why the match should *not* happen.

In Tulsi's case, however, her parents were forced to give in and reluctantly marry her to the boy she loved. The parents and many others in their biradari knew that she and the boy were from different family backgrounds (albeit both were Pandits) and were aware and concerned that there were many aspects of incompatibility between them.

Tulsi was a girl from a well-to-do family. She was outgoing, gregarious, and came across as being cheerful. She was tall and fair, but was not considered exceptionally beautiful. She had the features of a regular Kashmiri girl. But her manners, her charm, and her way of talking were such that she would attract the attention of one and all without any difficulty. She had a habit of making friends with persons belonging to any stratum of society, without being aware of any spoken and unspoken 'restrictions' that were associated with social interactions. This trait of hers, where her kindness and compassion were in evidence, was not liked by her family members, especially her mother. She had this nagging feeling that her daughter would put herself in such situations, from which it would be difficult to extricate and save her.

Tulsi's love interest was Pushkar Nath, who was living in her neighbourhood in an ancient part of Srinagar, only a couple of yards away from her home. Growing up together, they became friends in the first place. Then, with the passage of time, as they grew older, their friendship turned into deep intimacy. Pushkar Nath belonged to a poor family and that was one of the reasons why Tulsi's closeness to him was noticed. Yet the two of them would meet each other in secluded lanes, public parks, and on the nearby bridges that spanned the beautiful and fast-flowing Jhelum river. They would talk to each other for hours together, oblivious of and even forgetting that they were being watched constantly by nosey parkers and gossipmongers, whose only occupation was to make a mountain out of a molehill. Tulsi and Pushkar Nath's 'love affair' obviously didn't take long to become public knowledge in their locality, and very soon within the KP community in the city as well. It doesn't take much time to spread tantalizing and entertaining rumours of this nature!

The people of Kashmir are famous for spreading all sorts of rumours. Whether Pandit, Muslim or Christian, it's easy for them all to spread tales and exaggerate matters. For Kashmiris this is *real* entertainment. Slandering others through rumour-mongering also serves as a big whip with which to hit out and get even with one's detractors. Gossiping, lying, and ruining someone's reputation to settle scores with the people one doesn't like is therefore fairly common. If one wishes to take revenge on someone, this is the easiest way to do it.

Tulsi's love affair was talked about a lot. People, pretending to be well-wishers of the family, made her parents' lives impossible and miserable. The rumour mill was equally active. According to one of the rumours doing the rounds, Tulsi had secretly jumped from one of the windows of her home straight into the balcony in Pushkar Nath's home to meet him. She had ostensibly done this quite frequently. Obviously, this piece of slanderous gossip put the family to utter shame and made them vulnerable to being at the receiving end of people's comments and even harassment. Having a well-knit community, as the Kashmiri Pandits have traditionally been in the Valley, with close relatives living in Srinagar, it didn't take much time for everyone to know about everyone else's lives. A matter concerning a family would soon become a matter that concerned everybody, Hindus and Muslims alike. Shopkeepers, vendors, vegetable sellers, and passers-by would all get involved and add their perspectives to matters, adding to the general entertainment.

As far as Pushkar Nath's family was concerned, his parents and relatives were happy that a bright girl from a well-to-do and wealthy family had fallen in love with their only son.

Many people would envy Pushkar's parents and would tell his father, 'Pushkar has won a lottery, hasn't he? Now you needn't remain poor any more!' Or, they'd rub it in, 'Your son has managed a big catch. Very soon you too will be counted as being respectable people.'

Many others would taunt Pushkar Nath's family, 'You will not come to my shop to gossip any more. You'll be a big man soon!'

Tulsi's parents were very keen to marry their daughter into a family that would be at par with their own. But Tulsi had threatened that she would commit suicide if she were married to anyone except Pushkar. So, her parents and her close relatives were forced to give consent to Tulsi's marriage with Pushkar Nath. One silver lining in this match was that Pushkar was a bright boy and was pursuing a master's degree in sociology. He was tall and handsome, with a fair complexion and golden hair. He would attract anyone's attention towards himself. His parents were very proud of him and they were expecting a good match for him in spite of their relatively poor status in society. But with his love story, their expectations for a good dowry also grew considerably. They were imagining that Tulsi's wedding to Pushkar would jettison them into the circle of rich people in the city.

For Tulsi there were many matches that were available, but she was adamant to marry Pushkar. When her parents finally consented, they set a condition that before the marriage the house of Tulsi's would-be in-laws was to be done up and made liveable. This would ensure that Tulsi would not miss the comforts that she was used to after her marriage, when she'd have to move to Pushkar's house.

For the massive repairs that were needed, the money was given to Pushkar's family by Tulsi's parents, innocuously, and without anyone getting wind of the matter. This was a very thoughtful gesture and keeping the matter discreet was done so as not to embarrass Pushkar and his family within the community. Such sage actions were quite common in the community at that time. People used to help their close friends and kin financially on major occasions so that they wouldn't feel embarrassed or slighted in front of their better-off relatives.

Finally, Tulsi and Pushkar Nath were married with considerable fanfare. All the arrangements for the wedding were done by the parents of the girl. Pushkar's parents were boasting about the quantum of dowry that the bride had brought into their home and how they were so proud of their son. Many of their own relatives who were also not very well-off became quite jealous, and would tell Pushkar's parents on their faces, 'It's just because of Tulsi that you've became rich overnight! For that matter, we also know how you've managed to throw such lavish feasts and make other arrangements for the wedding. We know that all you wanted were the costly gifts that the bride would bring!'

The taunting that Pushkar's parents had to bear was immense. Nasty words of their own relatives and the actions of jealous friends from among their own social stratum would constantly remind them of their days spent in poverty, and how they could never get away from their past unless they moved to another locality.

So, they shifted to Karan Nagar, a relatively new area created in the 1940s by giving land on lease to people who were willing to move out of the congested inner city. Here no one knew them. No one taunted them any more. It was not only Pushkar and Tulsi who were going to start a new life together, but even for their elderly parents it was a chance to start a new life, *ab initio*, in a comparatively rich, modern environment. Moving from Habbakadal to Karan Nagar was a big leap forward, since in the Habbakadal area and other parts of the old city of Srinagar three to four families would share the same old house and manage in comparatively cramped spaces.

With the influence of his in-laws, Pushkar also got a good job in the administration of the post-Independence government. It was a white-collar job, which brought huge respect along with it. Their life became easier and it seemed that all was working out well with the family.

In their new neighbourhood, the family made new friends. Pushkar's mother too was feeling quite high and would behave like a rich woman, but would inadvertently spill the beans about her past with her clumsy ways and poor communication skills. Tulsi was always like a buffer between the people of higher strata and her in-laws. She would always save the situation in favour of her in-laws. However, this did not go down well with her in-laws because they would feel that their daughter-in-law was ridiculing them in front of her rich friends.

Due to the inferiority complex of Tulsi's in-laws and their gauche styles, Tulsi was beginning to be in a state of constant stress. This was also becoming visible as her gregariousness and energy were giving way to reticence and deteriorating health. Her parents were quite upset about her peculiar situation, but were also of the opinion that it was her own fault and therefore she had to handle the situation by herself.

Tulsi's condition, however, didn't get any better with time. Seeing her anxious, her parents wanted to wean her away from her in-laws so that she would breathe freely and be away from their toxic interference. Tulsi's father was a well-known person in society and had influence in the corridors of power. With a little help from his friends in the government, he managed to get his son-in-law transferred to Jammu. This brought great relief to Tulsi's parents. They lost no time therefore in helping Tulsi pack her belongings so that she could accompany her husband to Jammu.

In Jammu, the beautiful city of temples, Tulsi's life became better, smoother, and easier. She and her husband rediscovered their love, which had now matured and grown more intense and deeper. In her heart Tulsi was reassured that she had not made a mistake by marrying Pushkar, whom she loved very much.

Life became joyful for both of them. Away from the probing of their close families, they were both having a real honeymoon now. They began to understand each other's interests and likes and dislikes afresh, and knew that their love had blossomed ever since they had got married.

One evening, as they were relaxing on the terrace of their home in Jammu, admiring the bright moonlit night, Tulsi in an impulsive emotional manner asked Pushkar, 'Tell me, how much do you love me?'

'Don't you know? Do I have to prove this to you?' he answered, taken aback by the tone of her voice.

'I know, but I want to hear it from you. Tell me how much do you love me?'

'More than I love myself.' Pushkar paused a bit and continued, 'I love you more than anything in the world.'

'Are you sure?'

'Yes, absolutely!'

Thereafter, Tulsi would often ask her husband about the love they had for each other, and when he'd answer her—the way he had before—she would be reassured that they were on stable ground. The couple was in harmony with each other and with the world around them. For a while they forgot about their relatives and the norms of society that had almost kept them from getting married. They were truly engrossed in their own affairs, and had scant time to think about anybody else.

Pushkar, who also loved to be in Tulsi's company, often had to be pushed by her to go to work. He would rather spend as much time as was possible with his wife. They were sure that they could not live without each other.

One day, Pushkar got a severe headache and fever while at office and came back home early to rest. Seeing her husband in pain, Tulsi panicked, since she had never seen him so helpless before. Pushkar was in agony due to the headache and fever. She made him comfortable in the bedroom, but his fever was so high that he couldn't even rest properly. Being young and inexperienced, she was confused as to what had to be done to mitigate her husband's pain. Finally, she managed to reach one of her husband's colleagues, who got a doctor home to look at Pushkar.

Even after a week of treatment, Pushkar's fever showed no signs of abating. It was a matter of concern for all his colleagues and superiors. Doctors couldn't determine the reason for his high fever. Pushkar's office informed his parents and his in-laws about his illness. Tulsi was shattered and was in a state of utter confusion. But her neighbours were very considerate and helpful to her and provided considerable support in a variety of ways. Food for her was coming from the homes of friends in their Jammu neighbourhood. Friends were keeping a vigil on the patient, taking turns.

In those days people used to have very cordial relations. Even without having blood relations nearby, the community would go to any extent to help one another. Communication in those days was very poor. It would take quite some time to inform people living in the summer and winter capitals of the state about a problem that may have occurred in either Jammu or Srinagar.

At long last Pushkar's and Tulsi's parents arrived in Jammu. Tulsi heaved a sigh of relief when she saw them. She was desperate and didn't know what was happening with her husband. On seeing the condition of their son, Tulsi's in-laws poured out their wrath on the poor girl.

'What have you done to our dear Pushkar?' they shouted at her angrily. 'He was hale and hearty when he left Kashmir. Why didn't you inform us before? Now see what's happened to him!'

Pushkar's mother was weeping especially loudly, so that everyone should hear her sobs in the other rooms. Tulsi's parents, who were privy to the behaviour of the parents of their son-in-law, were very upset about the way poor Tulsi had been treated and spoken to. Pushkar's parents knew that he was sent to Jammu with the help of his father-in-law. So, to take revenge on Tulsi's parents, they couldn't have found a more opportune time. Which is why they took no time to pounce on poor Tulsi and directed their anger and hurt at the girl.

'You all hatched a conspiracy to send our dear boy to Jammu so that our son would be under your control and not have any connections with us!' they fumed.

Pushkar's father was shouting these bitter words, which were piercing Tulsi's heart. The loud conversations were audible to everyone present in the other room. Tulsi was weeping bitterly in a corner of the room, while her own mother was consoling her. Pushkar was too weak and barely conscious to fathom what was going on or to do anything about it. Even if he wished, the poor soul was so frail and helpless he could barely have spoken.

Again, with the help of Tulsi's father, the best medical facilities were made available and the best doctors were consulted. Whatever was available at that point of time was brought in to make sure that Pushkar was restored to normal health. Doctors finally diagnosed the patient and started treating him for typhoid. It was a long-drawn battle for Pushkar to get well. After many weeks, he was so frail that he could not talk properly or sit up at all. Most of the time, Pushkar's parents hovered around him, not allowing Tulsi to be anywhere near her husband. Tulsi was dejected to see the behaviour of her in-laws. She was upset, but could not do anything to change the situation in these trying circumstances. She didn't want to make an unpleasant scene when her husband needed rest and peace. She and her parents just wanted that Pushkar should get well soon. They were consciously ignoring the tantrums of Pushkar's parents, which would make things worse and provoke the uncouth couple to abuse Tulsi further.

Despite all the attention, Pushkar was not showing any positive signs of improvement even after a month. In fact, he was deteriorating. Every now and then the doctors would change the medicines but his fever was persistent. For Tulsi it was a long period of waiting for a miracle and watching over her husband, but as the illness continued beyond one month, Tulsi's patience got exhausted. She seemed to be defeated. She was gripped by apprehensions and didn't know what to do. She was possessed by negative thoughts.

'If something were to happen to him, what would I do? Everyone would blame me for choosing a husband like Pushkar. But is to fall ill in anybody's hands? Can't anyone fall ill? He has been a good husband. Very caring and loving ... oh, why doesn't he get well? He is getting weaker by the day. He can't even talk. His eyes are always chasing me, which shows his concern for me. I just can't face his gaze, which tells me that he wants to open his heart before me and say how much he loves me. I feel like hugging him and reassuring him that I too love him dearly and can't live without him. But how to tell him? His parents are not leaving him alone even for a moment. They are real leeches. But Pushkar is different, cultured, and wellmannered.'

Tulsi was praying for her husband's recovery day in and day out. She was not sleeping, eating, or resting properly. She was full of anxiety, which was visible on her face. Her health had deteriorated considerably.

One day, the attending senior doctor came to examine the patient. Upon checking his parameters, he made a long face and said:

'Don't know why he isn't responding to the medicine.' Tulsi, who was watching the whole scene and was observing the doctor's body language attentively, felt that her husband's illness was a very serious one. Watching the doctor's face, she was convinced that her husband wouldn't overcome the disease. To her, the situation suddenly seemed gloomy and devoid of hope. Members of her family too seemed gloomy.

That's when a dangerous thought bubbled in her mind.

'No, I cannot live without you. I have to die before you.'

Before anyone could even notice her leaving the room, she went to her kitchen, got hold of a canister filled with kerosene, and taking a box of matches with her, she procceded to the terrace to put an end to her life.

She poured the kerosene on her entire body and in a momentary impulse, set herself on fire.

It took just a few seconds for the flames to rise so high that the smoke was now visible in the entire neighbourhood. Seeing the smoke coming from the house, people thought that the house was on fire. So they rushed to the house and warned the householders about the fire, shouting, 'Your house is on fire! Your house is burning!'

They all rushed towards the terrace.

When they saw that Tulsi was more than half burnt, they were shocked, dumbfounded, and aghast. All of a sudden Tulsi's mother entered the scene and seeing her daughter burning, she also threw herself into the fire while shouting and crying, 'Why did you do this, my dear, my dear? Would you leave your aged parents behind? Oh God!'

Someone from the crowd dragged her out from the fire. She had been badly bruised, and fainted.

The atmosphere in the entire city of Jammu turned to that of a graveyard. Those people who didn't know the family also were shocked to know this gory story of a girl who was in love with her husband, and had chosen to finish herself in a terrible manner.

Despite the macabre plight of the girl, her story was something of a fairy tale. All sorts of rumours were doing the rounds in Jammu city. Some said that this was evidence of 'true love'. Others said that Tulsi was a foolish lady to have even thought of finishing herself like this. She should have waited for her husband to get well, a few others suggested.

Such a gruesome suicide was something unique, and had never happened before in the community. Such a terrible incident had never before been witnessed by anyone in Kashmir.

Tulsi's parents were shocked and shattered with the suicide episode. They were not able to understand their hot-headed daughter's choices, and were unable to reconcile with her. For them, their entire world had crumbled right before their eyes. They were so bruised and hurt with this tragedy that they lost their verve and any enthusiasm to face the world. There was no one else now for them to live for. The whole world seemed hostile to them. They left Jammu for Srinagar.

On the way to Srinagar, as they drove past the gigantic, majestic mountains they felt that the mountains too were weeping for their daughter. The dales, the brooks, and rivers too were shedding tears of pain to commiserate the loss of Tulsi's life. The blossoms of the trees that were shedding on the road were doing so with sadness. The river Chenab too was crying for Tulsi. It was a grief beyond what had ever been endured. Both the parents were like logs, experiencing great sorrow and pain.

It was springtime, a beautiful season. But as soon as Tulsi's parents reached Srinagar, all hell broke loose. Relatives and a host of people began to arrive at the home of the grieving parents to commiserate and help ease the pain for the family. People thronged to pay their condolences for nearly a month.

It's said that time is a great healer. After a month, Tulsi's father was persuaded by his relatives and friends to attend to his business. The day-to-day routine in Tulsi's parents' home was gradually resumed. But not a day would pass without a mention of Tulsi's name in the family. Her father would always blame Tulsi's in-laws for the terrible tragedy. Often the father would think that because Tulsi was very emotional and impulsive, she never listened to anybody. She always did what she wanted to do and fell prey to this mental state of hers.

A few months after Tulsi's death, a distant relative of the family entered the house and sat beside Tulsi's mother, who was cleaning spinach leaves for that evening's dinner. She didn't notice the presence of the visiting lady.

Finally, the lady spoke up.

'Have you heard something?' she said in a low tone, even as she was looking all over the room to be sure that they were alone.

Tulsi's mother was surprised to see her, and said, 'I just didn't see you entering. When did you come?'

'Did you hear something?' the lady repeated again.

'Hear what?' she lifted her eyes and enquired. Since Tulsi's mother was engrossed in her thoughts and preoccupied with the task, she hadn't heard her say anything.

'They say that he has married again,' the lady said mysteriously. The lady was sharing the news slowly to see the reaction of Tulsi's mother. The lady was adept in carrying tales, which would give her immense pleasure. Her gossip was rarely without basis. Whosoever saw her entering the compound guessed that some untoward thing had happened. She was known for being a gossip carrier. In fact, people used to add the phrase *badh khaber* to her name, because she invariably carried bad news (badh khaber) from one household to another.

'Who got married again? Who are you talking about?' Tulsi's mother left her work for a while and was curious to know more about this. She asked her once again.

'Who else, your son-in-law, yes, Pushkar. He has married again.' As soon as she uttered these words, Tulsi's mother felt as if someone had hit her with a hammer. She stammered, fumbled for words, and somehow managed to gain strength to say something. Finally in a weak and feeble voice she asked, 'Is he alive?'

'Yes, of course, he's hale and hearty. Her sacrifice didn't go waste.'

On hearing this, Tulsi's aged mother slumped on to the pile of spinach, and fainted.

20

Dramabāz Children and Lasting Friendships

There was a pattern in our family to involve all children in extracurricular activities, including activities in the outdoors. Initiatives by the older children of this household were encouraged and appreciated by the elders of the family. The older boys and girls therefore served as role models to the younger ones and set good examples for the younger generation to emulate.

Writing and performing plays and skits as also conducting group activities involving the children were therefore common, and added a unique charm to growing up in Rishi Vihar. Grandfather and his sons were of the opinion that the 'first school' of children was in the laps of their parents, as also the environment created within the home. Which is why a lot of emphasis was laid on the ambience within our home and the creative arts and crafts were given due importance.

There was even a mini-zoo for the children to interact with different animals and learn about the unique behaviour of each. There was a horse, a couple of cows, a goat, a sheep, rabbits, a pet dog, ducks, pigeons, parrots, and a number of small colourful birds. Small cages were made for the smaller animals and birds. The horse would also pull the family tonga and the cows were also tapped to provide pure milk every morning. The zoo was a big attraction for the relatives of the family, especially their children who used to have a lot of fun and would never get 'bored' while visiting our place.

The ducks were let loose early in the morning and they would forage in the Nalla Mar canal, which flowed barely ten to twelve metres away from our home. Children would especially enjoy watching the 'duck procession' walk towards the canal in a single file and then jump right into the canal, their wings flapping, as they would quack excitedly.

The Nalla Mar was a beautiful waterway that was used to transport grains, animal fodder, fruits, vegetables as well as construction material such as logs, bricks, and sand to all the localities that bordered the canal. Big wooden boats were used to ferry these goods and the boatmen responsible for the boats would use large punting poles to move upstream or downstream along the canal.

Sadly, the canal was filled up in the mid-1970s and now a road runs over it. I think that these old waterways and canals (*kols*), which connected the waters of the Jhelum and the lakes, served to regulate the flow of water from the Valley. Their wilful closure, along with the increase in Srinagar's population has contributed to more frequent floods and waterlogging in the expanding city.

The eldest daughter of Ram Chandra and Sukhmāl (Māl) was called Jiglāl. She was married into the Kaul family, and like her other sisters would visit her parents' home once in a while. Her son Nicklāl was especially fond of directing dramas and whenever he'd visit his maternal grandparents' home, it was a must that he perform some sort of play involving him as director that would serve to delight all the family members as well as the visitors. In preparation of the plays or the skits, all his cousins were ever ready to help. Nicklāl was always energetically involved and like an inspiring director would guide the actors and those involved with the sets and lighting on how he would like the play to unfurl. Even writing the script, finalizing the dialogues, and many other nuances of the play were his responsibility. He would do all this extremely well and was the perfect person to direct any skit. If there had been no taboo in KP families in those days about being in the world of theatre and movies, he would have made a great director. He became a doctor instead.

Nicklāl was born shortly after the end of World War II. When he started uttering a few words at the age of about one year, his parents were quite surprised and probably concerned when he would say, 'Me Shento.'

Initially, no one understood what he meant by this. In fact, when his loved ones would call him Nicklāl, he wouldn't like it, and would make his displeasure known by weeping and yelling. However, when members of the family would call him 'Shento', he would smile and be contented.

When he grew a little older and his speech got better and more coherent, he would say that he was a pilot and was killed in an airplane fight during the war. Nobody would have believed him, but every time he'd either see an airplane in the sky, or even if he just *heard* one, he used to get panicky and would close his ears and eyes. People would then say that in his past life he must verily have been a fighter pilot in World War II. Some guessed he might even have been a Kamikaze pilot.

I vividly remember the day when Nicklāl directed a beautiful play called *Khoje-bai*—The Khoja's Wife. A 'Khoja' is a wealthy Kashmiri Muslim businessman, a merchant. The play was based on the social milieu that prevailed at that point of time in the Valley of Kashmir. My sisters, Basha and Vijay, were playing the roles of the two main characters in the play. They had borrowed a couple of elegant dresses from our neighbours in the Peer family to look their respective parts. Other sisters, Indra and Gugi, were given supporting roles, which they managed very well.

Basha and Vijay were looking like real Khoja wives and when they started talking to each other and delivering their lines, the audience was in splits of laughter. The play was a satire on some ills that had crept into Muslim society, with appropriate dialogues. These girls had done the play in their school as well, and hence did a fairly good job of it under Nicklāl's direction. At school, Gugi was given the role of a mosquito. When Gugi mentioned at home that she was given the role of a mosquito in her school play, all her cousins made fun of her. 'Mosquito?' they exclaimed! 'What kind of role is this? Maybe because you're thin like a mosquito, that's why they may have chosen you for this role.'

This was too much for poor Gugi. During the casting for the home version of the play she refused to be a mosquito. Her mother, Benigashi, pleaded with Nicklāl to give her a 'respectable' role. Nicklāl was gracious and gave her the role of a butterfly. Gugi approved of this and she liked the way she looked in her costume. Everyone else liked her role as well.

As with many large families, there was tremendous competition between the cousins within our family too. Everyone would emulate the good points from each other. At the same time, they wouldn't hesitate to make fun of their brothers or sisters and pick on their weakness to tease them. In my childhood, I too was thin and gangly-looking. All my cousins would therefore make fun of me by calling me *loopzangi*. Lobzang was the name of a wise lama from Tibet who used to come to our home to stay for months together. He was also very thin and lanky. Since the word *zang* in Kashmiri means one's leg, my cousins creatively coined the name, *loopzangi*. I used to feel frustrated by this name, but had no 'weapon' to retort and get even. I used to complain to my father Bubji about this, but instead of scolding them he would always encourage me by saying, 'Having long legs is a compliment, isn't it? They are ignorant. With long legs one can walk fast and run to reach the top of the hill and be a winner in sports. Lobzang has long legs, and that's precisely how he manages to come to Kashmir from Tibet and Ladakh so often. If they try to tease you again, tell them boldly, "Yes, I have long legs." Remember, these inputs are really worth millions, because they help to build your character and make you strong and confident.'

The drama directed by Nicklāl was quite a hit with the members of the family and the invited guests from the neighbourhood, including the children from the Peer family, who had generously offered costumes for the event. Nicklāl was gracious enough to acknowledge their cooperation in making the play a success once it was over.

Out of so many children from the Dhar and the Peer families, Basha's and Momlāl's friendship lasted the longest. Momlāl was the daughter of Zainalal. One day it so happened that Momlāl went to meet Basha at her in-laws' (Munshi) home in Sopore. Momlāl's husband was a judge of the Jammu and Kashmir High Court at Srinagar. Basha's father-in-law, Munshi, too was a leading lawyer in Sopore town. This was the time when Basha's husband was studying away in Calcutta, so Basha was living with her in-laws in Sopore.

When Momlāl reached the Munshi home, there was a stir in the vicinity that the wife of a sitting judge of the high court had come to visit them. Momlāl had primarily come to invite Basha and her in-laws for the function of her son's circumcision, known as the *khutna* ceremony in Kashmiri. Basha's and Momlāl's mutual love, respect, and affection for each other brought many a tear to people's eyes.

Their friendship had weathered many personal and societal upheavals that affected not just their lives but also those of all the people in Kashmir. The last fifty-five to sixty years have seen very few periods of lasting peace and development.

During the violent period of chaos that started in the early 1990s, Momlāl got very ill and though not very old, she passed away. This was a jolt not only to Basha but to members of both the Dhar and the Peer families.

21

The Audacious Second Marriage

One of Ram Chandra and Māl's five sons was Manmohan. He was affectionately called Lalaji. At work his colleagues preferred to call him Mankak—an endearing term made from a shortening of his official name.

Lalaji's first marriage was done fairly early, as was the custom in those days, when he was barely in his teens. His wife Prabhavati was a beautiful, slim KP girl, who looked elegant and graceful. She was fair, her gait was elegant, and she made a positive impression on all those she interacted with. There wasn't anyone who wouldn't notice her presence and appreciate her overall beauty.

When she entered the Dhar home as a new bride, her mother-in-law, Māl, and father-in-law, Ram Chandra, were very happy and thanked their stars for getting such a beautiful and graceful lady as a wife for Lalaji. They presumed that she would be as talented and versatile as her looks. But, alas, that was not the case. The beautiful bride had so many physical problems and diseases that no one knew about before her marriage. In those days, because girls and even boys were not fully economically self-reliant, their parents would be under pressure to get them married off so that as they aged, they would be free from the responsibility of caring for them. For an unaccomplished boy, a marriage would broaden his scope for financial or other support and thereby better his prospects. But if a girl was somehow 'unfit' in any way for matrimony, many parents would hide their daughter's flaws or deficiencies. The blemishes could be diseases that afflicted a girl or a boy, or any other defect that was perceived to be a weakness.

It seems Prabhavati's parents had also successfully hidden their daughter's disability. She had epilepsy, which in those days (the 1930s) was a dreaded condition since nobody really knew why or how it occurred, or how to treat it. Besides, epilepsy attacks as and when they would occur would create panic and despair since no one knew how to deal with them.

Poor Prabhavati, who must have had fits before, experienced epileptic bouts in her new home soon after her marriage. Due to ignorance and the lack of medication, people would handle such patients quite ruthlessly and would depend on the prayers and potions offered by local *pirs* and *hakeems*. There was no permanent cure for this disease in those days and patients would have their fits while family members out of sheer helplessness and despair would often respond with rage and violence.

Patients would suffer the disease and people's wrath and together these conditions would result in the rapid deterioration of a patient's health. That's what happened in Prabhavati's case as well. Despite her in-laws being well-to-do and generally aware of advances in science and medicine, as far as this disease was concerned they were absolutely ignorant and clueless.

Lalaji had to suffer his wife's illness for years together. He had no family life. He was as good as a bachelor even after his marriage to

Prabhavati. In fact, she was mostly staying at her parents' home on the pretext of being treated, which suited both the families.

There were so many of Lalaji's relatives who wanted that he should get married again to have a normal family life. They were of the view that he needn't suffer on account of a marriage that was never consummated and must quickly remarry.

Lalaji's mother, brothers, and sisters were equally concerned about his situation. They felt especially bad since he was still in his early thirties and they knew, by then, that waiting for Prabhavati to get well was impossible. At the same time, the applicable laws in Jammu and Kashmir had already made bigamy in Hindus illegal, with stringent punishment for violators. For Lalaji to get married for the second time therefore, especially when the first wife was still alive, did not seem to be a convenient course of action. Yet the thought lingered and word did go around that Lalaji was looking for a decent woman to marry again.

Since Lalaji had an excellent job, was handsome, and came from a good family, many KP families were happy to offer their daughters in marriage to him even though they knew that it would be his second.

Soon the Dhar family also succumbed to the pressure of these families and went to the next step of choosing the bride with whose natal chart Lalaji's horoscope showed the most compatibility. Finally a suitable girl called Dulari was chosen.

Word of this also got around very quickly.

Lalaji was working as a government employee in the state of Jammu and Kashmir, in the Ministry of Panchayats as Commissioner for Panchayat Affairs. The state government, newly formed after Independence, was led by the towering young leader Sheikh Mohammad Abdullah. In his cabinet one of the ministers was Sri Kashyap Bandhu, a Kashmiri Pandit assigned the charge of the Ministry of Panchayat Affairs. Kashyap Bandhu was not only a minister but a social activist too, and stood for the rights of women and improving social justice (see Chapter 4).

When he got to know that Manmohan Dhar (Lalaji) was going to get remarried, even as his first wife was still alive, he began to ask questions of Lalaji and placed legal and other impediments in the way to stop his plans of remarriage. It is believed that Prabhavati's family had approached the minister, requesting him to stop Lalaji from even considering a second marriage. Being committed to social justice and having been an activist, Kashyap Bandhu took up this matter with alacrity.

Many weeks went by. Quietly, the preparations for the wedding of Lalaji with Dulari were under way. However, as the day of the wedding approached, on the orders of Kashyap Bandhu, the bride's home and the Rishi Vihar home of Lalaji were cordoned off with khaki-clad policemen armed with lathis. They had been instructed that neither the bride would be allowed to leave the house nor would the groom be allowed to leave his.

Interestingly, even Dulari's younger sister was to get married on the same day as her elder sister, only a few hours apart. Since the preparations for both the weddings had been done, everyone advised that apart from the wedding all other ceremonies be completed. Therefore, all the rituals, the essential pujas, and prayers were done for both the nubile sisters, and hence only the marriage was to be solemnized; first for Dulari and then a few hours later for the younger sister. But this would require the grooms to come to the house of the brides and go through the rituals.

Under the prevailing circumstances, it was next to impossible to send the elder sister's bridegroom with a baraat to his prospective consort's home to get married. Gloom engulfed the bride's family, as also the Dhars. Lalaji's mother was convinced that there was some sort of curse on Lalaji's married life, which seemed to explain why all sorts of hurdles were occurring even as the second marriage was about to happen. The bride's relatives and her brothers and the sisters too were deeply anguished about the unfortunate situation.

The parents of the brides had died when the girls were only infants. Their relatives, including their uncles and aunts, who had helped in their upbringing, began to shed all sorts of real and fake tears to express their concern about their family.

In KP society at that time, it was quite a big slur to have the younger sister get married first while the elder sister waited for an unknown length of time for her marriage. Yet, negotiations between the bride's family and Kashyap Bandhu had yielded a partial solution—the younger daughter would get married as scheduled. Only the elder daughter could not get married to Manmohan Dhar that day. This further added to the darkness about the future of their daughter Dulari. All the guests who had come to witness the two marriages were dejected and concerned about how they could be part of the younger daughter's marriage while the elder sister was still uncertain about her wedding.

Meanwhile, even in the Dhar family, the atmosphere was equally sad and a gloomy ambience seemed to have settled in. Māl was especially sad over the situation and was cursing the minister-activist who was hell-bent upon stopping the marriage of his senior official within his ministry, only to show his power and the might of the government.

Eventually, as the days went by and the original date of the wedding arrived, Mother and all the family members were of the opinion that the marriage of Lalaji was now off, forever. Everyone was now convinced that there was some hurdle in Lalaji's horoscope, which prevented marital happiness and well-being.

To get his mind off the fact that he was to get married that evening, Lalaji decided to go to work. Even his brothers attended their respective offices. Baiji, who was an advocate at the courts of law, attended to the clients in his chamber, but his despair at Lalaji's condition would have been visible on his face. A few of his clients remarked that he wasn't looking his best. Baiji smiled weakly and tried his utmost to divert his attention from the unpleasant situation that had engulfed his younger brother's life.

While still in his chamber, his bosom friend Mohammad Sidiq entered unexpectedly. Baiji was happy to see him, and he eagerly got up from the chair and welcomed him. Mohammad Sidiq was a successful businessman and trader who had known Baiji for many years.

'You were supposed to be in Baramulla, and return only this evening for my dear brother Mankak's marriage. Didn't you go to Baramulla to finish the work?' Baiji asked him. He was really happy to see his friend, especially at a time when his presence was most needed.

'I heard something regarding the marriage, so I cancelled my trip to Baramulla,' Mohammad Sidiq said. 'I can do that work some other time. What happened exactly? Why did you have to cancel the marriage?'

Both the friends sat down to talk for a while. Baiji narrated the whole saga to Mohammad Sidiq, and how the minister had made his brother's case an example to demonstrate that the writ of the law is to be upheld at all times.

Mohammad Sidiq got up from the chair and said emphatically, 'Baiji, do you want to say that we should succumb to the whims of the madcap? It's not a sin to get married again, especially when one's first wife hasn't been a wife at all. And then Mankāk has suffered for far too long. Enough is enough, no more suffering now!'

'The police have cordoned off our respective houses. Even the girl's house in Anantnag is under police protection. It would be impossible to enter the girl's home,' Baiji said dolefully. 'I don't think we can do much now.'

'Just tell me who's our contact person from the girl's side, who can help us to reach the bride's family,' Mohammad Sidiq said with emphasis. He was obviously working on a plan in his mind.

'Shamlāl is the girl's cousin and is working in the office of Mankāk. But he is quite busy today, because the girl's younger sister is also getting married today.' Baiji shared this information, not sure what Mohammad Sidiq was planning.

'Baiji, leave everything to God first, and then to me,' Mohammad Sidiq said with an unusual air of finality. 'I'll see what needs to be done under these circumstances. You needn't worry any more. We don't have to waste any time now. Don't divulge this to anyone, till we do something about it. You should go to Barzala to your sister's home and take your brothers Prathkāk and Mankāk along too.'

While saying this Mohammad Sidiq got up to leave. He paused and looking Baiji in his eye said, 'Inshallah Mankāk's marriage will be performed today evening, as scheduled.'

In those days very few people had cars of their own. The well-to-do families had horse-drawn tongas. Baiji owned a tonga, while Mohammad Sidiq owned a car.

After his conversation, Mohammad Sidiq wasted no time, and taking his trusted associate Assadullah along with him, he headed straight to Anantnag, urging his driver to drive as fast as he could all the way to the home of the bride-to-be, Dulari. Once he reached the bride's home, he pretended as if he had come to enquire about the arrangements of the marriages of the two sisters. The bride's cousin Shamlāl recognized him immediately and welcomed him into the house. He took him into one of the rooms of the house and as soon as they were alone Mohammad Sidiq came straight to the point, and said firmly—'We have to perform the marriages of both the sisters; otherwise it won't augur well for the other girl, who'll be left behind and will be unable to face anyone thereafter.' As soon as he uttered these words, Shamlāl's face suddenly lit up. It seemed that the girl's relatives also were extremely anxious, and had been unable to comprehend how they would deal with the crisis.

'What should we do now, sir?' Shamlāl almost jumped up with excitement.

'Listen carefully. You bring the girl to the hospital, which is next door. My car is parked there. We will perform Dulari's marriage in Srinagar. Simultaneously, the younger sister will get married here in Anantnag.'

By now Shamlāl was visibly elated.

'I'll take her out of the house and bring her to the nearby hospital. That's not a big deal. But who'll go to the city with her? I have to be here to look after the other girl's marriage arrangements. Is it all right if my younger brother were to accompany you today? Tomorrow morning I'll be there with all of you.'

Shamlāl was relieved and was now eager to share the good news with his relatives.

Mohammad Sidiq could see that Shamlāl was feeling extremely happy and relieved now that the plan about Dulari's secret wedding had been shared with him. But Mohammad Sidiq also felt that in his excitement he might spill the beans and spoil the entire scheme.

Mohammad Sidiq put his hand on Shamlāl's shoulder and said, 'You have to be quite cautious about this plan. Let the marriage happen. Then we can celebrate it together.' With these words he got up and left the place to await the bride-to-be at the nearby hospital.

Shamlāl went to see Dulari, who was lying on the bed, with swollen, tearful eyes. He put his hand on her head, and while stroking it, whispered, 'Get up, I've good news for you.' Then he put his finger on his lips and in a hushed tone said something in her ear. Finally, he whispered, 'We don't have much time to waste. Get up now. We've to leave.'

'Leave now?' Dulari whispered back, surprised. 'But for where?' She sat up on the bed, clearing her eyes, still bewildered.

'I'll explain everything to you on the way. We have no time to waste. You are also going to get married today after all. But hurry up. Change into a simple sari. The cops shouldn't doubt that you've suddenly taken ill. Pretend that you've got a tummy ache or something so that we can go to the hospital for treatment. Take this bottle for the medicines we need to get.' Shamlāl handed her an empty bottle, which Dulari held conspicuously in her hand.

When she, along with her cousin, came out of the house, Shamlāl began to announce loudly that Dulari had suddenly got a shooting tummy ache.

'I'll have to take her to the hospital urgently,' he said, looking at the policemen at the gate. As soon as he declared this there was a wave of sympathy from all the relatives in the house, and the cops as well.

'Poor girl, she must be in shock due to the cancellation of her marriage,' one of the cops said. 'Now the elder sister will be left behind while the younger sister will get married.'

'These girls are orphans. If only any one of the parents would've been alive things would have been different,' another person added. 'Dulari was supposed to get married into a very big and prestigious family. Don't know what will happen to her now. Poor girl.'

The poor bride, pretending to be in pain, was quickly allowed along with her cousin to walk to the hospital. Some relatives wanted to come along, but Shamlāl urged them to focus on the arrangements for the other girl's wedding that evening, reassuring them that they'd be back shortly.

As soon as they reached the hospital, Mohammad Sidiq's car was ready and the bride and her cousin left Anantnag town in a jiffy, so as not to waste even a minute on the way.

The party reached Srinagar city by around 5.30 p.m. that evening, well in time for the *muhurat* for the marriage. They drove to the Barzala locality, where Lalaji's sister, Jiglāl, lived with her husband, Mr S. N. Kaul, and their young girls, Pichru and Nani, and their boys, Kagga (aka Kagnath) and Nicklāl.

Jiglāl's home was already abuzz with people busy with tasks in preparation for the wedding. There was tremendous hustle and bustle around it. Two priests were already seated at a makeshift *mandap*, waiting for the bride and the groom to arrive. The marriage was to be performed at the auspicious hour.

Pichru and Nani, who were quite young at that time, took charge of decorating the bride. Jiglāl took out her best sari and also an approriate headdress to make Dulari look like a perfect bride. Mr Vakeel, a leading lawyer, who was Mr Kaul's friend, had been invited to perform the role of the bride's father and be a part of the ceremonies.

Baiji, Lalaji, Ṭāṭhāji, Mohammad Sidiq, and Assadullah were also present. Mr Kaul (affectionately called Papaji) had also invited a few of his friends, the Shahmiris and others, who were living in the vicinity of their home, to create the right ambience for the marriage ceremonies that were to begin shortly. Mohammad Sidiq had already arranged for a proper cook, who had commenced the preparation of all sorts of dishes to match the occasion. Kagnath and Nicklāl were so young they didn't quite grasp what was going on in their home. There were festivities going on, which they and other young children were enjoying. When they heard it was Lalaji's wedding they got curious about who'd be marrying him.

They were determined to know the name of the bride.

'What is her name?' Kagnath enquired. When they got no one to answer them satisfactorily, the children went to the room where the bride was being readied for the ceremony.

'What's your name?' they all asked her, curious to get to know her.

'Dulari. That's what I'm called,' the bride said shyly.

'Dulari, Dulari!' the children shouted, repeating the name again and again.

'Don't say Dulari,' Kagnath's mother Jiglāl suggested. 'Call her Dulabhabi.' The children checked again, 'Dulabhabi?'

'Yes, Dulabhabi.'

This was the name that Dulari got to be known by for the rest of her life—Dulabhabi.

The marriage was solemnized, and Lalaji and Dulabhabi were pronounced man and wife. Apart from the few guests and family members who had assembled at Barzala, nobody else knew of the secret wedding. Finally, Baiji, Ṭāṭhaji, and Lalaji—with the bride—left for their home late in the evening after the marriage was performed. Most people at Rishi Vihar were oblivious of the developments that had taken place at such a quick pace throughout the day.

En route, as Lalaji and his bride and his brothers were headed home, it had been decided that Mohammad Sidiq alone would break the news of Lalaji's marriage to all in the family the next morning. It was he who had made it possible, and he would announce it and share the good news with Mother and the family members at the break of dawn. Till then Lalaji and his bride would stay at a relative's house and Mohammad Sidiq would head home.

The next morning, the household was up as usual. Nobody knew of the momentous developments of the previous day. Nobody could guess that a significant turning point in the life of Lalaji had been navigated.

Outside the Dhar home, the guards and cops were sure that the marriage of Lalaji had been cancelled, since the auspicious muhurat was over. The constables who were on duty decided that there was no need to guard the house any further, so they all left the place lock, stock, and barrel.

As soon as it was confirmed that the guards had left, Mohammad Sidiq entered the house. He was ushered into the room when he indicated that he was there to meet Mother. Soon she could be heard coming down the stairs from her bedroom on the floor above.

'How come you're here so early, Sidiq? Is all well?' she asked, as she settled into her seat to speak with the visitor. 'I hope the administration and the police haven't put any more hurdles in poor Mankāk's life. They seem to be hell-bent on taking away his peace of mind! Aren't they satisfied that they've succeeded in scuttling the poor boy's marriage?'

Mother was visibly disturbed and annoyed with the behaviour of the government.

Mohammad Sidiq, however, went to where Mother was seated on the carpeted floor, and taking her hand in his, he gave her a handful of almonds and cardamoms and said, 'Mubārakh, Mubārakh, Mother, get ready to receive the new bride.'

'New bride? Which bride are you talking about, Sidiq? This is not an appropriate time for a joke,' Mother said, a little annoyed.

'Mother, I am not joking. Mankāk is indeed married!'

'Married, but how? Wasn't he here yesterday, sleeping in his room. How can it be?' She was dumbfounded and was in a state of utter disbelief.

'I've arranged for all the celebrations,' Sidiq continued. 'The cook will be coming any moment and all the guests also have been invited. Jiglāl and the children will soon be here along with Lalaji and the new bride. So don't waste any time, dear Mother. Please call everyone and ask them to be ready to welcome the new bride.'

While they were still speaking, the cook entered the room. When Mother saw the cook she knew that Sidiq wasn't joking after all. She spontaneously hugged Sidiq, even as he embraced her warmly. They both had tears in their eyes.

The house that had looked so gloomy from the day before was now abuzz with a host of joyful and pleasant activities. The entire mood in the house had changed. All the daughters-in-law were busy preparing to receive the new bride soon. All the gold ornaments to be gifted to the new bride along with a few traditional and new dresses were kept ready. There was an immense sense of anticipation and lots of curiosity to meet the newcomer.

Finally, Jiglāl along with her family, Lalaji and the bride reached home. They were all received in the traditional manner, with a *thāli* full of small *diyas*, sweets, and candy. Mother was immensely pleased to see the new bride and kissed her on the forehead. Then turning to her daughter, Jiglāl, she said knowingly—'This time you're here as an honoured guest from the bride's side, so we'll all have to be extra careful in our endeavour to please you.'

All the assembled relatives and family had a hearty laugh. The bride was fairly ordinary to look at compared to Prabhavati. But no one really cared about her looks. Everyone was wishing that she should prove to be a good wife for Mankāk, whose married life till then had been rather unlucky.

As news of the immense role played by Mohammad Sidiq went around, he became the hero in everyone's eyes. Soon even the government authorities knew about the secret marriage of Lalaji. It baffled the authorities that in spite of the police arrangements and the injunctions the marriage had taken place! This became the talk of the town and the security officials had mud on their faces.

Kashmiris get immense pleasure from being defiant. It's part of our nature to cock a snook at anyone in power, especially if those in authority are being high-handed and unjust. Denying Lalaji permission to marry again seemed to fall in the category of a rather harsh and unsympathetic decision, and people were therefore delighted that the wedding had gone ahead nonetheless.

After this episode, Mohammad Sidiq was treated as a member of the Dhar family, and almost like a son to Māl. All of us called him Chachaji. Given that he was a capable planner and organizer, the family would rely on his capabilities, his contacts, and his wide network to get big family events organized. Mother had chosen a special Persian phrase to describe him—*Rāzdar bā Ustād*—one who is talented, versatile, and above all a trusted confidant!

Chachaji would always tell Dulabhabi that she was his daughter-in-law. She would smile with loving gratitude whenever he said this, knowing that it was he who had brought her to the Dhar family in the most trying of circumstances.

22

The 'At Home' Blooper

My younger brother Surender had completed his MBBS degree from the Sarojini Naidu Medical College in Agra. My uncle's son, Gyan Nath, who was about the same age as Surender, had studied engineering. Like their elder cousins, their marriages too were performed more or less together, within the premises of the joint family home at Rishi Vihar. This was in the early 1960s.

Kashmir in those days was experiencing happy, resurgent times. The nation had become independent barely thirteen years prior, and the birth pangs that had affected the state for almost a decade were now subsiding. Bakshi Ghulam Mohammad, who had served as Sheikh Abdullah's deputy in the National Conference and who had taken over as the prime minister of the state of Jammu and Kashmir in August 1953 (after Sheikh Abdullah was dismissed and incarcerated by the Central government), was still the prime minister of Jammu and Kashmir at that time. He was a confident leader with a positive world view and a modern outlook, and he wanted the state of Jammu and Kashmir to join the national mainstream. Despite being from a poor family and not very literate, he had excellent political and rapport-building skills. He had even served as a bridge between Kashmir and the Central nationalistic leadership from as early as 1946.

Bakshi had been sworn in as the prime minister of the state by Dr Karan Singh, son of Maharaja Hari Singh, and the *Sadar-i-Riyasat* of the state. Bakshi Sahab, as the prime minister was called, knew that he did not have the mass base that Sheikh Abdullah had, and hence he gave a massive thrust to agricultural improvement and development and the initiation of rural welfare schemes. The improvements, which had a direct bearing on the economic well-being of the poor peasants of the state, yielded significant all-round benefits as well, and after long years the people of the state were feeling relaxed and aspiring to greater prosperity. The Central government continued to pump in money to meet the budgetary requirements of the Bakshi administration, so development initiatives during the ten years of Bakshi's rule continued with intensity.

With the people's mood being positive and wholesome, the marriages of Surender and Gyan Nath were performed lavishly. This was the era of rapid modernization as well, so new ideas and socially accepted customs were seeping into the social fabric of both Kashmiri Muslims and Kashmiri Pandits.

Tribhuvan, one of our uncles, who was serving at the ordnance factories in Pune, had suggested that Surender's and Gyan's marriages must be celebrated with a Western-style 'reception'. This must have been common in the metropolitan cities in the rest of the country where large numbers of guests were invited, but this format had not caught on in Srinagar at least. Tribhuvan must have been quite insistent, however, and his other brothers may have had to relent and play along with the idea of an 'At Home Reception' for the marriages of the young men.

The 'At Home' Blooper

The guests who came for the 'At Home' were all the elite of the state from not just Srinagar, but from Anantnag, Jammu, Baramulla and Sopore as well. There were judges, high-ranking officials from the government, ministers, businessmen, and professors, apart from friends, neighbours, and relatives. The organizers, I'm told, had planned for six hundred guests, but almost a thousand turned up! This overwhelming gathering, and the fact that the hired catering staff was also not completely trained, resulted in quite a situation. Furthermore, since the reception was held within Rishi Vihar, there was very little coordination between the 'trained' waiters and the normal house help who were also manning the kitchens and overseeing the cooking.

The result was that the 'At Home' was quite a chaotic situation. The crockery was insufficient, the food ran out, and the mismanagement of the event was glaring. Some people left without partaking of the many dishes that had been prepared. Nonetheless, the marriage ceremony was long remembered, not just for the faux pas during the reception but also because it had been a joyous few weeks of festivities and was a grand affair, overall.

23

The Rupa Devi Sharda Peeth Trust

Within the Kashmiri Pandits there was always an effort to ensure that matrimonial alliances were done between people who were socially, economically, and spiritually compatible. The 'spiritual' compatibility was gauged through the matching of the natal charts of the prospective bride and groom. In fact, this was always the first stage in the process of 'arranged marriages'. This was the reason for all KP families insisting that the natal charts of the prospects be matched by a learned astrologer and guru. Only when the charts matched would the other aspects be taken into account.

This happens even to this day. However, it is dispensed with if the boy and the girl have fallen in love even *before* the elders could have their charts matched! If KP boys or girls haven't identified someone suitable to be their spouse, especially by the time they are in their late twenties or early thirties, then the parents or the elders of the young adults would rely on their natal charts and the World Wide Web to identify suitable candidates.

Surender's father and uncles were keen that he should marry a woman who was also medically qualified. When the search was on, therefore, though natal charts were forthcoming from a wide catchment, there were extra points for the young lady who was beautiful as well as medically qualified. Surender was fortunate since the lovely woman he eventually married was not just medically qualified and beautiful—with lovely blue eyes—she was also from the affluent and well-known Mattoo family. Though her name was Vimla, she was known affectionately as Billieji because of her beautiful, blue eyes (*billė* in Kashmiri).

Billieji's maternal grandfather was Pandit Parmanand Bhat. He was a mathematical genius, and was highly learned in accountancy, Sanskrit and Persian as well. He was erudite and wise, and was largely a self-made man. His family owned large tracts of land in the Valley and many of his relatives were engaged in agriculture.

During Maharaja Hari Singh's regime, he served as accountant general of the state of Jammu and Kashmir. He was highly respected and a revered member of the KP community. Everyone used to call him *Tātėsahab* (pronounced as *tah-the-sahab*).

Parmanandji had been blessed with only one child—a lovely girl named Rupa. She was brought up in a very happy, congenial, and caring household. She actually personified her name, Rupa—she grew up to be a very pretty and grounded maiden. Since Parmanandji was aware of the adverse effects of parents doting on their children, Rupa was never pampered or spoiled by her parents. She was given a good education and the essential housekeeping skills that every young woman would need in those days. She was truly everyone's darling.

Due to her background there must have been a lot of requests for her hand in marriage. She was, however, destined to become part of the Mattoo family, and therefore got married to a brilliant lawyer, who later became a judge of the Jammu and Kashmir High Court.

In due course, Rupa gave birth to three children—two boys and a girl. These were Vimla (Billieji), her elder brother Moti Lal, and her younger sibling Ashok.

While Rupa's three children were still very young—with only the eldest, Moti Lal, attending school—Rupa was due to deliver again. While the delivery at home was under way, she started to haemorrhage profusely and lost her life. The newborn also did not survive. Her sudden demise shocked the entire community. Parmanandji and his wife were shattered beyond words at having lost their only beloved child. As they mourned her sudden and devastating passing, the whole of Kashmiri society was solidly behind them. Parmanandji and his wife took all the three children of his daughter under their wing and brought them up with utmost love and care.

Throughout history, childbirth has been one of the greatest contributors to the mortality of married women in Kashmir. All the way up to the early 1950s, there was not a single family in the whole of the state that had not been affected by the untimely passing of a mother, a sister, a spouse, or a daughter. It was only after the use of penicillin to prevent infections around the mid-1930s, as also improvements in obstetrics and gynaecological practices that maternal mortality began to decline in Jammu and Kashmir. However, as I write this, I'm still pained that every 180 seconds, somewhere in the world a woman dies due to pregnancy. Sadly, India still contributes (along with Nigeria) to almost a third of maternal mortality deaths worldwide.

In this context it's worthwhile to mention the extraordinary role played by Jagat Mohini Thussu, who happened to be the mother-in-law of my younger sister, Promila (Saraf). Jagat Mohini, who had her roots in Punjab, came to Kashmir as a young doctor in 1945, soon after she completed her medical education from the King George Medical College in Lahore. Energetic and enthusiastic, she was committed to bringing the latest advances in medicine as well as in obstetrics and gynaecology to the women of Kashmir. While in Kashmir, she married Dr O.N. Thussu, also a reputed doctor. Doctor Thussu had lost his wife, Rattan Rani, in a tragic accident in Tulla Mulla. Together Jagat Mohini and he established the Rattan Rani Hospital in Barbarshah, Srinagar. It was named after Dr Thussu's first wife, and in keeping with Jagat Mohini's interests, was focused on providing modern healthcare and treatment procedures to women. Till as long as she lived (Jagat Mohini passed away in 2009) she and the team that she had painstakingly trained and developed at the Rattan Rani Hospital made a wholesome difference to the reproductive health and well-being of thousands of Kashmiri women. Not only that, she was a feisty woman who also stood for the rights of women generally, ensuring that nobody was ever discriminated against on account of her gender. She was loved by those whom she served selflessly, and was endearingly called, 'Mummyji' by one and all.

Returning to Rupa Devi. Her passing was a terrible shock for Parmanandji. Yet, in order to keep the memory of his loving daughter alive, *Tātesahab* decided to create an educational organization in her memory that would benefit society, especially girl children. So he placed most of his savings in a trust that was named after his daughter and it was registered as the Rupa Devi Sharda Peeth. The Trust acquired proper premises for an institute and very soon children from the neighbourhood were admitted. The purpose of this educational institution was to teach girl students, especially from the poorer strata of society. They were taught Sanskrit along with a proper education and vocational skills consistent with the times. Soon the institute began to flourish. The library was expanded as books of all genres of literature—in Sanskrit, Pali, Persian, English, Hindi, Kashmiri, and Urdu—as also those of history and science were bought. A treasure trove of rare Sanskrit manuscripts and books was soon collected and other rare and valuable books of literature were brought in and preserved in the premises of the institute. After the demise of *Tātēsahab*, the rules of the Trust required that the role of the chairman of the Trust pass on to Rupa's three children, who would hold the position in rotation.

Thousands of girl students benefited from the education provided by the school run by the Rupa Devi Sharda Peeth Trust. However, as the Kashmir Valley saw fanatical *wahabi* ideas—riding in on petrodollars from Saudi Arabia and Iran—take root in Kashmir during the early 1980s, innocent Kashmiri families started to be berated by mullahs for sending their children to 'Hindu' educational institutions and not to madrassas instead.

When the terrorist violence in the late 1980s started, the stage had already been set for children to be kept away from schools if they were not madrassas. And as schools were targeted and set ablaze, so was the school run by the Rupa Devi Sharda Peeth Trust. With the burning of the school, some of the world's rarest books and manuscripts—in Pali, Sanskrit, Persian, Hindi, Urdu and English—all went up in smoke! The greatest treasure of Kashmir—the ideas and words of wise and erudite seekers over the ages—which had all been kept intact in the premises of school, were gone. There was nothing left. Everything was burned to ashes.

Part VI
Phases of Turmoil

24

The Surprise Attack

It was autumn of the year 1947. On 25 October, Bakr Eid was to be celebrated. People were therefore completing tasks in the orchards and the fields so that they could celebrate the festival happily.

Most people—Hindus, Muslims, Sikhs, and Christians alike—were unmindful of the political happenings outside their homes. They were not envisioning anything untoward or unexpected befalling them. Most people had peaceful lives and that seemed to have lulled everyone into a state of unhealthy unconcern. They were unaware that the enemy was already in their backyards, stealthily intruding into their placid lives even as they were attending marriage feasts and preparing for other festivities.

Over centuries, the topography of the Kashmir Valley and its relative inaccessibility have made the people of the region pretty relaxed and unconcerned about the rest of the world. For most Kashmiri people, anything and everything south of the ancient

Panchala Deva range (now known as Pir Panchal) was known as 'Punjab'. New things were adopted gradually and cautiously because disruption in the existing way of life was resisted.

When the first British Auxiliary Air Force bi-planes flew into Srinagar sometime in the late 1920s, there was immense excitement among the people of the city initially. Many flocked to the roofs of their homes along the river Jhelum to get a glimpse of the flying machines. In the excitement, many people fell off the roofs and hurt themselves badly or drowned in the river below. A poet recounted the sad events a few days later with a heartbreaking verse in Kashmiri:

Havai jahāz ha āv Mulki-Kashmīr
Yemi-yemi vuch temi kor tobé-taksīr

(Airplanes have come to Kashmir, but those who saw them were horrified and repentent)

Officers and soldiers from the newly formed Pakistani Army, along with expert mountaineers from amongst the tribals of the North West Frontier Provinces, formed the motley *kabalie* attackers who invaded the state of Jammu and Kashmir on 22 October 1947. The Maharaja was dreaming of keeping the state independent, and was therefore warding off pressure from both India and Pakistan to join them. The vacillating monarch obviously riled the tempers of the leaders in Pakistan because they had imagined that Kashmir—with about 66 per cent Muslims in the population at that time—would automatically be a part of the new 'Muslim' nation. Since that had not happened even two months after Independence from the British, the raiders made a surprise attack coming in from the west.

Baramulla was the first big city to face the brunt of the marauding soldiers and tribals. To the northwest of Srinagar, it was a bustling cosmopolitan town, with St Joseph's College, a convent, a mission hospital run by the Mill Hill Fathers of London, Hindu temples, gurdwaras, and many beautiful homes belonging to the citizens who were engaged in trade and commerce with regions to the west, north, and south of the state. Two days before Eid that month, a Chevrolet car carrying a young Pakistani Army officer directed the townsfolk to welcome the coming raiders and give them support. Then a day later the savage tribals descended from the mountains to the west and overran the town.

Baramulla witnessed immense brutality. Hindus, Muslims, and Sikhs were killed. The nuns in the convent were raped and killed. Those who had sympathies for Pakistan were horrified at the looting, the killing, and the destruction that they witnessed. More tribals descended on the town in lorries a day later and men, women, and children took refuge in the oddest of places. Many died after suffering terribly.

Pakistan's President Muhammad Ali Jinnah, who came to Kashmir for a period of almost three months in the summer of 1944, was accorded a series of massive receptions during his stay in the Valley. He also interacted with a host of people, especially those who were a part of the National Conference as well as those who still retained their allegiance to the Muslim Conference. Sheikh Mohammad Abdullah, who in 1931 had rejected the 'two-nation theory' and had opted for a more secular and broad-based, all-inclusive platform of governance, had carved out the National Conference from the erstwhile Muslim Conference, and had dissociated himself from the communal approach being pursued by the Muslim League (and the Muslim Conference in Kashmir).

I surmise that the meetings that Jinnah had with political leaders, opinion-makers, and members of the Hindu, Sikh, and Christian communities in Kashmir in 1944 gave Sheikh Abdullah a glimpse of how things might pan out—for him and his associates in the

National Conference—if he were to go with Jinnah's suggestion of joining Pakistan. It must have jarred his Kashmiri sensibilities to think of being a part of a nation based on something as non-monolithic as Islam. With an enormous following among the people of Kashmir, Sheikh Abdullah was clear that Kashmir's destiny would be determined by its own people and not a 'popular leader of Muslims' from Bombay.

The simmering animus between Sheikh Abdullah and Jinnah must have got worse, when in one of the public rallies that had been organized for Jinnah he compared Sheikh Abdullah to a rotten egg, saying that, 'He can neither be kept nor can he be thrown away because of the stink he'll raise.' This would not have endeared Jinnah to the Kashmiris either! In fact it is said that Jinnah's disdain for the Sheikh and his contempt for the popular leaders of his time (including the Maharaja) rubbed the people of Jammu and Kashmir the wrong way. There was no love lost for Jinnah thereafter.

When the monarch of Jammu and Kashmir took his own time to take a call on the accession of his kingdom, and when news of the raids by Pakistani soldiers and armed tribals in Baramulla spread, it was Sheikh Abdullah—the lion of Kashmir—who roared against the attack by the Pakistani raiders, and in a matter of days galvanized his party workers, students, schoolchildren, college girls, boys, men and women to protect the citizens of the state from the attackers.

The war cry of this citizens' militia was *'Hamlavar khabardar! Ham Kashmiri hain tayyar! Jo ham say takrayega, pash-pash ho jayega.'* (Beware warmongers! We Kashmiris are ready to fight you and throw you out). At that time, without concerns for caste, creed, colour, or religious affinity—all Kashmiris were united under the leadership of Sheikh Mohammad Abdullah. The entire population trusted him and his leadership. This was also a chance to put Jinnah in his proper place by demonstrating that the people of the state of Jammu and Kashmir demanded respect for themselves and those who represented them.

Sheikh Abdullah had a special relationship with Pandit Jawaharlal Nehru, the premier of the newly independent India. They were great friends. They both belonged to Kashmir and had a strong attachment with the place and its people. They had also known each other for a long time. When Sheikh Abdullah changed his party's name from Muslim Conference to National Conference in 1933, it is believed that it was as a result of his conversations with Pandit Nehru and the lofty vision of all-inclusive governance that they shared. They both rejected the two-nation theory, which was based on mere religious affinity

As the *kabalies* moved closer to Srinagar, and as the Muslim soldiers in the Maharaja's state troops in Poonch and elsewhere were siding with the Pakistani forces, Maharaja Hari Singh finally signed the Instrument of Accession with India on 26 October 1947. The people of Jammu and Kashmir, under the leadership of Sheikh Abdullah, also accepted this decision. As soon as the said document was signed, the first contingent of the Indian Army soldiers were flown into Srinagar in Dakota planes, and readied to repulse the invaders who were now dangerously close to Srinagar.

The distance from Baramulla to Srinagar would have been traversed by the *kabalies* much more quickly since there was very little opposition that they had to face. However, the raiders indulged in looting, vandalizing buildings and properties, plundering, and raping women. Wherever they put their hands they wreaked havoc. The *kabalies* had never seen so much wealth and gold and objects of value before, so they wanted to loot as much as they could carry. In this mad spree of chaotic looting and pillaging, they killed many innocent Kashmiri people who were patriots. They would label them as traitors and either put a bullet or a bayonet through them, or string them to gallows on the limbs of trees. People were scared to death to see such dreadful scenes.

The tribal soldiers had a notion that in Kashmir they would find lots of gold. It was told to them that each Kashmiri (Hindu) woman wore thousands of rupees worth of gold on her neck, in her ears, and on her head. So these raiders were searching for Hindu ladies in particular to get the gold. So much so that they mistook the bronze samovars in the houses they entered as gold, and began to collect as many as possible to hoard. Bronze samovars were used by Hindu families whereas copper samovars were used by Muslims. By the time the *kabalies* collected their loot and were done with the killings along the way, the Indian Army had advanced well ahead and was marching towards Muzaffarabad, pushing back the raiders along the way. It was rumoured that the attack on Kashmir, by Pakistan, was instigated by the British army officers in the Pakistani Army, while telling their British counterparts in the Indian Army about what they were doing! Quite an unusual situation for any army to be in!

Each one of the key people and dramatis personae were playing the game according to the best of their abilities and desires. We, humans think we are the doers. With bloated egos we think we can conquer the world, fight wars, and build walls of hatred and divisiveness. In the process we make hellholes for ourselves to fall into. Like a silkworm making its own cocoon, we too are caught and trapped in the self-woven web, never to find even a tiny opening to come out of the terrible conditions that we create. But the will of God is supreme, and in spite of thousands of hurdles, it is His will that always prevails.

25

The Unexpected Return

Sidha, our help, was sprinting down the lane leading to the entrance of Rishi Vihar. Anyone who saw him knew that he was dying to convey an important message to the senior members of the family before anyone else had a chance to do so.

As he barged through the door, and as he headed to where Māl was seated, he was heard shouting, 'He has returned home, safe and sound! Can you imagine? He is back!'

Sidha was breathing fast and it was clear that he was speaking in dead earnest. 'Who has returned home? Whom are you talking about?' Māl asked, intrigued. 'Who else, but Mr Nerkāk Vāriku? There is a big feast on at his home. I caught a glimpse of him myself.' 'Is he alive? Are you sure about what you're saying? How come you went there all of a sudden?' Mother wouldn't believe him at first, and so she began to question him, and speak aloud. 'If true, then he's back after nearly eleven months! Isn't it a real miracle, because I believe they didn't spare anyone? We all thought he too might have been killed a long while back. They have been brutal and didn't allow anyone to run away, but how has he been able to come out of the clutches of those murderous *kabalies*?' Mother was as intrigued as she was relieved with the news. She knew Sidha was reliable and trustworthy and unlikely to spread rumours.

'Did you share this news with Benji?' Māl enquired a few minutes later. 'After all, Mr Vāriku is her sister's brother-in-law?' Mother was looking towards Sidha appreciatively, and it was evident that Sidha would be rewarded for bringing this good news to the family.

―⚬⚭⚬―

The news of Mr Vāriku's return spread throughout the household in a jiffy. All the members of the family quickly assembled in the large *vattoo* (sitting room), where the ladies, men, and children would all sit together and catch up with the day's events. This room was a sort of a club, which was used by members of the household to busy themselves with activities during their free time. While the men were at work the ladies would complete chores and a host of tasks, such as knitting, mending, and chopping vegetables for the next meal. This room was an all-purpose room. However, the office work of adults or children's studies and college work were never done in the *vattoo* since it was always noisy.

'Have you heard about Nerkāk Vāriku? He's been freed by the *kabalies*.' Mother was looking towards her daughter-in-law, Benji, as she was saying this.

'Freed by the *kabalies*? How come?' Benji asked, really astonished. Looking at her mother-in-law incredulously, she queried, 'Who told you about this?'

'Sidha has seen him with his own eyes,' Mother said affirmatively. 'There's no reason not to believe him.' Then she continued, her eyes gleaming.

'You, along with Sati, Shobawati, Gauri and Uma, should go there to congratulate them. This is really a new life, a new *janma* for him. This is not a joke! Do you remember how everyone thought that he'd never come back again? But when God is kind, miracles do happen.'

As instructed, all the ladies got dressed up to visit the Vāriku home. The younger ones wore saris, while the older women wore the traditional Kashmiri pheran. This was a happy visit after all, and they all wanted to look their best. Sidha accompanied them as the driver of the tonga that the family owned, but also to carry and present to the Vārikus the large wicker basket that had been filled with rogini breads, sugar candy, dry fruits and nuts in honour of Mr Vāriku's safe return.

Along the way, Sidha filled in the details of Mr Vāriku's miraculous escape. All that he shared were obviously rumours because nobody still had a clear idea of how a simple man like Mr Vāriku, with no military training whatsoever, had succeeded in coming back home alive after almost a year with the Pakistani raiders. As was his habit, he spoke with such confidence it would seem as if he were a witness to the events leading to his freedom.

'Who told you these stories? Are these the creation of your rich imagination?' the ladies admonished him.

'This time it's not a joke at all. Do you know Hassana? The man who serves as the caretaker of the Vāriku lands in Mirgund? He is a distant cousin of mine, and it was he who told me that Vāriku sahab was made a *maulvi* by the *kabalies*. He used to perform all the practices of Islam. He became a very effective imām and would even lead the faithful in prayers.' Sidha was speaking earnestly.

'Now that we'll all be meeting Mr Vāriku, we'll get to know the real story,' the ladies said, indicating that they didn't entirely buy Sidha's version.

When the women reached the Vāriku home, they were warmly welcomed by Benji's sister, who was known to all the younger ladies by her pet name, Maciji. They all exchanged greetings and congratulated and hugged each other warmly. Sidha kept the big wicker basket on the floor of the room, where all the guests were ushered and requested to sit. All the guests sat on the floor, which was covered with thick carpets and woollen namdahs embroidered with colourful *ari*-work. Along the sides were huge round bolsters, which the guests reclined upon to be comfortable.

On one side of the room there was a big sofa chair that was kept exclusively for Nerkāk Vāriku to sit upon. It was for him that the guests had come, and they all wanted to congratulate him and his wife on his safe and unexpected release from the clutches of the enemy.

After a while Nerkāk (who was also affectionately known as *Nain-saeb*) entered the room along with his wife and all the visiting ladies and a few men got up to welcome and congratulate them. Nerkāk sat on the sofa while his wife sat on the carpeted floor with the guests.

'This is a new lease of life for you, dear Nain-saeb! We are so happy to see you!' Sati, the elder of the Dhar daughters-in-law, said on behalf of all the others. 'It's all because of your loving wife dear Janki dyaed's prayers that you are here with your family once again. You may have done some good deeds in your life, otherwise it's nearly impossible to come out of the clutches of a treacherous enemy such as the *kabalies*. And of course, dear Janki dyaed's prayers have been answered.'

Nerkāk smiled gratefully. 'Yes, I'm very fortunate indeed to be alive and in your midst once again. The prayers of my dear wife and all the loved ones have given me a new life,' he said, as his eyes filled with tears.

As tea was served and everyone settled down, many more people came in to visit and congratulate Mr Vāriku. A fairly big group of well-wishers was now requesting Nain-saeb to narrate the whole story of his capture and release from the clutches of the Pakistani raiders dressed up as tribals, *kabalies*, from the beginning to the end. Nain-saeb smiled, and even though he had narrated the saga of his adventures a number of times already, he was gracious enough to oblige.

―∞―

It was the last week of the month of October 1947, and the season of harvesting the crops and fruits across the Valley of Kashmir. Mr Vāriku, who was responsible for the upkeep of the lands that belonged to his family, had set out early in the day on his horse-driven tonga to oversee the harvesting of the paddy crop on the lands situated around the village of Mirgund, northwest of Srinagar, on the road to Baramulla. The distance to the lands in Mirgund is no more than twelve kilometres but it was late morning by the time Nerkāk went there.

Mr Vāriku was completely oblivious of the fact that in the months of dithering that engulfed the Maharaja of Jammu and Kashmir since 15 August 1947, when he was unable to firmly decide whether to join India or Pakistan, the Pakistanis had been getting restive (they wanted Kashmir to be a part of Pakistan) and had been making secret plans to capture Kashmir by force.

By 22 October 1947 the Maharaja still hadn't made up his mind. That's when the newly minted Pakistani government—with a British army chief—sent in a contingent of soldiers dressed up as Pathan tribals to launch a surprise attack on the state. It was this contingent of soldiers who were given the name of *kabalies*—tribesmen.

Apparently, that morning, a group of heavily armed *kabalies*, who had commandeered a number of civilian lorries in Baramulla, had driven towards Srinagar the night before and had entered the village of Mirgund. Nerkāk Vāriku, completely clueless about the attack, was looking around for his manager and the villagers who'd work on his land. He was totally surprised to find the whole village empty. There was absolutely no one to even welcome him. 'The whole village is always happy to receive me. Today not a soul is visible. Where have all the people gone?' Nerkāk was deep in thought.

The tonga driver, Assada (an affectionate short form of the name Assadullah) was well built and muscular. He was referred to as *pehelwan* by all those who knew him. Today, even he looked like a mouse—frightened, confused, and perplexed to find the village completely devoid of people.

The whole village was deserted. The windows of the homes were shut, the doors of some homes were ajar, and there was an eerie silence. There were neither adults nor children visible anywhere.

Nerkāk and Assada suspected that something untoward had befallen the village. But whom could they ask? They were perplexed and scared as they ventured towards the interior of the village, on the tonga, but at a gentle pace. Assada finally stopped the tonga next to a narrow village lane, as he and Nerkāk got down to explore the rest of the village on foot.

As soon as they moved past one of the larger houses in the lane, a group of about ten coarse and gruff-looking strangers emerged who shouted at the two men and then quickly caught hold of Assada and his master. Most of the men who held Assada and Nerkāk were tall, loutish, and had the crusty, bearish look of rowdies. They sported black unkempt beards and wore long kurtas with pyjamas. On their heads they had donned rough, large, and dirty turbans. Long guns with sharp bayonets were slung on their shoulders and they looked menacing. Assada and his master were trembling with fear and were completely tongue-tied. Not a word could come out of their mouths.

'What is your name?' one hefty person, who seemed to be the boss, shouted at the two trembling men. But out of sheer fright neither of them could utter a word. Assada, fearing the worst, had closed his eyes and hung his head down.

'Kill them both. They're both *kafir*,' another said menacingly. This phrase, however, galvanized the pehelwan.

'We're Musalmans, we're Musalmans! Please don't kill us!' Assada fell on his knees, his hands folded, in an abject entreaty for clemency. His voice was cracking as he repeated, 'We're Musalmans, have mercy!'

'I asked you your name, you blabbering idiot! Do you think you can get away with this charade?' said one of the persons as he pointed his bayonet at poor Assada, kicking him with his torn shoe.

'We want your name! Don't you hear us? Are you deaf?'

'My name is Assadullah. I'm also called Assada and he, he is my master.'

Assada's voice was feeble with fright and now his whole body was shaking with fear. Mr Vāriku was equally frightened and was quavering like a leaf on a windy day. He was sure that this encounter was going to be his what.

'We'll have to kill them both, they're traitors, kafirs. Let's not waste any more time.'

'No, we'll have to move ahead. Leaving dead bodies behind in the village is not wise. Tie them both with a rope and take them along as prisoners.' The man who spoke seemed to be the leader of the group.

Assada and Nain-saeb were tied with thick ropes and taken along as prisoners. As the *kabalies* moved from one small hamlet to the next, looting whatever they could lay their hands on and burning what was left, hefty Assada and the lean Nerkāk were made to stand where they could be seen—all tied up and bedraggled—by anyone caring to peer from behind closed windows. The *kabalies* thereby terrorized the locals, and made sure that they were met with no resistance on their onward journey to Srinagar.

The events of the last few days of October, and November 1947 are indelibly etched in the minds of Kashmiris. The *kabalies* who had entered the valley, as well as those who attacked and overran the cities to the west of the Valley, unleashed unprecedented violence on the hapless Kashmiris. Hindus and Muslims alike suffered. Kashmiri-speaking people, who worked in business establishments, schools or other small organizations in cities such as Rawalpindi, Naushera, Abbottabad, and Muzaffarabad, fearing for their lives and those of their accompanying families, endeavoured to return to their homes in the Valley. Many got killed in the process. Families were separated. There are stories I've heard of younger men and women who couldn't travel hiding in abandoned houses in Muzaffarabad and Rawalpindi until things became safe again. Thousands lost their lives.

In these circumstances, Nerkāk and Assada were fortunate. As the Maharaja signed the Instrument of Accession with India on 26 October 1947, India sent in troops to defend the state. The Indian battalions were able to successfully repulse the *kabalies* even as the enemy had reached the Shalteng locality to the northwest of Srinagar, on the old Muzaffarabad road.

Nerkāk and Assada therefore found themselves in the clutches of the enemy—alive, but as prisoners. They were taken westwards by the *kabalies* and lodged as prisoners in either Rawalpindi or Abbottabad.

Meanwhile when Nerkāk and Assada failed to return even after a few days, the Vāriku family used all their connections in Srinagar and Delhi to determine the whereabouts of Nerkāk and his associate, and to secure their freedom if they were alive. The family eventually learned that the two had been taken in as prisoners by the marauding tribals.

In September 1948 there was a swap of Kashmiri civilian prisoners who had been missing since the *kabalie* raid, and were held by forces in India and Pakistan. Nerkāk and Assada were also fortunate to be among the prisoners who were released and returned home to their respective families in Srinagar, safe, sound and grateful.

26

The Loss of the Moh-i-Muqaddas

It was the bitter winter of 1963, late in the month of December. The time when Kashmiris declare that the *chill-ai-kalān*—the coldest of the cold season—has begun. Because of the subzero temperatures, waterbodies freeze, the taps get blocked, and the roads become dangerous with the deadly *kaṭhish* or black ice that is the cause of many a fall.

It is a matter of necessity to stay well stocked and provisioned for the three months of winter. Most Kashmiri families spend much of the preceding months collecting firewood and charcoal as well as rice and lentils to last the winter. The firewood was for cooking in the traditional and still prevalent (in the 1960s) dān, and heating. The charcoal was for use in the traditional kāngris that all adults and children would carry under their pherans. There was always a concern that the roads that allowed for commodities and food items to be brought in from Jammu and the rest of the northern states would get blocked (as they often did, due to landslides and excessive snowfalls) and hence people would prefer to have more items at home than less.

It was morning and I was sitting in the living room of my home, where a *bukhāri* (a wood-burning stove) was radiating enjoyable warmth all around. All of a sudden, our gardener, Hassan Bhat, entered the room. His face was sullen and he looked visibly sad and depressed.

'Is all well, Hassan Bhat?' I asked, sensing from his body language that something was wrong.

'A great big theft has occurred,' he replied dolefully.

'Theft? What's been stolen and from whom?' I was curious.

'It's something priceless and really beyond any value. If the thieves had stolen a huge big treasure, people wouldn't have minded at all. But what is lost is priceless.'

'What's priceless, Hassan Bhat? What has been stolen, pray tell me.' I was getting impatient with his riddles.

'The *Moh-i-Mubarak* in the Hazratbal shrine has been taken away by some devil,' he finally said, anguished.

While Hassan Bhat was speaking, my husband, Omkar, entered the room. He had overheard Hassan Bhat's words.

'This is really very bad,' Omkar said. 'Who could do such a dastardly act? Besides, who told you about this? This may just be a rumour.'

'No sir, this is authentic news. People have come out on the roads.'

Hassan Bhat was right. The Holy Hair (Moh-i-Muqaddas in Persian, but also called Moh-i-Mubarak in Kashmir), a strand of hair from the beard of Prophet Muhammad was indeed missing from the Hazratbal shrine, at Naseem Bagh, not far from Srinagar. The news spread like wildfire. People in large numbers came on to the roads, shouting slogans and beating their chests. Everyone was united in this calamity and there was great grief at this unusual and highly abhorrent and distasteful occurence. There were rumours aplenty, and all sorts of allegations were cast on the government agencies in general and politicians in particular.

Those who knew something about the relic, and those who knew nothing about it, were all swept by the collective outpouring of heartbreak and melancholy. This kind of thing had never ever occurred in the history of Kashmir. Not since the relic was acquired in 1699 in Bijapur by a wealthy Kashmiri merchant, called Khoja Nuruddin Ishbari, who gifted it to the Hazratbal shrine for the people of Kashmir.

People began to extol the many qualities of the relic to show that they had touched it, felt it, and experienced its grandeur.

'It's not an ordinary hair,' they'd say.

'It's a golden hair.'

'Yes, real gold.'

'It was guarded by snakes.'

'It's the *paigamber's* [the Prophet's] hair from his beard.'

'It is kept in a golden box that makes rounds with the sun and the moon constantly.'

'It's eternal, and doesn't perish or burn if put into fire.'

There was enormous faith that the people had in the holy relic, even though it had been brought into Kashmir a mere three hundred years ago. On three Fridays and on one additional special occasion, the custodians of the holy shrine of Hazratbal would bring the Holy Hair out of its safe box, and show it to those assembled beneath the pulpit. People in thousands, and from far-flung areas, would throng to have a glimpse of the relic of Prophet Muhammad. Looking at the relic was the next best thing after Hajj, and many Kashmiris considered it even as important as going to Mecca. So be it summer, autumn, winter or spring, crowds of people would go to Hazratbal for just one glimpse of the holy relic, which was brought out for *deedār* no more than four times a year.

As the day wore on, all communities—Muslims, Hindus, Sikhs, and Christians—in Kashmir joined their Muslim brothers and sisters in commiseration, and took part in the spontaneous processions that had been taken out across localities. It was truly an unplanned, yet combined outpouring of pain and despair at the loss. Without being concerned about one's caste, creed, colour, or religious affinity, everyone had come out to show solidarity with one another and demand an immediate retrieval of the Holy Hair.

The whole episode was indeed intriguing. People were asking simple, pertinent questions but had no answers. How could such a theft have happened? What benefit would the thief derive from the relic? Who was behind this shocking act? These questions were bothering people and answers were being demanded from the administration.

As the days went by, big processions of agitated people began to meander through localities and bazaars across the Valley. There was complete communal harmony and a beautiful solidarity.

The Hindus were chanting, 'Har-har-Mahadev! The culprit must be punished!'

The Sikhs in the same procession were saying, 'Jo bole so nihal, Sat Sri Akal! The thief should be caught immediately and brought to book!'

The Muslims were chanting, 'Allah-o-Akbar! La-illaha-ilallah, Muhammad Rasul Allah!'

In Kashmir nothing remains a secret for long. In no time the rumour mill was abuzz with the news that the theft was the act of the Bakshi brothers. Bakshi Ghulam Mohammad, who had been the prime minister of Kashmir till only a couple of months earlier, and his brothers were being stealthily blamed for the theft. Bakshi sahab was removed from his position under the Kamaraj Plan that was put into effect in the middle of 1963. The idea was to revitalize the Congress party, as also to take out long-serving chief ministers for party work. The prime minister of Jammu and Kashmir was one of the state heads recalled, as was Kamaraj himself (who was the chief minister of Madras state).

In Bakshi sahab's place, Khwaja Shams-ud-din Katta was made the chief minister of the state of Jammu and Kashmir. He was Bakshi's trusted confidant and many saw his appointment as a proxy for the continuation of the former prime minister's influence. Going by the hierarchy within the National Conference party, G.M. Sadiq—another key political associate of Bakshi sahab—was supposed to take charge as the chief minister of Jammu and Kashmir. But due to personal rivalries and squabbles in the party, and Bakshi's support, it was Shams-ud-din who was made the chief minister and that too out of turn. He was therefore seen as being just a rubber stamp in the hands of Bakshi.

Despite being the head of the Intelligence Bureau of the Government of India, Bhola Nath Mallik was rushed to Srinagar soon after the crisis erupted, and it took a while for him and his team to get to the root of the matter. A few days into the theft, as the holy relic was still not found, all the schools, colleges, and universities in the state were closed indefinitely. Business establishments and government offices too were closed. Roads were deserted in all the cities and towns of the Valley. There was only one cry from everybody—the holy relic had to be recovered come what may, and the thief brought to book.

Kashmiris were feeling rudderless, as if the pivot of their happy, productive lives had been taken away. People were concerned. Whom would they kneel before? Who was going to heed their woes? Who was going to hear their prayers? Who was going to heal their wounds and their heartaches? Everyone was desperate and lost. Simultaneously, there was tremendous anger of the people directed towards the establishment. The administration was charged with being ineffective and unable to apprehend the culprit.

The agitation lasted for days. The rumour mills in Kashmir were hyperactive as always. Everyone was apprehensive about the outcome. Many knew that there was politics and treachery and deceit at the heart of the theft, but nobody dared say anything. Since schools were closed, all the children were at their homes, with nothing much to do. Someone from the neighbourhood suggested that the children should make and hoist black flags on top of their homes to show the solidarity in grief. The children got enthused with this idea and in a jiffy there were small black flags fluttering on the rooftops of all the houses.

Late in the evening one day, almost a month after the loss of the holy relic had been discovered, there was such a commotion on the streets outside our home. It was evident that people were on the streets and there was an excited babble of voices. We could sense that some news regarding the theft had been received. More people from other localities were joining in.

This time the people were jubilant and ecstatic. They were shouting, 'It's been found! It's been found!'

'It was deliberately taken by the rascal,' someone from the crowd said out loud.

'He should be punished!' Another person from the crowd suggested.

'He should be hanged for this heinous crime.'

'The bastard!'

'We will lynch him alive! How dare he!' People's emotions were getting aroused.

'We won't rest till the culprit is booked and punished.'

While there was happiness that the relic had been found and it was safe, tempers were running high because nobody had been apprehended for the crime. Again, in a jiffy, big processions of people began to move through the bazaars of Srinagar. Now there were cries that the culprit be exposed and punished.

Meanwhile, another rumour surfaced soon after the Moh-i-Muqaddas was found. It was being said that the genuineness of the relic would have to be ascertained by some religious, pious persons.

'How can we be sure that this is indeed the Moh-i-Mubarak?' some people had begun to say.

Other people had doubts too.

'If someone can steal it, he could as well exchange it. What stops him?'

It was a very tricky situation for the Government of India, and Mallik, the head of the Intelligence Bureau of the Government of India, is believed to have called a meeting of all the police and civilian officials of the state administration in Srinagar just to ascertain how best to ensure that the relic was genuine. Meanwhile, tremendous apprehensions about this new problem had erupted. 'What will happen if its genuineness is jeopardized? What if some mischief-monger declares it fake?' Mallik enquired.

'Disgruntled politicians could play foul and arouse the tempers of the masses,' L.D. Thakur, the inspector general of police, said. 'There could be violence if the relic is found to be fake, right?'

Nobody responded to Mallik's question. Everyone knew that Kashmiris are known to be emotionally sensitive, especially when it comes to matters of faith.

While the government was trying to determine a credible and reliable way out of the mess, the processions continued unabated. People's lives were in a state of flux. Their minds were agitated and they wanted to know that 'all was well' with their beloved holy relic.

Finally, a day and a date were fixed for the assessment and verification of the holy relic. To declare its identity was a very sensitive matter. With utmost care many *maulanas* who were the opinion-makers had been identified. All other religious heads, respected senior citizens, and, above all, the mystic Mirakh Shah—who was revered by Hindus and Muslims alike—were also called to identify the relic and ascertain its authenticity. The prime minister of India, Pandit Nehru, had sent his deputy prime minister, Lal Bhadur Shastri. Shastriji had Nehru's trust and was known to be wise and firm.

On the appointed day, the whole city of Srinagar was kept under police surveillance just to avoid any untoward acts of mischief by miscreants.

I vividly remember that day, because we had a few plumbers repairing our home plumbing, and when they turned up much earlier for work, I struck a conversation with them.

'How come you're here so early. Is all well?'

'We haven't come to work here today. We're going to Hazratbal.'

'Yes, of course, I understand. This is an important day.'

'I want that you should give us some *baksheesh*?'

'Baksheesh?'

'You've misunderstood me. I mean you should pardon me and my friends.'

'Pardon you for what?' I was getting more and more puzzled with his talk.

'Today we're ready to die for our religion. If the holy relic isn't genuine, blood would flow like a river. Who knows who is going to live. That's why I am asking for your and Sahab's pardon.'

'All will be all right. Rest assured,' I told him, but deep within my heart sank.

Thousands of people had thronged outside the Hazratbal shrine. From women with babies, to children and adults, everyone seemed to be there. All ages were represented. The whole area was jam-packed with the crowd of people. Everybody was tense and apprehensive. No one knew the outcome of this exercise. Meanwhile, in the shrine the process was on. Everyone was sitting in a line on the carpeted floor of the large hall, according to their status in society. With the presence of the mystic Mirakh Shah, the whole atmosphere was spiritually charged. All present in the hall were in prayerful mood.

The holy relic was kept in a shiny golden tray, which was decorated with a green piece of velvet cloth, with elegant gold brocade. The person who was carrying the tray was doing so with utmost reverence and was carefully carrying it from one person in the line to the next.

Shastriji and others were also meditatively praying on the side as the process was on.

The relic was first shown to the saint Mirakh Shah, the only mystic present and hierarchically at the top of the spiritual journey. Mirakh Shah held up the Moh-i-Muqaddas, kissed it, and put it on his eyes. As he did this, he wept joyous tears of ecstatic reverence.

After him, everyone followed suit and by turns they touched the relic, kissed it, and put it to their eyes. All were overwhelmed by its genuineness. As soon as this was done, the news was carried forward to the people who were waiting for the momentous news. There was jubilation on the streets and people were dancing with happiness.

Although the culprit was never brought to book, the town was agog with the theory that the relic was taken to give deedār to Bakshi sahab's mother, who was on her deathbed. This may have been her last wish. This act could have been done in a normal, peaceful way, but since there was a political rivalry underlying the transfer of power in the state, the act of requesting the clerics to loan the relic apparently backfired, taking Kashmir through another dreary winter of discontent.

27

The Vicissitudes of Kashmiri Life

Life in the Valley of Kashmir has always been intertwined with moments and timelines of peace, interspersed with periods of disturbance, anxiety, and tumult. When the going is good, people almost *expect* some sort of upheaval or unrest to arise and afflict their minds and well-being.

The 1950s saw the era of Prime Minister Sheikh Abdullah coming to an abrupt end on 9 August 1953, and the start of the Bakshi Ghulam Mohammad era thereafter.

The late 1950s and early 1960s, however, saw relative peace in the Valley, and the people too were mentally relaxed. The Bombay film industry (now known as Bollywood) was also in overdrive, and hundreds of colour feature films were shot in the many beautiful, picturesque, and unseen locations in the Valley of Kashmir. That also gave a fillip to tourism, since many people were able to appreciate the stunning natural beauty of Kashmir and adjoining regions for the first time since Independence. A host of company events were also held in different parts of the state, with support and help from the administration of Bakshi.

There were also stories doing the rounds that Prithviraj Kapoor—one of the pioneering actors and producers of Hindi films—was always on the lookout for talented and beautiful Kashmiri girls whom he could cast in his forthcoming films. It is true that the senior Kapoor would be invited to plays and theatrical productions organized by colleges and the many fests that were organized by the state government as also by Radio Kashmir (as the Srinagar station of All India Radio was known). In fact the Jashn-i-Kashmir was an initiative of the state government that brought talented poets, playwrights, actors, *bhands* (traditional Kashmiri performers), and singers together for a theatrical and cultural show that lasted a few days, and was well attended by people from the city of Srinagar and the villages around it.

Bollywood scouts would reach out to the parents of some of the more accomplished men, women, and student artistes they discovered in Kashmir. But as far as I know, the image of Bollywood as a place for young women—in the minds of Kashmiri people—was not a very good one; and no woman from Kashmir ever ventured there, until the 1970s.

When Sonia Sahni was discovered by I.S. Johar in 1959 or so, it became the talk of the town for a while because Sonia then was a teacher at Burn Hall School (where my sons studied as well). Her rise to stardom soon after was quite a story!

As for schools, they too were busy giving their students exposure to a variety of sporting, outdoor, and cultural activities. The Tyndale Biscoe School, where my siblings studied, had an active programme of taking their boys camping and hiking in the mountains. My brother Surender was especially fond of treks and he continued doing them with his family even after he became a successful doctor. Many other children were involved with regattas in the Dal lake, and swimming across the lake and becoming 'Dal-cross Swimmers'.

There were also annual sporting events held in the Bakshi Stadium, and school plays and elaborate magic shows, which were held in the Tagore Hall, also built during the regime of Bakshi.

Interestingly, sometime in 1966 or so, even the Indian Air Force organized a special 'Aero Show' at Srinagar airport that was attended by a host of civilians. The children in the audience were full of excitement and many young boys and girls decided there and then that they'd become pilots!

The months of October and November 1962 caused considerable anxiety among the people of Jammu and Kashmir once again. In a month-long conflict, Chinese soldiers of the People's Liberation Army (PLA) attacked military posts in the Ladakh regions and along the North Eastern Frontier Agency region of India, and even crossed the disputed borders. This was done, as the Chinese Premier Zhou Enlai and others said later, to teach India a lesson for unilaterally 'altering' the borders as drawn by the McMahon Line. As I write this, the bloody 15 June 2020 skirmish in Ladakh continues to dominate the news. Even fifty-eight years later, China claims that India is 'unilaterally' altering the borders!

The war of 1962 caused consternation and anxiety across the state of Jammu and Kashmir, especially as it became evident that India was ill-prepared to deal with the aggression and that the Chinese were well entrenched in the upper reaches of the Ladakh, and Aksai Chin areas. Some say that Pandit Nehru was so lulled by his own desire for India and China to be like brothers (*Hindi–Chini bhai bhai* was the slogan that Pandit Nehru and Chinese leaders used a lot in those days) that he was taken for a royal ride by the shrewd and cunning Zhou Enlai.

As has been shared in the story of Moh-i-Muqaddas in an earlier chapter, during the bitter winter of December 1963, Kashmiris again experienced a month of turmoil. The holy relic—a strand of hair from the beard of Prophet Muhammad, called the Moh-i-Muqaddas or Moh-i-Mubarak by Kashmiris—was stolen along with the glass vial it was stored in, from the Hazratbal shrine near Naseem Bagh in Srinagar.

Fortunately, a month later the relic was found and though it was never revealed who the thief or thieves were, rumours at that time suggested that the former prime minister of Kashmir, Bakshi sahab, had probably requested the custodians of the Hazratbal shrine to lend it to him for a few hours, so that his ailing mother could have a deedār (a glimpse) of the holy relic. However, when the matter was reported to the senior cleric at the shrine, he chickened, and soon political forces swung into action, probably to discredit the longest-serving prime minister of the state. In fact, Bakshi had relinquished his post just a few months prior to the incident and Khwaja Shams-ud-din Katta was the chief minister of the state of Jammu and Kashmir (not prime minister, since that change was brought about after Bakshi). Which is why the matter was quickly hushed up after the relic was restored to the shrine.

There was another war with Pakistan in 1965. This war too started with the erroneous notion within the Pakistani Army and their planners that by sending in units of their Ghaznavi Force—a special operations group that would infiltrate into Jammu and Kashmir, dressed up as locals—they would be able to incite and motivate the Muslims of the Valley and the rest of the state to start a rebellion against India. However, neither in 1947 nor in 1965 did this strategy develop any traction. Instead, the people of Kashmir—as one—rejected the infiltrators' attempts at sabotage and instigation, and the force was quickly neutralized. As a result of this, and the many more small and big provocations by Pakistan—that had started soon after the snows along the mountain ridges in the West had melted—India retaliated strongly in July 1965. The Indian attack blunted the Pakistani operation (code-named Gibraltar) and by September that year the war was over.

The people of Kashmir were quite unnerved by this war though. Life had begun to settle into a happy groove of peace and development, and yet Pakistan was not letting them rest. The propaganda from across the border was relentless, but this was very effectively blunted by the extraordinary work done by Radio Kashmir. They had special programmes, such as the *Vādi-ki-avāz* for people in the Valley as well as across the border, which were extremely popular and had a great fan following even in Pakistan-occupied Kashmir! However, some Pakistani money kept flowing into the few obliging and accommodating quarters within the state—who had been identified for Operation Gibraltar—even after the war ended in India's favour. The result was that one would occasionally encounter poorly and hurriedly written graffiti on walls, especially on those of randomly chosen Hindu homes, which said, 'Indian Dogs Go Back', or 'Pakistan Zindabad'.

Yet another war with Pakistan in 1971 resulted in the creation of a new nation, Bangladesh, out of erstwhile East Pakistan. The human tragedy in that region, which had preceded the war, and which had resulted in millions of refugees pouring into India, was well reported in all the two main Urdu papers of the Valley, the daily *Srinagar Times* and the daily *Aftab*. Radio Kashmir also broadcast regular bulletins that demonstrated the growing clout of India in comparison to Pakistan. What had a major impact on the psyche of most people was that even the Seventh Fleet of the United States Navy—which had menacingly placed aircraft carriers and battleships in the Bay of Bengal at the behest of President Nixon—had no effect on India's strategy for the entire duration of the war.

Sheikh Abdullah signed an accord with Indira Gandhi in 1975, and returned—amidst much jubiliation—to serve as the chief minister of the state of Jammu and Kashmir. With this, the *shers* felt emboldened while the *bakras* felt let down. Overall however, until the demise of Sheikh Abdullah in 1982, there was relative peace in Jammu and Kashmir. After the Sheikh's demise, with Farooq Abdullah now at the helm of the state, the decline, amidst intense jockeying for power, started—creating a period of uncertainty and turmoil.

In February 1986, there was a serious attack on temples, Hindu homes, and the properties and businesses of Hindus and Sikhs in Anantnag. The unprovoked and unusual anti-Hindu violence spread rapidly towards Baramulla, as well as towards cities and hamlets in south Kashmir, and was reminiscent of the *kabalie* raids by Pakistani tribals in 1947. The difference this time was that the looting, the desecration of temples, and the burning of homes of KPs, Sikhs, and Hindus in the affected cities was done by Kashmiris, instigated, funded, and supported by people inimical to the state and to India.

Within the Rishi Vihar families, life moved on. I lost my uncle, Baiji, in 1969 while I was in Germany. His younger brother, Ṭāṭhāji, had passed on a few years earlier after a long illness. My father, Bubji, left his body in October 1970. My youngest brother, Ranaji, who was still unmarried at the time of our father's passing, got married in the mid-1970s. Life moved on. Children were born, even as the older generation gave way to the new. My generation of siblings and cousins were all in the midst of their respective professional journeys—some in Kashmir, but many others in different parts of India and the globe.

At this time Rishi Vihar continued to reflect some of its old grandeur, although many things had changed over the years. With the passing of Māl in the latter part of the 1950s her adult children decided to have separate kitchens and independent living spaces within the same overall premises. So while the family would interact and live as before, each brother's family was now in an independent home of their own. The common lawns and the gazebo were the places where all—including neighbours—would meet and share stories and jokes and family gossip, just like in the earlier days.

28

The Kashmiri Pandit Agitation

For centuries the Pandits of Kashmir have placed considerable attention and emphasis on being educated, skilled with languages, and in a position to be useful to society. As has been mentioned elsewhere in this book, when the Hindu samaj that the Pandits depended upon for their sustenance and to whom they would provide spiritual and ritualistic guidance were converted to Islam, from the thirteenth century onwards, the economic condition of the community became dire. That's when the community decided that in a family, the elder brother would continue to pursue the traditional vocations of puja and Vedic studies, and become a guru (*gor*) while the younger brothers would acquire the skills needed to be useful in governance and administration, and would be called karkuns.

This division eased the economic standing of the community as a whole, but created a sad division as well. Since the guru-brothers were not as well-off economically as their karkun brothers (because the karkuns were the ones supporting them), they began to be treated with disdain and in a short span of a few hundred years, the daughters of karkuns were not married to the sons of gors!

The ethos within the community, to this day, has therefore been to focus on the acquisition of knowledge and skills that would make them useful. Even in difficult times Kashmiri Pandits would do anything to get educated. No matter how arduous the process, they would not leave the task of learning skills halfway. In the community, educated persons were respected and revered. People used to emulate them and learned people served as role models.

Whoever ruled the Valley, Pandits would always be ready to serve that administration, doing whatever jobs were needed, and for which they had the requisite skills and capabilities. From simple jobs to high-ranking positions, they filled roles across the board. Due to their education, skills, and their work ethic, their services were always needed. The Pandits received benefits in return. Lands, known as *jagirs*, were gifted to accomplished Pandits for them to use to feed themselves and their families. As the Pandits were in jobs that required their full attention, they would offer the land to sharecroppers who were mostly Muslim peasants, and give them rights to till the lands on their behalf.

With the passage of time, the Pandits also acquired proficiency in the changing court languages. First the court language was Sanskrit, and Pandits were adept in this language. Their proficiency in the language enabled them to contribute to producing some of the most beautiful Sanskrit works in India—from Kalhana's Pandit's *Rajatarangini* to the writings of Kshemendra and Sudraka to the spiritual treatises of Abhinavagupta.

As the rulers changed, so did the court language. To stay relevant, it was necessary to learn the alien language and to master it. After Sanskrit, Afghani Pashto, then Persian, Urdu, and English became the languages of governance and administration. The skills and capabilities of the Kashmiri Pandits made them (the Pandits), in the words of one of the viceroys of India, 'the greatest export of Kashmir'.

Within the Valley, the Pandits managed to eke out a living with some members in paying jobs and with rice coming in from the small parcels of lands that they might have had, if they were fortunate. However, from the 1930s onwards, as Sheikh Abdullah was leading his political movement aimed at bettering the lot of poor Kashmiris, he also directed his attention to the exploitative nature of the manner in which *asaamis* (landowners in Kashmir) were using sharecroppers and tenant tillers to pay the state revenue on farm produce. Maharaja Hari Singh, in fact, had a commission led by an Englishman, B.J. Glancy, look into the matter, and a recommendation was put up to the Maharaja for the tenants to be made owners of those government lands that they were tilling with the permission of His Highness's administration.

With Independence, the aspirations of the people of Jammu, Kashmir, and Ladakh began to rise. All of a sudden everyone became aware of their rights. People were eager to better their lot and to get good paying jobs became an avenue to further their desires.

Post-Independence, the administration of Sheikh Abdullah was conscious of the fact that despite his efforts with the Maharaja's administration, the sharecroppers who were tilling lands that didn't belong to them still needed to better their lot. To effect a change in their conditions, the state government, in 1950, passed the Big Landed Estates Abolition Act. This Act provided land to the tillers without the payment of any compensation to the erstwhile owners, and ended the rights over the lands of those who had never cultivated them.

The Kashmiri Pandits and Dogras were obviously affected by the Land Act. Lands that they had received in lieu of their services from grateful administrations that had been served well were given to the tillers, but with no compensation to the original owners. Yet, apart from seeking a greater share of the jobs in the state government, the affected Kashmiri Pandits went along with the Land Act of 1950, hoping that it would genuinely improve the lot of the tillers.

The educated Muslims also demanded a greater share of jobs in the state government. They indicated that since they were numerically larger in the state's population, they should get a greater share than before. The Pandits, already smarting under the adverse economic impact of the Land Act, were also feeling the pressure on jobs, with many more Muslims joining government jobs in Jammu and Kashmir. In fact, the government actually made it a rule to reserve a large chunk of jobs for the socially, educationally, and economically backward sections of the state. The Pandits were given a nominal reservation of 10 per cent of government jobs at that time. Simultaneously, the representation of KPs, Sikhs, and Hindus in the Valley, in the state legislature, also began to decline. As KPs started to go outside the state for better prospects the numbers left behind were fewer, and not sufficiently large a group to be able to elect their own representatives. Elected lawmakers had many different priorities, and scant attention was therefore paid to the needs and grievances of the Pandits, Sikhs, and Hindus in the Valley.

Even the admission to professional institutes, colleges, and universities was affected. In the race for admissions, and with limited seats offered each year, Pandit boys and girls even with very high marks and ranks in the examinations and entrance tests could not get admission due to their small proportion in the state's population. In government organizations, a gradual but discernible bias was depriving Pandits and Hindus of promotions and appointments to senior positions.

These trends caused serious anguish in the KP community. By the mid-1960s, Kashmiri Pandits felt that they were being treated as second-class citizens in independent India, even though the state of Jammu and Kashmir was an integral part of it. The refrain was that it was of no use to work hard and be meritorious and top one's class because it yielded no opportunities for work or further education within the state.

The value and the honour that Kashmiri Pandits had assigned to erudition was fast eroding. Cynicism was taking root and many young men and women left the state in disgust.

With this mass feeling of injustice towards the entire community on the rise, Kashmiri Pandits nurtured a festering wound within themselves. As more evidence of discrimination and indignities—right from the time of the Land Act and all the way to the time of the war with Pakistan in 1965—was forthcoming, Kashmiri Pandits were experiencing extreme frustration.

The Pandits of Kashmir were well aware of their tragic history and of the trauma emerging from the brutalities and indignities suffered by all the people of Kashmir. As a community, they did not wish to have to experience any such tragic events again and would do whatever they could to resist being pushed to the wall.

As the anguish in the minds of the Kashmiri Pandits grew, a particularly gruesome incident dating to the early part of the thirteenth century was recounted, and people were reminding one another that something would have to be done to prevent the annihilation of the community. Deep generational trauma that was etched in the Kashmiri psyche, but was hidden and dormant, suddenly began to raise its frightening head, adding to the sense of fear and fuelling further frustration.

The incident that people would refer to was the one where Zulju—a Turkic-Mongol invader—and his armed horsemen attacked major towns and villages along the river Jhelum one evening. He chose sundown for his attack because as dusk descended on the Valley, thousands and thousands of men, women, and children, from Khanabal to Baramulla, were happily celebrating the 'birthday' of the river Vitastā (also known as the Vethvothur river in those times, and now called Jhelum river). As people from all strata of the Hindu samaj were lighting little lamps and floating them into the divine river on either side of the river's banks, the horsemen emerged and attacked the helpless and unarmed people, killing thousands and prompting many more thousands of women and children to jump into the river and get drowned. Men, women, and children could be heard screaming and running to save their lives, as the attackers used their swords and axes to decollate the hapless people.

Thousands perished. Family members got separated and no one knew who was alive or dead. In a matter of hours, dead bodies were seen floating downstream of the Jhelum river. The water became red and then black with the blood of those slain. Whoever was alive didn't dare to look for their loved ones, or recover their bodies, lest the attackers find them and execute them all. The whole land was terrorized.

In a matter of days after the brutal attack by Zulju and his marauding troops, the waters of the Vitastā downstream turned into a macabre red and black from the blood of those slain. Hundreds of lifeless bloated bodies, along with sooty lamps floated downstream, creating a sense of horror and intense fear in the minds of people downstream. The Lohara king of Kashmir at that time, an ineffective Raja called Suhadeva, simply fled the moment he got wind of the attack by Zulju, leaving the kingdom in utter despair and turmoil.

Such savage attacks on Kashmir by Zulju, and then by other zealots and kings, such as Renchen and those who followed him, changed the religious affiliation of the people of Kashmir to Islam. The simple people of the Valley followed the faith that gave them an assurance of security and which even the rajas began patronizing. All these developments, over a span of a few centuries, reduced Kashmiri Pandits to a powerless group, deprived of the many sources of economic and political authority that they had been enjoying for centuries. The treacherous history also affected the mode of thinking of all Kashmiris—Kashmiri Pandits as well as other denizens of the Valley. The emphasis was on survival and on defending oneself. Ensuring one's survival became an animal-like instinct. The generational trauma and the deep-seated emotional scarring from brutal events from the past have ensured that the devious traits of Kashmiris—Pandits and Muslims alike—can be found in almost all of them, to this day.

Such thoughts and concerns, reinforced by memories of past distress, were once again emerging in the collective mind of the community in 1967. It was clear that this time, however, the Kashmiri Pandits were determined to stand up for their rights, and put up a fight if need be.

The pent-up frustration of the Kashmiri Pandits that was simmering for long exploded as a collective reaction when a KP girl, Parameshwari Handoo, first converted to Islam, and then eloped with a Muslim boy to get married. Remember, this was 1967 and the term 'love jihad' was a term that had not been coined and nobody had ever heard about it. But something about the manner in which the girl ran away with the Muslim boy, and got married to him, opened the floodgates of KP anger. The KP community in the Kashmir Valley felt deeply anguished, agitated, and angry at the insensitive provocation by the Muslim community. They felt that the government agencies too were playing foul, and were wilfully shielding the man's claim.

The girl's parents insisted that the girl was a minor and was not yet able to take critical decisions, either about her marriage or her future, on her own. Their argument was that since the girl was a minor, she could only have been kidnapped. The girl's 'abductors' pushed back, and asserted that the young girl had willingly chosen to elope with the man. There were several rounds of deliberations at police stations, where the girl was questioned in the presence of her parents and other members of the community. The police finally established that the girl was indeed an adult and was therefore free to choose whom she married.

This whole episode turned into an ugly agitation. Men, women, young boys and girls, and children of the Pandit community assembled in the historic grounds of the Sheetal Nath temple. Tempers were quite high. Thousands of Kashmiri Pandits assembled in the audience were visibly angry, and they were shouting slogans, decrying the government for its blatant inaction in the matter. Ghulam Mohammad Sadiq, who was the chief minister of the state at that time, was stridently denounced. A KP leader, Durga Prasad Dhar, called D.P. Dhar by those who knew him and who was a part of Sadiq's cabinet of ministers, along with a few other ministers of national repute were abused. The restive crowd was addressed by a number of community leaders and members of the political party, the Jana Sangh. The polarization of the communities and a hardening of their respective positions were in evidence. Many hundreds of young Kashmiri Pandit men boycotted work and protested in the city centre. The police would round up these young men and take them to jail.

The agitation even spilled over to some parts of Jammu. Some Muslim girls were married off to Hindu men there, creating a backlash in the Valley. The chief minister, Sadiq, suggested that the trouble was the handiwork of mischievious elements that were bent upon starting communal riots in Jammu and Kashmir. There may have been some truth in this because even then Pakistan was using whatever levers it could, to create unrest and turmoil in the Valley and other regions of the state.

The agitation lasted for nearly three months. Amidst this, select government emissaries from New Delhi parked themselves in Srinagar to initiate a dialogue between those aggrieved and the state government. A dialogue was started. Both the sides began to dwell on all matters, including the grievances that had piled up during these past years. However, the rallying event for the agitation, namely a minor girl's abduction, was soon forgotten. More issues were added to the list of demands by the community members. There were some agreements, and in September 1967 about 4000 KP men who had been jailed were released.

But, through willful and inadvertent governmental prevarication, the agitation fizzled out.

29

Radicalization and Ethnic Cleansing

In the spring of 1979, Pakistan's Prime Minister Zulfiqar Ali Bhutto, who had been the president of his country when Bangladesh was carved out of its eastern part, was hanged. The charges against him were partly real and partly trumped up at the behest of the then President, General Zia ul Haq. Zia declared himself as the president of Pakistan in 1978, and fast-tracked the controversial trial of Bhutto. Simultaneously, Zia, who was used by the US to blunt the Russian occupation of Afghanistan, stepped up the Islamization of Pakistan even as he curbed civil liberties and curtailed the rights of women and minorities.

The hanging of Bhutto created tremendous anger in the Kashmir Valley towards the military régime of that country. People came out openly to lash out at Pakistan and its president, General Zia ul Haq. Kashmiris felt that he was a cruel and inhuman fellow, considering that he got the prime minister of a country executed so brutally and brazenly.

The people of Kashmir thereby lost faith in the Islamic military regime of Pakistan totally, and abused Zia publicly with considerable anger and contempt. People in large numbers came out in protest. Huge processions were taken out to show solidarity with the people of Pakistan, especially those who were not with the military ruler. For once in the Valley of Kashmir the people thought that their decision to merge with India was a wise step taken by the leaders at the time of independence.

Many bizarre events came to be witnessed on the streets of Srinagar. Placards with foul words of abuse for Zia were hung on the necks of street dogs to show people's feelings of hurt and anger towards the despicable and loathsome military rulers of Pakistan. There was deep-rooted hurt and anguish in the hearts of the people. The image in their minds of the Islamic Republic of Pakistan was shattered beyond repair.

Since Zia relied heavily on the Muslim clergy and used them to bring about the Islamization of Pakistan, the people of Kashmir began to associate local members of the Jamaat-e-Islami (all of whom were predominantly bakras) with whatever they found wrong and inappropriate with what was happening in Pakistan.

The result was tragic. Some especially angry people took the law into their own hands and maltreated and hurt those people who were known members of the Jamaat. The houses of many were burned down, others were forced to have their heads and beards shaved off, and many others were beaten up. It is said that those party members of the Jamaat who were wronged took an oath to destroy the fabric of brotherhood, harmony, and coexistence that Kashmiri communities had experienced for hundreds of years. They pledged to grab power and rule the state according to their own whims and fancies.

Around this period, Ayatollah Khomeini's rise and the fall of Shah Reza Pahlavi of Iran was also watched with interest in the Valley of

Kashmir. Due to Khomeini's orthodox ways and his insistence on a return to the conservative dress code and hijab for the women of that country, many felt that a shunning of 'Western' values was a way out of all the problems that Muslim societies were facing globally. The new leaders in Pakistan and in Iran were forcing a return to the illiberal ways of orthodox Islam, and this seems to have resonated with some of the conservative imams and mullahs in the Valley of Kashmir as well. Taking a cue from Iran (which predominantly has people following the Shia faith of Islam), some Shia imams and elders in the Valley also issued fatwas to their womenfolk to observe the Iranian dress code for women. As a result of this desire within Srinagar city and neighbouring towns to be identified with the 'trends' in Iran and Pakistan, all of a sudden there were hundreds of women and girls wearing headscarves while going to their schools and moving about with their friends.

These developments also coincided with a very large influx of money from the mid-1970s onwards from charities in Saudi Arabia. The administration of Sheikh Mohammad Abdullah, who had signed an accord with Indira Gandhi in 1975 and had thereafter assumed the position of chief minister of the state of Jammu and Kashmir, was liberal in allowing funds from Islamic organizations being brought into the Valley. The quantum of funds also saw a major uptick from 1973 onwards when oil prices (as determined by the OPEC) moved up from a low $1.8–2.8 per barrel to a whopping $11 per barrel that year! This increase yielded enormous amounts of surplus funds within the Saudi regime, and a large part of the monies were systematically moved—as a means to also keep the Muslim Brotherhood within Saudi Arabia happy—to regions with sizeable Muslim populations.

Much of the funds from Saudi Arabia came in for 'religious' purposes and resulted in the wanton construction of new mosques in the Valley, and the expansion and renovation of existing ones. Madrassas too sprang up, and young children from poor rural families especially were taken into these well-funded 'Islamic schools' for learning and propagation of the Quran. Many more Islamic institutions also sprang up all over the Valley. Orphanages received funds, Islamic literature was published in large numbers and distributed freely and widely, by proselytizers of the *tabhliqi jamaat*. New printing presses were set up to publish pamphlets, papers, and magazines covering Islamic themes.

Slowly and gradually, Kashmiri Islam, which was a tolerant, mystical, and love-based version of the religion that had evolved in its own beautiful way in Kashmir and which was an amalgam of the Islamic ideas brought in from Iran, Arabia, and Central Asia, was changing into a new and hardened Sharia-dependent doctrine that left no scope for the liberal, free-thinking ideas of Kashmiris.

The radicalization of the people in the Valley was thereby under way, with the Wahabi/Salafi brand of conservative Islam being pushed into Kashmiri Muslim societies and communities, supported and bankrolled by the streams of foreign funds coming in. Mullahs and preachers, now with significant funds at their command, were doing all that they could to have the simple people of Kashmir fall in line with their imported ideas of Islam. There were many questioning the traditional Kashmiri mentality of visiting the graves or *asthans* of mystics, sufisaints, and spiritual men and women. This was not the 'real' Islam, these propagators of the conservative version kept emphasizing. There was peer pressure used, as well as intimidation and violence to make people acquiesce.

All this was a completely new phenomenon for the people of modern-day Kashmir. Young people, who were now 'warriors of Islam' and were forcing people to be compliant with the strict rules of the conservative dogma, were attracted towards this new forceful ideology because it gave them 'power' over others, and if anybody resisted them that person was an apostate and therefore worthy of being bullied, beaten, and intimidated.

The geopolitical developments in the Middle East, and the local pressures of mullahs and young 'warriors' of the faith, brought about a spurt of Islamization in the Valley. In the first place, it was in evidence in certain sections of Muslims and localities, such as the Shias. Later on due to other factors, including the desire of preachers to demonstrate their clout and influence, the tentacles of the Wahabi version of the faith spread all over the Valley. By mid-1985, the radicalization was significant.

By the early 1980s, as Saddam Hussein too was emerging as Iraq's brutal strongman, it was apparent that he would continue to hound the Shias and Kurds of Iraq, despite their substantially large numbers within the population. The poor treatment of Ayatollah Khomeini while in exile in Iraq (before he was sent to France in 1975) also rankled the Shias of the world, and hence when the mullahs took over power in Iran, hostilities between the Shias of Iran and the Sunni leader of Iraq (Saddam) soon resulted in a terrible war between the two nations.

Whether it was Saddam's 'strongman' image or his hostility against Israel, the West, and Shias in general, something about him resonated with a section of the Sunnis of Kashmir. His photos began to be hung in busy marketplaces, especially in the semi-rural towns of the Valley. Shia areas began to hang portraits of Ayatollah Khomeini and other clerics of the Shia faith of Iran. In Saddam Hussein and Ayatollah Khomeini, people found new heroes to emulate, especially those who were tough and firm and who could take on bigger nations such as the USA and the UK.

All these developments and a lack of an effective, credible, and a truly secular and non-communal leadership in the state of Jammu and Kashmir took the Valley down the path of terrible violence from the autumn of 1989. The Valley was engulfed in a hurricane of hatred, mayhem, looting, killings, arson, and the selective abduction and killing of Kashmiri Pandits and of Muslims who were seen to be working against the communal agenda of the radicalized forces. In December 1989, Rubaya Sayeed—the daughter of India's first

Kashmiri home minister (and first Muslim, since Independence), Mufti Mohammad Sayeed—was kidnapped by armed mercenaries demanding the exchange of a number of imprisoned armed terrorists locked up in the jails of Jammu and Kashmir. This opportunity was leveraged to bring about the swift release of five incarcerated militants. With the capitulation by the Central government it was felt that even a powerful nation such as India could be brought to her knees. There were bomb blasts, fires, and killings all over. Newspapers carried sinister advertisements and notices asking Hindus to leave Kashmir or face a volley of bullets and be killed. The loudspeakers on mosques were used to blare out hate-songs and warnings to Hindus, Sikhs, and others opposed to violence that they should leave the Valley, or be killed. The hate-filled propaganda from loudspeakers emphatically warned that KP women were to be left behind, if the men-folk fled. The collective fear in the minds of the KP community as well as others who feared the madness unleashed by the armed terrorists was so intense that on the night of 19 January 1990, thousands and thousands of KP families just locked their homes and fled to Jammu and other parts of the country.

In the run-up to this terrible exodus of the KP community, many prominent Kashmiri Pandits—men and women—were murdered brutally in broad daylight. Unarmed paramilitary personnel and air force officers were slain in a shower of gunfire. Armed militants were openly roaming in the lanes and the interior parts of the city of Srinagar, brandishing their Pakistan-issued, Chinese-made AK-47 rifles. Shankaracharya Hill was dotted with the flags of all sorts of communal, separatist groups. Every nook and cranny was infested with armed groups showing off their weapons and intimidating people with their bombast and bravado. They would of course kill as well, but with a bizarre logic that nobody could comprehend.

The common, poor Kashmiris were told that the armed mercenaries were *mujahideen*—fighters of a holy war, in the same frame as the brave fighters who got rid of the Russians from Afghanistan. The gullible Kashmiris actually thought that these armed fighters would bring prosperity for the poor, under some imagined Islamic regime. Kashmiri Pandits and the leaders of mainstream political parties became the first targets of these terrorists.

Tikka Lal Taplu, a Kashmiri Pandit leader, Justice Neelkanth Ganjoo, and a National Conference leader, Mohammad Yusuf Halwai who was pro-India, were among the first few targets. Neelkanth Ganjoo, as a sessions judge in the late 1960s, had presided over the trial of Maqbool Bhat—the founder of a secessionist outfit called the Jammu Kashmir Liberation Front (JKLF)—for the murder of Police Inspector Amar Chand, and had sentenced Bhat to prison. Mohammad Yusuf Halwai had dared to leave the lights of his house on despite a call by the armed terrorists to maintain full 'darkness' on India's Independence Day on 15 August 1989. Simultaneously, handbills and advertisements started to appear in newspapers and as messages pasted on the walls of KP homes—'Join us, get killed, or run for your lives' the threatening messages said. Papers began to justify the violence, suggesting that those who were killed were 'informers' or 'agents' of India. As darkness set in, mosques would play 'jihadi' music and lyrics, the kind that incited further violence, and which eventually resulted in lakhs of KP families fleeing the Valley with next to nothing of their possessions.

People were terrorized and scared to death. But they couldn't say anything against the armed mercenaries because of the fear of the gun. Those who dared to criticize what was happening were branded as traitors or 'informers' of Indian agents, and were murdered in cold blood. Hordes of men and women—of all faiths—were killed in this fashion. The Pandits were specifically targeted as well, and wilfully frightened out of their wits. It was like when one from among a group of crows that are all perched on a wire in a row is hit with a stone, and falls down dead, all the others fly away to safety. This is what happened to the entire community of Pandits. As people were targeted in their neighbourhoods, and simple, innocent persons were killed brutally, it resulted in Kashmiri Pandits leaving their homes and hearths en masse. They went to unknown places, clueless about the conditions, and not knowing how to cope with the harsh, hot weather of those climes. It was for the first time that Kashmiri Pandits, Sikhs, and many Muslim families as well, encountered the harsh life in the plains. They left Kashmir for safety, but in the alien places that they took refuge in, they succumbed to heatstroke, scorpion bites, and snakebites. But those who survived the tragic onslaught of armed mercenaries had to work terribly hard to earn two meals a day. With festering wounds in their chests and unimaginable pain, hurt, disgust, anger, helplessness, and hatred towards those who had compelled them to leave their homes and hearths, they carried on with their tragic lives. Hundreds of families couldn't bear the heat of the plains and left India for good, seeking refuge and help in foreign lands.

30

Armed Violence and Abductions

In the winter of 1992, the demolition of the Babri structure was used by those involved in the radicalization of Kashmiri Muslims to demonstrate that living in India would always be dangerous for Muslims. They went about vehemently preaching that there was no guarantee that Muslims would be allowed to practise their religion freely in India. This kind of propaganda was also actively fuelled by Pakistan's ISI (Inter-Services Intelligence), which by now had already spent many years arming, training, and sending in mercenaries to kill Hindus as well as pro-Indian Muslims in Kashmir, and generally disrupt life and institutions in Jammu and Kashmir. Rumours loaded with venom and hatred and the kind that fomented mistrust between the communities were injected through willing preachers, and young, and by now armed, 'warriors' into the psyche of Kashmiris. There was a conscious movement to resort to lies and half-truths in creating a narrative that would make it seem as if Islam was in danger in India. The pre-Independence agenda of the Muslim League was once again being resurrected with ample support from Pakistan, and funds from overseas Islamic charities. The resultant fear in the hearts of Kashmiris caused unrest and anguish in many quarters. Stone pelting was an easy way to show anger towards the authorities. Those leaders who were in mainstream politics also were considered as their enemies.

As if the killings and the terrorization of innocents were not tragic enough, those families that stayed put in the Valley were not spared. Kidnapping, extortion of money, and abduction of young boys for forcible recruitment into the ranks and file of terrorist gangs became the order of the day. Many Muslim families, concerned about the lives of their young sons and daughters, had to leave the Valley for their own safety and security. So many girls were kidnapped, while many—in a fit of Islamic fervour—eloped with gun-toting militants. Many a pregnant woman was left behind with no help or economic support as the terrorists they had eloped with were either shot dead by security forces or liquidated in intra-militant gang wars. So many orphans too, were left behind.

My husband, Omkar, and I were abducted by armed militants of the Hizbullah group in September 1991. Our travails during the forty-five days that we were in captivity have already been recorded in our book, *Kidnapped*, which was published a few months after we were rescued from the clutches of our captors by the Indian Army. Even as we were coming to terms with these developments, and the unspeakable tragedy that had befallen Kashmiris, my brother, Doctor Surender Dhar, was also abducted a few months later from the Chest Diseases Hospital, where he worked. The Kashmiri Pandits who'd stayed behind in the Valley were obviously soft targets and the mercenaries made full use of access to them to terrorize people further.

Much like my husband and I, even Surender was taken by his abductors from one place to another to avoid detection by the police and the armed forces. The militants knew that he was a doctor, so wherever they took him he was asked to treat patients. Surender, who was compassionate and a caring doctor, would do so readily. Besides, he was a renowned physician and his patients came from far-flung areas. Therefore, news of his presence with armed terrorists spread like a fire, even in those remote areas where his captors had taken him.

One day he was asked to treat a patient who was almost dead due to a severe fall in a nearby gorge. Somehow, with Surender's treatment and medications, the man survived. It turned out that the injured man was a local leader of a terrorist gang, who had jumped into the gorge to save himself from his armed rivals from another group. The fact that the man was healed resulted in further respect for the doctor. As a token of their gratitude and by way of a reward for his deed, Surender was gifted an old, albeit working, transistor radio. Surender was happy to have it because now he could tune in to news from the outside.

One evening, as Surender was listening to the news, there was mention of the number of schools that had been torched and gutted by militants in Srinagar city over the past few days. One of the schools mentioned was Rupa Devi Sharda Peeth (see Chapter 23). When Surender heard this news, his heart sank, and tears of sadness rolled down his eyes. He was crying, and thinking of his dear wife, Vimla (Billieji), in whose Mother's name the school had been established and who now played an active role in its management. Surender's anguish was heightened since he was still a captive; and Billieji was all by herself.

The more Surender thought about his wife's well-being, the more anxious he grew. Seeing him crying, one of the militants came forward and asked: 'Why are you crying, doctor sahab? Has anyone said something insulting to you?'

'No, no one has said anything to me,' he replied. Then turning to the open window and looking out into the darkness, he added, 'I'm crying because our land has lost its soul.'

Epilogue
Another August Date with Destiny

The month of August has always been a harbinger of change for Jammu and Kashmir. India and Pakistan, of course were formed in August 1947, impacting Jammu and Kashmir significantly. Sheikh Mohammad Abdullah, once honoured with the sobriquet 'The lion of Kashmir', was imprisoned on 9 August 1953. The initial skirmishes that led to the 1965 war with Pakistan also started in the month of August.

Who knew that August 2019 too would bring about an unprecedented change in the very structure of the state of Jammu and Kashmir! Unimaginable events took place, in a matter of days, and in a manner that took everyone by complete surprise.

The months of June and July 2019 were relatively peaceful in the Valley despite the tragic suicide attack by a local terrorist on a security convoy in the Pulwama area just a few months earlier. The calm and the excessive and oppressive heat of the plains brought in a large number of toursits, and hoteliers and houseboat owners were beginning to view the summer season as a positive one, after a long spell of sluggish and sporadic tourist inflows. The Amarnath *yatra* too was going on smoothly. One could feel that the shadow of terrorism was lifting steadily. The famous Dal lake was buzzing with happy and excited tourists traversing the placid lake in *shikaras*. The people in Srinagar were once again feeling relaxed, and were looking forward to having a productive and peaceful summer season after decades.

All of a sudden, however, in the last days of July, the government of the state (with the governor in charge) issued an order, which was promptly announced on radio and television, that the pilgrims, the *yatris* headed to Amarnath, were to leave the Valley as soon as possible. At the same time a very big contingent of the army too was brought into Kashmir. The troop movement was also announced on the news bulletins of AIR (All India Radio). Hoteliers were directed to vacate all tourists from their properties with immediate effect.

There was another government order suggesting that people should store food and essential items for at least three months. Even as these developments were taking place, the government simultaneously kept announcing that there was no dearth of food items, gas, and other essential commodities in the Valley. Furthermore, the government emphasized that it had made all the necessary arrangements for the upcoming Eid festival, which was just round the corner and was scheduled to be celebrated on 6 August.

The Eid celebration this time (Bakr Eid) involved the sacrificing of sheep and goats. Which is why even as people were wondering what the government (especially the Central government in New Delhi) was planning, one would witness hordes of sheep and goats being taken to the *mandis* for selling in the run-up to the Eid celebrations.

Most people took the announcements from the government as indicative of a possible war with Pakistan. Since the Kashmiri brain is fertile and loves exaggeration and embellishment, word also went around that maybe a world war was about to commence! People derived tremendous pleasure out of such gossip. This time, however, behind the hyperbole, there was also a tinge of fear arising from the lack of information about what was *really* going on. Some mischief-mongers floated a dreadful rumour that there would be bombardment by the Indian Army to annihilate all the Muslims of the Valley! People were genuinely scared, and the last few days of July had people bewildered and worried.

Many had the apprehension that even if Pakistan initiated a war, and there was indeed aerial bombardment, it would still be the Muslims who would be killed. So, the people of the Valley actually began to see themselves as losers in the geopolitical game between India and Pakistan.

On August 3, as I was working on something in my sitting room, two persons entered unannounced. I could see that they were trembling with fear. I too got alarmed upon seeing them.

'What has happened?' I asked, recognizing them as acquaintances from my neighbourhood. 'Why are you both trembling like leaves in the wind?'

One of the persons showed me a picture on his mobile phone with trembling hands.

'Madam, please see this,' he said, thrusting the screen of the smartphone towards me.

'What is this?' I asked, as I took the phone from him.

'Yasin Malik has been beheaded. See, this picture that I've just received shows his head and body separated.'

The other man piped in. 'Who could have done this dastardly act?'

'The Indian Army, of course. Not only this, four more people have been killed,' the first man responded.

As they were speaking, I noticed that their faces were ashen, and they were truly afraid.

For a moment I was struck by how real the picture looked on the screen. I knew from my sons that deep fakes were a big part of the Pakistani propaganda industry, and I knew deep down that this just could not be true.

'This photo is all fake,' I said boldly, albeit not really sure. 'All that you've heard is nothing but rumours. If anyone from the security forces intended to kill him, why would they have been treating his medical condition over all these past years? These are all rumours. You should never believe these things.'

I was very sad that vicious rumours that could incite the emotionally charged Kashmiris were being spread and *believed* by people living not far from where I stay.

The same day, some more of my neighbours came to meet me. They wanted to know more about the goings-on and were endeavouring to find out what was really under way. They too were frightened, not knowing what might befall next. On the government's side there was absolute secrecy and very little information was emerging, apart from the fact that essential supplies were available. On the night of 3 August, however, Governor Satyapal Malik addressed the people on radio and television simultaneously and reassured the people to stay calm and peaceful. In his broadcast he even reiterated that Article 370 would not be lifted at all. So people presumed that war was the reason for all the preparations.

The next morning, people were quite busy with purchases for Eid. As the government had been announcing over the past few days, all the items needed for the celebrations were indeed available in abundance. Sheep, chicken, eggs, vegetables, sweets and confectionery, the latest clothing, and whatever else might have been desired, was all there to be bought. All were thronging the markets to purchase as much as was possible. Irrespective of their religious affinity, Kashmiris love good food, good clothes, and whatever else gives them pleasure.

So, war or no war, they didn't want to spoil the Eid festival in any way at all.

The next morning, on 5 August, everyone in Kashmir was glued to their televisions in anticipation of an announcement of the war. TV channels were also speculating and flinging jingoistic rhetoric and bombast, raising concerns in the hearts of Kashmiris.

Yet, it was in Parliament in New Delhi where a 'big bang' occurred! The much-talked-about and temporary, Article 370 of the Indian Constitution was abrogated and made null and void, even as the state of Jammu and Kashmir—comprising the regions of Jammu, the Valley of Kashmir, and the Himalayan districts of Ladakh—was bifurcated into two union territories. Jammu and Kashmir became one, and Ladakh the other union territory. This meant that the administration of the regions would now be directly under the Centre.

Interestingly, the first flush of reactions from the common folk of the Valley was not negative at all. They had no clue how the Article was benefiting them! Although curfew was imposed soon after the deliberations in Parliament, the government had given the permission for Eid prayers to be performed in the local mosques only. People went about peacefully and returned quickly to perform the ritual sacrifice of sheep and goats. This ritual goes on for two and a half days after the Eid day. The sacrificial meat was distributed amongst the relatives of the people without any hassle, because even private transporters were allowed to ply their buses from day one. Overall, therefore, there was a neutral response. Besides, since Eid had come right then, everyone was eager to have a good time.

After the happy celebrations of Eid got over, the rumour-mongers got overactive. They began to spread rumours that people from other states of India would now come to snatch the lands from Kashmiris by force. For that matter, there was even a rumour that the Ambanis were going to purchase the whole of the Gulmarg Tourist Resort, depriving simple Kashmiris of their businesses. These rumours and many of the apprehensions were quelled by the government by announcing on local television networks that all the rumours were false propaganda. Simultaneously, Internet services, especially social media and mobile phone services, were stopped or curtailed. With these steps the rumour mills and their free access to spreading lies and half-truths were restricted, and the spreading of fake news was definitely curtailed. Local newspapers were closed for one week. All political leaders from top to bottom were either kept under house arrest or moved to jails. The government on its part was continuously sharing the narrative that the 'leaders' had robbed the masses—for the past several decades—of the fruits of real progress. The leaders, now under house arrest or in jails, the government informed, had amassed wealth and riches, all of which were meant for the people of Jammu and Kashmir.

The narrative that Article 370 was a big impediment in the way of progress, overall development, and the creation of employment gained traction over the following weeks. The fact that the sons and daughters of leaders and 'high-ups' in the bureaucracy were studying in or were already graduates of universities and colleges in the rest of the country or overseas was also highlighted. The common man too started to question why the children of leaders would leave Kashmir, while theirs were left behind to be killed by the terrorists or become terrorists themselves. This information campaign was a strong one and resonated with the masses. People would openly say that it was better that the leaders were locked up, otherwise they would have orchestrated the bloodshed of poor, innocent people.

As I write this, towards the end of 2019, the events of the past few months and the saga of change reminds me of the terrible months of December 1989 and January 1990, when terrorism was at its peak in Kashmir. People were gagged, choked, and killed. Initially, one section of society was targeted and Kashmiri Pandits especially were singled out in a bid to brutally terrorize them to the extent that they would leave the Valley for good. The random killings were spine chilling. Later, and all through the next three decades, the killings became routine and commonplace, with armed terrorists liquidating anyone who dared speak against the terrorists.

Fear is scarier than death. It can make a person die by inches within. One's soul is scarred with fear, and as I've mentioned elsewhere in this book the trauma is passed on from one generation to the next, and to the one after. Although Kashmiris by and large have a great capacity to adapt to even the toughest of situations, they believe that their survival is assured if they align with the stronger side. This trait, cultivated for the survival of the community over centuries of brutality, historical upheavals, and violence that has been endured by Kashmiris as a whole, has also made them resilient in the face of sudden and unexpected changes. Today this trait manifests in the principle best enunciated in the Hindustani phrase 'Jo jeeta vahi Sikandar'. Implying of course that if the change is beneficial and brings no harm, why not give it a try?

Index

Abdullah, Farooq, 101–02
Abdullah, Sheikh Mohammad, 100–02, 103, 105, 201–02, 274, 285–86, 297–99, 318, 322–23, 327, 336, 347
Abhinavagupta, 326
Afghanistan, Russian occupation, 334
Afghans, xiv, 3, 13–14, 157
Aftab, 322
Ahad Bub, 209
All India Radio (Indian state broadcasting service), 65
All State Kashmiri Pandits' Conference (ASKPC), 99
Allahditta, 180–81, 183–85
Amar Chand, 340
Anantnag, 63, 277–80, 286; violence against Hindus and Sikhs, 323

Anglo-Sikh wars, 96
Appaji, 245, 250–52
Assadullah, 278, 281, 306–08
Azad Conference (political party), 100

Babri mosque demolition, 342
Bandhu, Kashyap, 98–99, 274–76
Bandudattā, 60
Bazaz, Prem Nath, 99
Bangladesh, creation of, 322, 334
Baramulla, 277, 286, 296–300, 305, 323, 330
Beejān, 186–95
Bhan, Uma (Didā) née Dhar, 170, 233–35, 237–39, 246–47, 302
Bhat, Hassan, 310
Bhat, Justice J.N., 99
Bhat, Maqbool, 340

Bhat, Parmanand, 289–90, 291
Bhutto, Zulfiqar Ali, 334
Biddulph, John, 64
Big Landed Estates Abolition Act, 1950, 327–29
British Auxiliary Air Force, 296
British East India Company, 62, 96, 160
Buddhism, 59, 210
bukhāri (a wood-burning stove), 310

Central Asia, 59, 64, 337
China–India war, 1962, 320
Christians, 295, 312
Congress, 312
Constitution of India, abrogation of Article 370, xv, 351–52
conversion of Kashmiri Hindus to Islam, 61, 157, 226, 330–31
Cossacks, 64
culture shock, 47

Dattatreya clan, 182
Ḍeke Dæd, 210
Devi Singh, General, 63
Dhar, Bal Bhadra, 4, 5–14, 16, 26–40, 48, 52, 55, 57
Dhar, Benigashi, 88, 90, 116, 166, 170–72, 175, 248–50, 269
Dhar, Benji, 88–90, 115–16, 138–40, 166, 170–74, 178–83, 214, 222, 248–50, 302–03
Dhar, Bibi, 85–90
Dhar, Bulla, 86, 229, 230
Dhar, Dulabhabi (Dulari), 90, 122, 166, 169–73, 175, 235, 274–75, 278–81, 284

Dhar, Durga Prasad, 332
Dhar, Gasha, 83, 233–35, 237
Dhar, Gyanji, 229–30
Dhar, Gyanṭoṭh (Gyan Nath), 166, 285–86
Dhar, Heemal (née Tikku), 3–6, 11–14, 15, 26, 41–42, 43–55, 57, 95–96
Dhar, Jaya, 227–29
Dhar, Kashi Nath, 4, 5–14, 15, 26, 28–45, 46–54, 56, 95–96
Dhar, Manmohan (Lalaji), 88, 194, 272–84
Dhar, Niranjan Nath (Bubji), 81, 88, 104, 106–08, 111, 114–15, 122, 177, 182–83, 270, 323
Dhar, Prabhavati, 273–75, 284
Dhar, Prathkāk, 83, 278
Dhar, Prem Nath, 116
Dhar, Prithvi Nath, 107
Dhar, Rajinder (Rajṭoṭh), 160–62, 221–30
Dhar, Ram Chandra, 4, 5–10, 26, 41, 44–46, 48–51, 54–55, 57, 77, 78, 83, 85, 97, 103–04, 111, 114, 117, 132, 140, 156–57, 158–59, 160–61, 186, 209, 210, 231–34, 248, 267, 272
Dhar, Ranaji, 323
Dhar, Sati, 88, 90, 115–16, 166, 170–74, 212–15, 240, 248–50, 302, 304
Dhar, Shambhu Nath (Baiji), 23–24, 25, 83, 85, 87, 99, 104, 106, 111, 115, 143–53,

Index

155, 194, 210, 212, 230, 240, 276–78, 281–82, 323
Dhar, Sondhlal, 221–30
Dhar, Sukh Māl, 78–83, 85–87, 89–91, 114, 116–17, 129, 131–37, 140–41, 152–55, 156–57, 166, 168–69, 174, 193–95, 211, 232–34, 236–41, 248, 251–52, 267, 272, 276, 282–84, 301–02, 323
Dhar, Surender (Sardar), 133, 138–41, 173, 177–84, 229, 230, 250, 285–87, 289, 319, 343–44
Dhar, Tāṭhāji, 88, 194, 212–13, 281–82, 323
Dhar, Tribhuvan Nath, 78–91, 286
Dhar, Vimla (née Mattoo), 289–90, 344
Dogra rule in Kashmir, Dogras, 78, 96, 100
Duleep Singh, Prince of Punjab, 96
Durrani Afghans, 3
Dvitiya Rajatarangini (Jonaraja and Srivara), xi

economic hardships of Kashmiri Hindus, 226

Farooq, Maulvi, 101–02
Fateh Kadal Reading Group (FKRG), 100
Fotedar, Jigri, 118–20, 122
Fotedar, Prakash Joo, 98

Fotedar, Shiv Narain, 98–99, 103–10, 111, 115–20, 122

Gandhi, Indira, 322, 336
Gandhi, Mohandas Karamchand, 75
Ganjoo, Justice Neelkanth, 340
geopolitical developments in the Middle East, 338
Ghaznavi Force, 321
Ghulam Mohammad, Bakshi, 285–86, 312–13, 318–20
Gibraltar Operation, 321–22
Gilgit, 63–74, 232
Gilgit river, 69
Glancy, B.J., 327
Graṭè Bub, 210–17
Gugi, 269
Gulab Singh Dogra, Raja of Jammu, 62–63, 96
Gul-e-Bakavali, 118

Hafiz, 116
Halwai, Mohammad Yusuf, 340
hamāms, 241
Handoo, Parameshwari, 331–32
Hari Singh, Maharaja, 66–68, 112, 286, 289, 298–99, 305, 327
Hazratbal shrine, 310–11, 316, 321
Hindus, xii, 60–61, 63, 157, 199, 226, 255, 275, 294, 297, 307, 312, 315, 323, 328, 330, 339, 342
Hizbullah group, 343

housing of Kashmiri Pandits, 222–24
Hussein, Saddam, 338

Imamuddin, Sheikh, 62
Indra, Peshin, 269
Indus river, 63, 69
Instrument of Accession with India, 26 October 1947, 299, 308
Ishbari, Khoja Nuruddin, 311
Islam, 60, 157, 336, 342
Islamic Brotherhood, 336
Islamization: in Jammu and Kashmir, 334–41; of Pakistan, 334–35

Jamaat-e-Islami, 335
Jammu and Kashmir Constituent Assembly, 77, 105
Jammu Kashmir Liberation Front (JKLF), 340
Jan Mohamed, 174
Jana Sangh, 333
Jashn-i-Kashmir, 319
Jindan Kaur, Maharani of Punjab, 96
Jinnah, Muhammad Ali, 297–98
Jivaka, 59
Johar, I.S., 319

Kabir, 116
Kafiristan, 63
Kahluria, Zorawar Singh, 62
Kak, Keshav Lal, 57–58
Kak, Ram Chandra, 58
Kalhana, *Rajatarangini*, xi, 326

Kalidas, 116
Kamaraj Plan, 312–13
kāngri, 167–68, 205, 236, 241–43, 309
Kantha Ram, 6–7, 8, 166–67, 170–72, 176
Kapoor, Prithviraj, 319
Karan Singh, Dr, 286
kārkuns, 226, 325–26
Kashkāk, 210
Kashmiri Mohalla, Lucknow, 16, 28, 48
Kashmiri Pandits (Battas), xiv, 20–25, 29–34, 60, 65–66, 68, 74, 78, 95–98, 104–06, 109–10, 167, 172–73, 182, 203–04, 226, 234, 254–55, 268, 274, 276, 286, 288, 289, 323, 331, 339–40, 341; agitation, 325–33; smart and knowledgeable, 14–16, 60, 66, 99

Katju, Kailash Nath, 105
Katta, Khwaja Shams-ud-din, 313, 321
Kaul, Brij Lal, 115–16
Kaul, Gwasha Lal, 111–15, 117–18
Kaul, Hargopal, 97, 98–99
Kaul, Jiglāl, 89, 267, 280–81, 283
Kaul, Kagnath (Kagga), 86, 229, 230, 280–81
Kaul, Nani, 131–32, 187, 229, 280–81
Kaul, Nicklāl, 267–70, 280–81

Kaul, Pichru, 131–33, 134–37, 229, 280–81
Kaul, Saligram, 97
Kaul, Sumali, 16–21, 26–28, 29, 31–40, 42–43, 49–55, 57
Kauls, 16–17, 182
Khalila, 138–41, 144–55
Khayyam, Omar, 211
Kheer Bhavani temple, 5–12
Khema, 119, 178, 229
Khoje-bai, 268–70
Khomeini, Ayatollah, 336
Kilam, Justice Jia Lal, 98–99
Kishni, 187–88, 192–94
Kokernag spring, 121–22
Kshemendra, 326
Kumārajīva, 59–61
Kumārāyana, 59

Lalleshwari (Lalded), 121, 150, 214
land to the tiller, 78
Landed Estates Abolition Act, 77–78
Lassa Joo, 129–31, 134–37
love jihad, 331

Mahadev Ram, 150
Maheshwar, 55–56, 57
Maheshwar Nath, 66–76
Malaviya, Madan Mohan, 105
Malik, Satyapal, 350
Malik, Yasin, 349–50
Mallik, Bhola Nath, 313, 315
marriages and celebrations among Kashmiri Pandits, 221–30
Martand, The, 99

maternal mortality in India, 290–91
Mattoo, Ashok, 290
Mattoo, Moti Lal, 290
Mattoo, Rupa (née Bhat), 289–90, 291
McMahon Line, 320
Mirakh Shah, 315–17
Mithan Lal, 116
Moh-i-Muqaddas, loss of, 309–17, 320–21
Momlāl, 270–71
Mughal system of administration, 97
Munshi, Basha, 268–71
Muslim Conference, 100–01, 297, 299
Muslim League, 297, 342
Muslim rulers of Kashmir, 226
Muslims, 63, 100–02, 286, 312, 315, 321, 328, 331, 341, 342
mystical traditions, 199–208, 209–17

N.D. Radha Krishan and Company, 82
Nabha, 120
Nalla Mar, 267
Nanḍe Lāl Bab, 199–208, 210
Nanga Parbat, 69
National Conference, 101–02, 285, 297, 299, 313, 340
Nav-sheen (first snowfall of the season), 231–43, 248–50
Nehru, Jawaharlal, 298–99, 315, 320

Nimlāl, 212–16
Nixon, Richard, 322
Noor-ud-din, 202–03
North West Frontier Provinces – (NWFP), 296
Nunde-rishi, 121, 214

Organization of the Petroleum Exporting Countries (OPEC), 336

Pachhin, 241
Padmavati (Benijigri), 97–98, 103, 117–19
Pakistan: Army, 296–300, 321; creation of, 101; India war, 1965 and 1971, 321–22, 329; Inter-Services Intelligence (ISI), 342; invasion on Kashmir, 1947, 295–300, 305–08, 323
Pant, Govind Ballabh, 105
Partition of Indian subcontinent, xv
patri, 241
Peer, Qamar-uddin, 250
Peer, Shareif-uddin, 250
Peer, Sidhlal, 251
Peer, Zaina (Zainlal, 245–47, 251
Peers and Dhars, 244–52, 270, 271
Peshin, S.N., 99
Pestonjee Transport, 82
Prasad Ram, 6–7, 8, 44, 46, 49, 51, 53, 55, 56, 91
Pratap Singh, Maharaja of Kashmir, 57

Prema, 172–73, 174, 214
Pulwama terrorists' attack, 347–48
purity and defilement, concepts, 172–73
Pushkar Nath, 254–65

Quit Kashmir, 105

radicalization and ethnic cleansing, 334–41, 342
Radio Kashmir, 319, 322
Raina, Raja Narendra Nath, 105
Rajatarangini (Kalhana Pandit), xi, 326
Ranbir Singh, Maharaja (1856–1885), 3, 47, 63–64, 96–97, 100
Ranjit Singh, Maharaja of Punjab, 62, 97
Ratan Rani Hospital, Srinagar, 291
Ratni, 187–90, 192–94, 195
Razdan, Krishna Joo, 209
Razāq, 146, 153, 175
religion and identity, xiii
religious bias, 328
Renchen, 330
Reshi-Ver, xiv–xv
Reza Pahlavi, Shah of Iran, 336
Rinpoche, Kushok Bakula, 209
Rumi, Jalaluddin, 116, 211
rumour-mongering, 255
Rupa Devi Sharda Peeth Trust, 291–92, 344
Russia, 64; Russian occupation of Afghanistan, 334, 340

säd makkārs, 127–37
Sadiq, Ghulam Mohammad, 313, 332
Sahni, Sonia, 319
Sanatan Dharam Yuvak Sabha (SDYS), 99, 104, 105–06, 108
Sapru, Tej Bahadur, 105
Saraf, Gowri (née Dhar), 246–47, 302
Saraf, Promila, 291
Sarvanand (Sarva), 7, 8–10, 44, 46, 49, 51, 53, 89, 91, 150, 172, 193, 240
Sati Dæd, 210
Saudi Arabia: funding to charities in Jammu and Kashmir, 292, 336–37
Sayeed, Mufti Mohammad, 339
Sayeed, Rubaya, 339
Shah, Mehmooda Ali, 202–03
Shah, Mohammad Yusuf, Mirwaiz of Jama Masjid, 100–1
Shamlāl, 178–79, 278–80
Sharga, Pandit, 29–32
Shastri, Lal Bahadur, 315–17
Sheetal Nath temple, 99, 108, 332
Shias, 336; and Kurds of Iraq, 338
Shishur, 242–43
Shobawati, 302
Shyam Nath, Pandit, 48–51
Sidha, 89, 91, 172, 175, 192–93, 301–03
Sidiq, Mohammad, 277–84
Sikhs, xiv, 295, 297, 312, 323, 328, 339, 341
Sita Ram Bazar, Delhi, 16

snowball fight, 249–51
social reforms and education in Kashmir, 95–99
social taboos about love marriage in Kashmiri society, 253–55
Sona Bub, 210
Srinagar Municipal Corporation, 105
Srinagar Times, 322
Sudraka, 326
Suhadeva, the Lohara king of Kashmir, 330
Sullā, 146, 153
Sultan Sæb, 210
Sunnis of Kashmir, 338

Tajikistan, 59
Taklamakan, 59
Taplu, Tikka Lal, 340
Thakur, L.D., 315
Thomas, 67–68, 75–76
Thussu, Jagat Mohini, 290–91
Thussu, O.N., 291
Tikaram, 133–34, 148–50, 165–66, 170, 176, 235
Tikku, Divan Nand Ram, 3–4, 12, 13, 27, 28, 42, 44, 47, 48, 56
Treaty of Amritsar, 1861, 62
Tulsi, 253–65
two-nation theory, 297
Tyndale Biscoe School, 319

Vādi-ki-avāz, 322
van Buḍini, 138–55, 156
vanėvun (Kashmiri marriage songs), 205
Vāriku, Janki, 304

Vāriku, Liljigri (Maciji), 116, 303
Vāriku, Nerkāk, 301–08
Vashnavi, Amar Nath, 99
Vijay, Kachru 268–69
Vitastā, 330
Wahabi/Salafi conservative Islam, 337
Wakhlu, Omkar, 310, 343, 344
wars; India–China, 1962, 320; India–Pakistan, 1965, 321–22, 329, 347; 1971, 322

Wazir, Shyama, 118, 122, 212, 214–16, 229
women in Kashmir, xii, 66, 88, 95, 97–99, 157–58, 232
World War II, 200, 268
Wular lake, 69

Zap Khan, 182–83
Zhou Enlai, 320
Zia ul Haq, 334–35
Zulju, a Turkic-Mongol invader, 329–30

Acknowledgements

This book is the result of the generous encouragement and support received from a large number of people over the years. I would like to express my gratitude to them collectively—especially to my near and dear ones who form the extended Rishi Vihar family—knowing that it would not be possible to mention them all, individually, by name. Your loving presence in my life has been a source of great joy and enrichment.

I must specifically mention my dear niece, Aruna Wazir Kar, for some of the stories that she shared with me, and which I have been happy to include in this book. Thank you, Aruna, for your suggestions and your warm affection.

My husband Omkar, who passed away as I was working on this book, was ever my inspiration and guide. Early on, he had discovered that I wrote well, and his encouragement thereafter was sustained and purposeful. I truly wish that he could have been by my side to see how this book finally turned out.

My immense thanks to Krishan Chopra and Sachin Sharma and their wonderful team at HarperCollins. In his role as my commissioning editor, Sachin took my raw manuscript and transformed it into this neat book. It has taken considerable time, and effort, including sending the draft manuscript back and forth a few times between us, to get it into this form. I'm deeply appreciative of Sachin's efforts, and of Krishan's support. The pandemic disrupted the regular flow of life, and yet they never lost sight of the goal of getting the book without much delay. With this book, I'm now reassured that future generations of children from Jammu and Kashmir will appreciate the kind of lives their forebears lived; and the many hardships they braved to improve their lot—and that of their families.

My son Bharat deserves kudos for his consistent encouragement and constructive suggestions as I was writing the book. It was he who helped me in the run-up to completing this book. He and his lovely wife, Savita, have both been there with me in this rather long journey of writing, and I'm ever grateful to them. To my elder son, Arun, and his dear wife, Anu, my appreciation for always cheering me in my efforts. You all have my love and blessings.

Finally, my immense gratitude to Anu Aga, Lila Poonawalla, Pran Kishore Kaul, Rakesh Kumar Kaul, Dr Mallika Sarabhai, and Siddharth Kak for their gracious compliments and advance praise for this book. I feel truly overwhelmed with their kindness, and thank them most heartily for their friendship and their appreciation.

About the Author

Khem Lata Wakhlu is a writer, a political leader and a social worker, who has devoted the past forty-five years to improving the lives of the people of Jammu and Kashmir. She has held important political positions in the National Conference, the Awami National Conference and the Indian National Congress, and has served as a Member of the Jammu and Kashmir (J&K) Legislative Assembly for twelve years, and as the minister of tourism in Jammu and Kashmir from 1984 to 1986. She was the chairperson of the state's social welfare board, with the status of a minister of cabinet rank, from 2010 to 2014. She continues to serve as senior adviser to the Jammu and Kashmir Pradesh Congress Committee.

Apart from holding public office and serving on the boards and governing committees of many public and social organizations, Wakhlu has been a prolific writer of novels, plays, poems and short stories, in Hindi, English and Kashmiri. Her first novel in Hindi, published in 1968, was *Jheel aur Kamal*. This was followed by *Kashmir ki Dharti* (1970), *Khila Phool Murjhaya* (1979) and *Dehekte*

Angarey (1980). In 1992 she collaborated with her husband, Dr O.N. Wakhlu, to write the widely acclaimed non-fiction, *Kashmir: Behind the White Curtain*. This was followed in 1993 by *Kidnapped: Forty-five Days with Militants in Kashmir* and *A Matter of Fact* in 2001. She was awarded the first prize by the Jammu and Kashmir Sahitya Akademi for *Kashmir ki Dharti*. Her plays, *Kayamat* in Hindi and *Lale Saab* in Kashmiri, were both adapted for television and aired on Doordarshan in the state. Her latest compilation of poems in Hindi and English is entitled *Jeevan Ek Paheli* (2016).

Besides her contribution to public service and literature, Khem Lata Wakhlu has also been a proficient sitar player since she was a young girl. She divides her time between Srinagar and Pune.